PRAISE FOR THE SECOND EDITION

"A comprehensive and practical guide to the Small Claims Track. Dominic Bright has set out a clear and extensive guide which will be invaluable to all practitioners who deal with Small Claims; as well as those in the voluntary sector.

t Judge & Recorder Pollard
South Eastern Circuit

"The seco the Small Claims Track con- *tinues to* nvolved in conducting small *claims. Written in a clear, accessible style, Dominic Bright's detailed yet concise guide sheds light on all aspects of the small claims procedure. With up-to-date information on changes in practice precipitated by the Covid-19 pandemic, this book is an invaluable resource particularly for litigants in person and those who are unfamiliar with the court process."*

– District Judge Dias
South Eastern Circuit

"In this book, Dominic Bright has managed to produce a detailed and comprehensive guide to dealing with all aspects of a case in the small claims track which is both easy to understand and to navigate. Although small claims cases are normally for less than £10,000, the amounts claimed and in dispute can still be life changing for parties. The book will assist practitioners and litigants in person in preparing and presenting cases in the best and most effective way."

– District Judge James Britton
Western Circuit

"Mr Bright has written a thorough, detailed yet easy to follow guide to all using the small claims procedure in the County Court. It will be an invaluable aide to litigants in person, practitioners and the newly appointed District Judge, and I cannot commend it highly enough."

– District Judge Bishop
South Eastern Circuit

PRAISE FOR THE FIRST EDITION

"Dominic Bright has balanced a thorough, careful review of the Small Claims Track procedure with a helpful analysis of the most common areas of law the County Court sees. The wealth of sensible, practical advice for those coming to court helps further set this book apart."

– District Judge Cridge
South Eastern Circuit

"… it has the potential to be a genuine game-changer in the pro bono sector … Despite its small size, [it] takes in everything from the pre-action stage right the way through to costs and appeals. … It seems inevitable that [it] will quickly become the go-to small claims book for practitioner volunteers (and junior practitioners generally), especially those unfamiliar with handling claims allocated to the small claims track, as well as an indispensable self-help guide to LiPs."

– Richard Pitkethly
In-house counsel and head of learning & practice at LawWorks
'A pro bono game-changer' in the *Law Society Gazette*
Five Stars

"Barrister Dominic Bright comes from Lamb Chambers and he has written a masterful account of what to do when you are faced with dealing with a small claim."

– Phillip Taylor MBE
Reviews Editor of *The Barrister*
Five Stars

Dominic is a barrister at Lamb Chambers, registered civil and commercial mediator at Resolved Online, and former judicial assistant to Sir Brian Leveson, then President of the Queen's Bench Division.

His recent articles include: 'COVID-19, International Commercial Contracts & "Breathing Space": Further Encouraging ADR; Developing Common Law Doctrines; & An Implied Term of Good Faith'; 'UK Autonomous Sanctions System: Substantial Increase in the Costs of Compliance'; and 'Climate Change & the Judiciary: Europe; the United States; & the Indian Subcontinent'.

He is a member of the British Institute of International and Comparative Law, Chatham House, Civil Mediation Council, Commercial Bar Association, Property Bar Association, and Technology and Construction Bar Association.

A Practical Guide to the Small Claims Track

2nd Edition

A Practical Guide to the Small Claims Track

2nd Edition

Dominic Bright
Barrister, Lamb Chambers

Law Brief Publishing

Published 2020 by Law Brief Publishing, an imprint of Law Brief Publishing Ltd
30 The Parks
Minehead
Somerset
TA24 8BT

www.lawbriefpublishing.com

Paperback: 978-1-913715-62-5

For my father.

FOREWORD TO THE
SECOND EDITION

A litigant in England and Wales is most likely to come into contact with the civil courts, principally the county court, in connection with a claim proceeding on the Small Claims Track which, despite the name, is the track to which nearly all the cases worth up to £10,000 are allocated, a very significant number of cases every year. Such litigants are often faced, for the first time, with a set of rules of practice and procedure and legal principles which they will never have seen before and which some might find somewhat bewildering. They need not fear. In the Second Edition of his book Dominic Bright has provided a comprehensive, step-by-step, guide to the Small Claims track which will take the litigant by the hand and lead them through the process from beginning to end. In the course of that journey the author addresses everything which the reader might want to know about the court, the system, the processes and the participants, including what technology the litigant might need to be familiar with and how to "break the ice" with the other side. The book is learned, practical, readable and useable.

I think that no one will doubt that 2020 has been a challenging year for everyone, including the courts, HMCTS, the judges and all the court users, professional and lay. Each has had to adapt to ensure that cases can continue to be heard and, as Her Hon Judge Walden-Smith commented in the Foreword to the First Edition of this book, to ensure that there is the proper system for the judicial resolution of disputes between citizens and that the rule of law can continue to be upheld. The proper functioning of the Small Claims Track is crucial to the maintenance of the rule of law. The author has addressed the challenges which 2020 has brought to those courts with specific sections dedicated to remote hearings and C-19. It is to be hoped that C-19 will not need to appear in what I am sure will be a Third Edition of this splendid book in due course.

The book is, in my view, essential reading not only for litigants in person, but for all practitioners who handle small claims (whether as advocates or in the earlier stages of the case). I also have no doubt that the judges of the county court (whether salaried or fee-paid) would benefit considerably by reading this book and keeping it by their side when giving directions or trying cases on the small claims track or hearing the occasional appeal from a decision made on the track. The Practical Guide to the Small Claims Track is an excellent book.

His Honour Judge Marc Dight CBE
Senior Chancery Circuit Judge
Designated Civil Judge Central London and
Mayor's & City of London Courts
Lead Diversity and Community Relations Judge
Royal Courts of Justice
London

PREFACE TO THE SECOND EDITION

Fully revised and updated.

Clearer. More comprehensive. More concise.

Guidance on remote preparation, conferences and final hearings; new authority on bias, unfairness and litigants in person; and step-by-step advice for efficiently working from home.

The law in England and Wales is stated as at 1 November 2020.

Dominic Bright
Working from home
November 2020

FOREWORD TO THE FIRST EDITION

Over recent years, a succession of Lord Chancellors and Ministers of Justice have been keen to emphasise their commitment to protecting judges and upholding the rule of law. Such commitments are not without meaning and while the rule of law is a phrase often said, it is rarely examined. It is not an arid legal doctrine but is the foundation stone of much that creates a fair and just society.

It may be thought that the rule of law is of no relevance to a foreword about a book giving practical guidance to claims within the small claims track in the County Court. On the contrary, the rule of law is front and centre. It is because people with a dispute, however low in value and lacking complexity, can bring a claim before an impartial judge, that we can function as a civilised society where business can be done and wrongs remedied. The small claims procedure is a very real example of the rule of law in operation.

The District Bench across England and Wales is under pressure as it has never been before, with both the volume and variety of work that judges are obliged to hear. Added to that, judges generally, and the District Bench in particular, has to be able to reach both legal and factual decisions often without the benefit of the parties having legal representation. In order to fulfil their role properly and in order to continue with their duties to uphold the rule of law, without fear or favour, both full-time and deputy District Judges need to be able to manage heavy lists of both civil and family cases. A sizeable part of the daily diet of the District Bench will be civil claims which are allocated to the small claims track.

As Dominic Bright sets out, small claims account for approximately 60% of all allocations of civil work in the County Court and three-quarters of all civil claims disposed of by way of final hearing. The financial value of a small claim is now £10,000 or less and the track is designed to provide a proportionate procedure by which the most straightforward of these relatively low value claims can be decided without substantial pre-hearing preparation and without the formalities of a traditional trial. Of course, most people with a claim worth £10,000 or less are unlikely to consider the sums involved to be "small" and the title given to this track must not be seen to belittle the importance of the dispute to the parties involved. What is important is that the track provides a proportionate means of resolving a dispute between parties which can be of considerable practical importance and, despite the categorisation of small, considerable financial worth to the individuals involved.

In this comprehensive guide to the small claims track, Dominic Bright has set out all that a practitioner could possibly need to know about how to deal with a small claim, from allocation to judgment and through to any potential appeal. He covers the court's duty to manage cases actively and the overriding objective and, in doing so, points out the duty of the court to take into account the fact that a litigant is without representation when exercising powers of case management albeit that all rules, practice directions and orders apply equally to represented and unrepresented litigants. It is, of course, incumbent upon a practitioner, as well as the court, to act in furtherance of the overriding objective. An unrepresented litigant is not only entitled to a fair hearing, he is entitled to understand that he is obtaining that fair hearing.

Further to the specifics of how the court will deal with a small claim, including the pleadings, the allocation and the hearing itself, Dominic Bright has included guidance on a wide range of matters, such as ethics and ways to behave when in court, which will be of assistance to any junior practitioner appearing in a civil case at an early stage of their career. The inclusion of the civil procedure rules and practice directions relating to the small claims track, and also to pre-action conduct and protocols and to the overriding objective and the court's duty to manage cases, means that this guide provides a useful toolkit of relevant rules and practice directions.

This Practical Guide to the Small Claims Track will be of benefit to practitioners, particularly those new to practice. It will therefore be of benefit to the District Judges and their deputies who hear small claims. Undoubtedly, the better informed and prepared the representatives are, the better it is for the judges who hear such claims to enable them to concentrate on reaching the correct legal and factual conclusions in furtherance of upholding the rule of law.

HHJ Karen Walden-Smith
Senior Circuit Judge
Designated Civil Judge for
the County Court in East Anglia
November 2019

PREFACE TO THE FIRST EDITION

My aim is to shine light upon the 'what', 'when', and 'how' of the small claims track. This practical guide is written with junior *barristers* and *solicitors* in mind, however, *litigants in person* may also find it of some assistance. This is because the *special* procedure for dealing with these claims is designed so that *litigants* may conduct their *own* case.

It purports to be *clear*, *comprehensive*, and *concise*.

'Clear' because *short*, *descriptive* sub-headings are used to marshal content, often comprising just a few sentences; and sometimes, only one, *importance* sentence, containing a *single*, but *key* point.

'Comprehensive' because the full timeline of a claim is covered: from *pre-action*, through *final hearing*, to *appeal*. There are many, more comprehensive, authoritative texts on civil procedure in general, advocacy, and on the small claims track within the Intellectual Property Enterprise Court.

'Concise' because every effort has been made to remove jargon unencumbered with merit, unwarranted primary authority, and unnecessary secondary sources.

It aspires to be well-thumbed, throwing a beacon of light onto issues, *before*, and *when* they arise, so that they can be dealt with *confidently*, to the benefit of *lay* and *professional* clients, and enabling *the court* to achieve the overriding objective to deal with cases justly, and at proportionate cost.

The law in England and Wales is stated as at 1 November 2019.

Dominic Bright
Lamb Chambers, Temple, London
November 2019

"It is not the critic who counts; not the man who points out how the strong man stumbles or where the doer of deeds could have done them better. The credit belongs to the man who is actually in the arena, whose face is marred by dust and sweat and blood; who strives valiantly; who errs, who comes short again and again, because there is no effort without error and shortcoming; but who does actually strive to do the deeds; who knows great enthusiasms, the great devotions; who spends himself in a worthy cause; who at the best knows in the end the triumph of high achievement, and who at the worst, if he fails, at least fails while daring greatly, so that his place shall never be with those cold and timid souls who neither know victory nor defeat."

– Theodore Roosevelt
Sorbonne, Paris
April 1910

CONTENTS

1. Overview

This chapter summarises the special procedure for dealing with claims that have been allocated to the small claims track.

Specific reference is made only to those that are of fundamental importance. The remaining chapters go further, providing guidance as to when to rely upon specific rules, and when to deploy authority interpreting them.

a. Small claim

The rules of civil litigation in England and Wales are prescribed in the Civil Procedure Rules ("CPR").

Part 27 of the CPR is entitled: 'The small claims track'.

A "small claim" is a claim that: falls under this Part which sets out the procedure for dealing with small claims; and limits the amount of costs that can be recovered (CPR 27.1(1) and (2)).

The special procedure for dealing with claims that have been allocated to the small claims track 'is intended to provide a proportionate procedure by which most straightforward claims with a financial value of not more than £10,000 can be decided, without the need for substantial pre-hearing preparation and the formalities of a traditional trial, and without incurring large legal costs' (Practice Direction ("PD") 26 at [8.1(1)(a)]).

It is regrettable that these are referred to as "small claims".

First, they make up about three-quarters of all civil claims disposed of by way of final hearing. Secondly, many would not accept that £10,000 is a "small" sum. Thirdly, the claimant bringing the claim, and the defendant defending against it, are likely to disagree that the importance of their dispute is "small".

b. Context

In April to June 2020, 14,000 cases were allocated to the small claims track. This is more than 60 percent of all allocations.

Of the claims that went to a final hearing, about three-quarters were allocated to the small claims track. This is a five percent increase when compared to the same quarter in the previous year.

A claim takes about 42 weeks to go to a final hearing (Ministry of Justice, *Civil Justice Statistics Quarterly, England and Wales, April to June 2020,* 3 September 2020).

c. Allocation

The small claims track is the "normal track" for three types of claim (CPRs 26.6 and 27.1(2)).

First, any claim with a value of not more than £10,000. In practice, this forms the overwhelming majority.

Secondly, a 'claim for personal injuries' where: the value of the claim is not more than £10,000; and the value of any claim for 'damages for personal injuries' is not more than £1,000.

A 'claim for personal injuries' is one in which 'there is a claim for damages in respect of personal injuries to the claimant'.

'Damages in respect of personal injuries' means 'damages claimed as compensation for pain, suffering and loss of amenity and does not include any other damages which are claimed'.

Thirdly, any claim which includes a claim by a tenant of residential premises against a landlord where: the tenant is seeking an order requiring the landlord to carry out repairs, or other work to the premises; and the cost is estimated to be not more than £1,000.

If a tenant is claiming a remedy in respect of harassment, or unlawful eviction, it will not be allocated to the small claims track.

d. Civil Procedure Rules

CPRs and PDs apply, except if they provide otherwise.

CPRs relating to the following do not apply (CPR 27.2):

1 interim remedies (except as it relates to interim injunctions);
2 disclosure and inspection;
3 evidence (except the power of the court to control evidence);
4 miscellaneous rules about evidence;
5 experts and assessors (except the duty to restrict expert evidence; experts' overriding duty to the court; the court's power to direct that evidence is to be given by a single joint expert; and instructions to a single joint expert);
6 further information (although the court may, on the court's own motion, order a party to provide further information if the court considers that it is appropriate);
7 Part 36 offers to settle; and
8 hearings (except the general rule that hearings are to be in public; and those regarding communications with the court).

e. Final remedy

The court may grant any final remedy that may be granted if the proceedings were allocated to another track (CPR 27.3).

f. Preparation

After allocation, the court will do one of the following (CPR 27.4).

Give *standard* directions, and fix a date for the final hearing.

Give *special* directions, and fix a date for the final hearing, or direct that the court consider what further directions are to be given, no later than 28 days after the date that special directions were given.

Fix a date for a *preliminary* hearing.

Give notice that the court proposes to deal with the claim *without* a hearing, and invite the parties to notify the court by a specified date if they agree.

"Standard directions" means: 'a direction that each party shall, at least 14 days before the date fixed for the final hearing, file and serve on every other party copies of all documents (including any expert's report) on which he intends to rely at the hearing'; and any other standard directions prescribed in PD 27.

"Special directions" means 'directions given in addition to or instead of the standard directions.'

The general rule is that the court will give the parties at least 21 days' notice of the date fixed for the final hearing. The exception is where the parties agree to accept less notice.

In any event, the court must inform the parties of the amount of time allowed for the final hearing.

g. Experts

No expert evidence may be given at a hearing without the court's permission (CPR 27.5).

h. Preliminary hearing

A preliminary hearing may only be held in three circumstances (CPR 27.6).

First, *special directions are needed* to ensure a fair hearing, and it appears to the court that it is necessary for a party to attend at court, so as to ensure that that party understands what she must do to comply with the special directions.

Secondly, *to dispose of the claim*, on the basis that one of the parties has no real prospect of success at a final hearing.

Thirdly, to enable the court to *strike out a statement of case*, or part thereof, on the basis that it discloses no reasonable grounds for bringing, or defending, the claim.

When deciding whether or not to hold a preliminary hearing, the court must have regard to the desirability of limiting the expense of the parties that will be incurred by attending court. The parties must be given at least 14 days' notice of the date of such a hearing.

If all parties agree, the court may treat the preliminary hearing as a final hearing.

At, or after, a preliminary hearing, the court will do three things.

First, fix the date of the final hearing (if it has not already been fixed), and give the parties at least 21 days' notice of the same, unless the parties agree to accept less notice. Secondly, inform the parties of the amount of time allowed for the final hearing. Thirdly, give any appropriate directions.

i. Additional or amended directions

The court may add to, vary, or revoke, directions (CPR 27.7).

j. Final hearing

There are six rules for the final hearing (CPR 27.8).

First, the court may adopt any method of proceeding that it considers to be fair. Secondly, hearings will be informal. Thirdly, the strict rules of evidence do not apply. Fourthly, evidence need not be on oath. Fifthly, the court may limit cross-examination. Sixthly, the court must give reasons for its decision.

k. Non-attendance

If a party does not attend the final hearing, but satisfies the following conditions, the court will take into account that party's statement of case, and any other documents that she has filed when the claim is decided (CPR 27.9).

First, at least seven days before the hearing, written notice ("notice") that she will not attend has been filed with the court, and served on the other party. Secondly, at least seven days before the hearing, she has served any other documents on the other party that she has filed with the court.

Thirdly, in the notice, she has requested that the court decide the claim in her absence, and she has confirmed her compliance with the first and second conditions.

Otherwise, the court may strike out the claim (CPR 27.9(2)).

The court may decide the claim solely on the evidence of the claimant if two conditions are satisfied (CPR 27.9(3)).

First, a defendant does not attend the hearing, or give notice. Secondly, the claimant does not attend the hearing, or gives notice that she will not attend.

The court may strike out a claim, defence, and counterclaim, if neither party attends, nor gives notice (CPR 27.9(4)).

l. Disposal without a hearing

If all parties agree, the court may dispose of the claim without a hearing (CPR 27.10).

m. Set aside & re-hearing

Where the following are met, a party may apply for an order that judgment is set aside, and that the claim is re-heard (CPR 27.11).

First, she was neither present, nor represented, at the hearing of the claim. Secondly, she has not given notice, in accordance with the rule for non-attendance at the final hearing. Thirdly, the application must be made not more than 14 days after the day on which notice of the judgment was served on her.

Where these conditions are satisfied, a court may grant an application, but only if the applicant satisfies a further two conditions.

First, she had a good reason for not attending or being represented at the hearing, or giving notice in accordance with the rule for non-attendance at a final hearing. Secondly, she has a reasonable prospect of success.

If judgment is set aside, the court must fix a new date to hear the claim. This may take place immediately after the application. It may also be heard by the judge who granted the application.

An application to set aside cannot succeed, however, where the claim was disposed of without a hearing.

n. Costs

There are three overarching rules.

Pre-allocation. After allocation. Re-allocation.

i. Pre-allocation

CPRs 46.11 and 46.13 apply before allocation (CPR 27.14(1)).

In general, once a claim is allocated to the small claims track, the rules that apply to costs on this track apply to the periods *before and after* the claim was so allocated (CPR 46.11).

The exception is where the court, or a PD, provides otherwise.

Any cost orders made before a claim is allocated to the small claims track will not be affected by allocation.

In general, where a claim is allocated to the small claims track, and the court subsequently re-allocates the claim to a different track, any special rules about costs in relation to the first track: apply up to the date of re-allocation; and in relation to the second track, apply from the date of re-allocation.

This is unless the court orders otherwise (CPR 46.13(2)).

Where a case settles before allocation, and assessment of costs is on the standard basis, the court may restrict costs to those that would have been allowed on the small claims track if the claim would in fact have been so allocated (CPR 46.13(3)).

ii. After allocation

The only sum that one party can be ordered to pay to another, in respect of another party's costs, fees, and expenses, including those relating to an appeal (CPR 27.14 and PD 27 at [7.3]), are:

1 fixed costs, attributable to issuing the claim, which

1.a are payable under the rule prescribing fixed costs (CPR 45) or,

1.b would be payable under that rule if it applied;

2 in proceedings including a claim for an injunction, or an order for specific performance, a sum not exceeding the amount specified in PD 27 for legal advice and assistance;

3 any court fees paid by that other party;

4 expenses which a party, or a witness, has reasonably incurred in travelling to, and from, a hearing, or staying away from home for the same purpose;

5 a sum not exceeding £95 for any loss of earnings, or loss of leave, by a party, or a witness, due to attending a hearing, or staying away from home for the same purpose;

6 a sum not exceeding £750 for an expert's fees;

7 such further costs as the court may assess by the summary procedure, and order to be paid by a party who has behaved unreasonably;

8   Stage 1, and where relevant Stage 2, fixed costs (CPR 45.18), where

    8.a the claim was within the scope of the Pre-Action Protocol for Low Value Personal Injury Claims in Road Traffic Accidents, or the Pre-Action Protocol for Low Value Personal Injury (Employers' Liability and Public Liability) Claims,

    8.b the claimant reasonably believed that the claim was valued at more than the small claims track limit, in accordance with [4.1(4)] of the relevant protocol, and

    8.c the defendant admitted liability under the process prescribed in the relevant protocol, but did not pay those Stage 1, and where relevant, Stage 2, fixed costs; and

9   in an appeal, the cost of any approved transcript that was reasonably incurred.

"Behaved unreasonably" does not necessarily include a party who has rejected an offer in settlement. The court may take this fact into consideration, however, when assessing reasonableness.

The limits on costs also apply to any fee, or reward, charged by a person exercising rights of audience as a lay representative, for acting on behalf of a party to proceedings.

iii. Re-allocation

When allocated to the small claims track, and subsequently re-allocated to another track, the rule prescribing costs on the former will cease to apply after the claim has been re-allocated (CPR 27.15). Fast track or multi-track costs apply from re-allocation.

2. Overriding objective

The overriding objective is to enable the court to deal with cases *justly* and at *proportionate cost* (CPR 1.1(1) and appendix A).

This includes six *factors*. One is to deal with the case in ways that are proportionate. This, in turn, includes four *aspects*.

When an application is heard, or a case management decision is made, the following can be effectively deployed.

They are often simple, persuasive, and decisive.

a. Duty

The CPR imposes *different* duties on the court and the parties.

i. Court

The *court* must seek to give effect to the overriding objective when exercising any power, or interpreting any rule (CPR 1.2).

This includes actively managing cases, so as to further the overriding objective (CPR 1.4(1)), chapter 3 and appendix B).

ii. Parties

The *parties* must help the court to further the overriding objective (CPR 1.3). This is not a duty to help another party.

A party ("A") does not have to assist another party ("B") to remedy B's procedural mistake, unless there is a genuine misunderstanding, relating to a material matter, to which A has contributed.

A is entitled to take a good procedural point. In doing so, A should act "in a proper professional manner in researching the position, advising the client and taking their instructions". It should not be capable of being recast as "technical games" (*Woodward & Anor v Phoenix Healthcare Distribution Ltd* [2019] EWCA Civ 985 at [50]).

In *Piepenbrock v Associated Newspapers Ltd & Ors* [2020] EWHC 1708 (QB) at [64], Nicklin J said that: "Providing s/he has done nothing to mislead or obstruct, a [party] could hardly be criticised if s/he decided to follow Napoleon's advice not to interrupt an enemy when s/he is making a mistake."

There is an important distinction, however, between a good procedural point and *adverse authority*. Advocates are under a duty to draw the court's attention to an authority that: undermines the case that she is advancing; and has not been cited by the other party (see chapter 13(b) (ii)(2)).

b. Factors

Dealing with a case justly and at proportionate cost, so far as is practicable, includes considering six factors (CPR 1.1(2)).

First, ensuring that the parties are on an equal footing. Secondly, saving expense. Thirdly, ensuring that the case is dealt with expeditiously and fairly.

Fourthly, allotting an appropriate share of the court's resources to the case, while taking into account the need to allot resources to other cases. Fifthly, enforcing compliance with CPRs, PDs, and court orders. Sixthly, dealing with the case in proportionate ways.

They are not: exhaustive (which is clear from the word 'includes'); expressed to be hierarchical; or absolute requirements (which is demonstrated by the caveat 'so far as is practicable').

i. Equal footing

There are two important components.

First, recognising that unrepresented litigants may justify such procedure as the court considers appropriate to further the overriding objective. Secondly, procedural and substantive correspondence with the court should be served on the other side.

1. Litigants in person

Where a party is unrepresented, the court *must* have regard to this fact when *exercising any power of case management*.

The court must adopt such procedure at any hearing as it considers appropriate to further the overriding objective.

This includes the following.

First, ascertaining from an unrepresented party the matters about which a witness may be able to give evidence, or ought to be cross-examined. Secondly, putting, or causing to be put, such questions as may appear to the court to be proper (CPR 3.1A).

This does *not* lower the standard of compliance with CPRs, PDs, or court orders. In practice, it usually means that, when making *case management directions*, they should be clear, understandable, and achievable, to unrepresented litigants.

CPRs, PDs, and court orders, apply to *all* litigants.

This is clear from *Barton v Wright Hassal LLP* [2018] UKSC 12, [2018] 3 All ER 487 at [18], where Lord Sumption (with whom Lords Wilson and Carnwath agreed) said (with emphasis added):

"... Their lack of representation will often justify making allowances in making *case management decisions* and in conducting hearings. But *it will not usually justify applying to litigants in person a lower standard of compliance with rules or orders of the court.* The overriding objective requires the courts so far as practicable to enforce compliance with the rules: CPR rule 1.1(1)(f). *The rules do not in any relevant respect distinguish between represented and unrepresented parties.* ... Unless the rules and practice directions are *particularly inaccessible or obscure*, it is reasonable to expect a litigant in person to familiarise himself with the rules which apply to any step which he is about to take."

Lord Briggs (with whom the then President of the Supreme Court agreed) said at paragraph 42 (with emphasis added):

"... Save to the very limited extent to which the CPR now provides otherwise, *there cannot fairly be one attitude to compliance with rules for represented parties and another for litigants in person*, still less a general dispensation for the latter from the need to observe them. ..."

The court must approach non-compliance by *un*represented parties in the *same* way as non-compliance by *represented* parties.

Otherwise, there is an unjustifiable disturbance in the balance struck by the CPRs, PDs, and court orders.

The exception to which Lord Sumption referred does *not* carve out a general exception for claims allocated to the small claims track.

Relevant CPRs and PDs are unlikely to be inaccessible or obscure.

2. Correspondence

As a general rule, any communication with the court on a matter of *substance* or *procedure* must be disclosed to, and served on, the other party (CPRs 27.2(1)(h) and 39.8).

Failure to do so, so as to deprive the other party of an opportunity to respond, amounts to "a serious procedural irregularity" (*National Westminster Bank Plc v Rushmer & Anor* [2010] EWHC 554 (Ch), [2010] 2 FLR 362 at [35]).

ii. Proportionality

Consideration should be given to the following, so that a case is dealt with in ways that are proportionate (CPR 1.1(2)(c)).

First, the amount of money involved. Secondly, the importance of the case. Thirdly, the complexity of the issues. Fourthly, the financial position of each party.

In cases arising out of road traffic collisions, for example, insurers are often named parties, so their financial position cannot usually be described as modest. The first three, however, are always likely to be modest for the following reasons.

First, the amount of money involved is usually not more than £10,000 (see chapter 11(b)(i)).

Secondly, the importance of the case to the *parties* will likely be modest because: disputed allegations of dishonesty will not usually be suitable for allocation to the small claims track (see chapter 11(a)); and the value of a claim for damages for personal injuries will not be more than £1,000 (see chapter 11(b)(ii)).

Thirdly, the importance of the claim to *persons other than the parties* is likely to be modest because, in general, county court authority may not be cited (see chapter 13(b)(ii)(3)).

Fourthly, the complexity of the issues is likely to be modest because: if the facts, law, or evidence, are complex, the claim is unlikely to be allocated to the small claims track (see chapter 11(b)(iii)); and it will not normally be allocated to the small claims track if it is likely to take more than a day (PD 26 at [8.1(2)]).

3. Court's duty to actively manage cases

The court must further the overriding objective by actively managing cases (CPR 1.4(1) and appendix B).

There are 12 prescribed considerations.

They are not exhaustive or expressed to be hierarchical.

First, encouraging the parties to co-operate with each other in the conduct of proceedings. Secondly, identifying the issues at an early stage. Thirdly, deciding promptly which issues need full investigation, followed by a final hearing, and disposing summarily of those that do not.

Fourthly, deciding the order in which issues are to be resolved. Fifthly, encouraging the parties to use alternative dispute resolution, if appropriate, and facilitating the same. Sixthly, helping the parties to settle the whole, or part, of the case.

Seventhly, fixing timetables, or otherwise controlling the progress of the case. Eighthly, considering whether the likely benefits of taking a particular step justify the cost. Ninthly, dealing with as many aspects of the case as it can on the same occasion.

Tenthly, dealing with the case without the parties needing to attend court in person. Eleventhly, making use of technology. Twelfthly, giving directions to ensure that a final hearing proceeds quickly and efficiently.

They can be deployed whenever the court has to exercise a discretion, so as to persuade the court that: the way in which you invite the court to exercise a discretion is in accordance with the court's duty to *actively manage cases;* and, therefore, the *overriding objective*, which the court *must* seek to further.

a. Encouraging co-operation

Where there is no pre-action letter, a party fails to reply to sustained correspondence over a prolonged period, or unreasonably refuses to consider an offer of alternative dispute resolution, the court should take this into consideration.

Failure to do so is incompatible with the court's duty to actively manage cases, so as to further the overriding objective, which the parties are obliged to help the court to achieve.

These arguments can, perhaps, be best deployed in an application for costs on the basis that a party has behaved unreasonably.

With the increasing use of remote, telephone and audio-visual hearings, the court may direct the parties to cooperate in arranging the hearing. Directions requiring the parties to agree an electronic bundle before a hearing are increasingly common.

Failure to comply may result in the hearing not going ahead, the claim being decided in the absence of one or both of the parties, or imposition of some other (likely costs) sanction.

b. Early identification of issues

The *key* documents should be disclosed *before* a claim is issued (PD – Pre-Action Conduct and Protocols at [6(c)]).

Particulars of claim must set out the claim in a clear, coherent way. They must conform to PDs (CPR 16.4(1)(e)).

In a claim based upon a written agreement, this includes attaching a copy of the contract (or documents constituting the agreement) to, or serving them with, the particulars of claim (PD 16 at [7.3]).

Where a party ("A") fails to do so, an application should be made by the other party ("B") to strike out A's statement of case. The basis is failure to comply with CPRs and PDs (CPR 3.4(2)(c)).

In the alternative, the application should invite the court to make an unless order. That is, unless the written agreement is provided within a specified time period, the claim will automatically be struck out (see chapter 22(a)(iv)).

The submission is that: the court is under a duty actively to manage the case; the issues have not been identified at an early stage; so that the court has been unable to further the overriding objective, which includes enforcing compliance with CPRs and PDs.

c. Summary disposal

Where particulars of claim disclose no reasonable grounds for bringing a claim, or a defence discloses no reasonable grounds for defending against a claim, an application should be made for strike out and / or summary judgment (CPRs 3.4(2)(a) and 24.2).

The issues in these statements of case do not need to be decided at a final hearing. They do not even need full investigation.

If allowed to proceed, they would be bound to fail. The case would not be dealt with expeditiously. An inappropriate share of the court's resources would be allocated to the case. Summary disposal is appropriate. It is required by the overriding objective.

In a claim for credit hire, for example, if there is no evidence of basic hire rates, it is hard to foresee a need to cross-examine on the issue of impecuniosity, so as to establish whether or not the claimant is impecunious. The court will award the credit hire rate, as there is no alternative evidence (of the basic hire rate).

As it is unlikely to have any effect on judgment, there may be no need to resolve the "issue" of impecuniosity. The defendant may accept that the claimant is impecunious, so that this issue falls away, court time is saved, and the case is dealt with expeditiously.

d. Order of resolution

The obvious example is that liability should be resolved before quantum. If liability is not established, quantum is academic.

In the credit hire example, where disputed, whether or not there was a need to hire should be resolved first. This is because, if there was no need to hire, a claim for credit hire should be dismissed. The question of quantum relating to credit hire is purely academic.

e. Alternative dispute resolution

All parties must agree before the case can be referred to the Small Claims Mediation Service.

This is why section A1 of the directions questionnaire is so important. It asks whether a party agrees to the claim being referred to the Small Claims Mediation Service.

The directions questionnaire must be completed and filed. Upon receipt, and the request of the parties, the court will stay proceedings for one month to allow for settlement (CPR 26.4(2)).

f. Helping settlement

On the day of the final hearing, where the parties consider that there is a real prospect of settling the claim, or even narrowing the issues, the court should grant an appropriate amount of time.

This is in accordance with the overriding objective to allot an appropriate share of the court's resources to the case, while taking into account the need to allot resources to other cases.

g. Controlling progress

Where a statement of case does not have a statement of truth, for example, the court should make an 'unless' order. That is, unless verified by a statement of truth, filed and served before a certain date, it will automatically be struck out (see chapter 22(a)(iv)).

This is an example of the court fulfilling the duty to actively manage cases, through fixing a timetable, so as to control the progress of the case, without waiting for a party having to make (and pay the issue fee for) an application. In this way, the court ensures that a case progresses. Even if the parties fail to do so.

h. Cost / benefit analysis

Where the claimant fails to attend a final hearing without giving written notice in accordance with CPR 27.9 (see chapter 19(c)(i)), or a good reason for failing to attend, the court should consider whether the likely benefits of adjourning the case justify doing so.

Where the amount in dispute is modest, and counsel for both sides have attended, the court will weigh up the following.

Unfairness to the defendant occasioned by granting an adjournment, including: the expense of attending that hearing; the additional expense of attending a further hearing; and that the case is not being dealt with expeditiously.

Balanced against this, the court will weigh any unfairness to the claimant if an adjournment is not granted: liability may be admitted;

the defendant may have a substantial counterclaim; and the financial circumstances of the claimant may be dire (she may be an impecunious individual, as opposed to an affluent insurer).

Also, the court will factor in the need to allot an appropriate share of the court's resources to the case, while taking into account the need to allot resources to other cases.

i. Efficiency

Special directions may be needed to ensure a fair hearing.

If so, the court may order a preliminary hearing where necessary for a party to attend court, so as to ensure that she understands what she must do to comply with the special directions (CPR 27.4).

The court must, however: have regard to the desirability of limiting the expense to the parties of attending court; and make use of technology, in the form of remote hearings.

At a preliminary hearing, the court will deal with as many aspects as it can at that hearing. This includes considering whether to fix a date for the final hearing (if it has not done so already), and giving any other, appropriate directions (CPR 27.6(5)).

j. Technology

The COVID-19 pandemic 'necessitates the use of remote hearings wherever possible ... so as to minimise the risk of transmission' (Civil Justice Protocol Regarding Remote Hearings ("the Remote Hearings Protocol") at [1] and [2]).

Although the Remote Hearings Protocol is a temporary measure, there are three reasons to suspect that, having largely resolved the teething troubles, remote hearings are here to stay.

First, they further the overriding objective to deal with a case justly and at proportionate cost, so far as is practicable. They save expense, and deal with cases in ways that are proportionate to the amount of money involved, the importance of the case, and the financial position of each party.

Secondly, they further the overriding objective by actively managing cases, including considering whether the likely benefits of an in-person hearing justify the cost, dealing with the case without the parties needing to attend court, and making use of technology.

Cost includes the expense of the *parties* travelling to court, and the *public,* in relation to the risk of transmission of COVID-19.

Thirdly, the Lord Chief Justice and the Chief Executive of HMCTS support the use of remote hearings beyond COVID-19.

The Lord Chief Justice is reported to have told the Select Committee on the Constitution that: "Moving towards virtual hearings … will continue to be an extremely important tool for the future" (Parliament Committees, 13 May 2020).

The Chief Executive of HMCTS is reported to have said that video hearings are "a crucial tool in maintaining our justice system during the pandemic and beyond" (HMCTS, 29 July 2020).

k. Directions

The court also has a general power to add to, vary, or revoke, directions (CPR 27.7). This should be used to further the overriding objective by actively managing cases.

A party may invite the court to make a particular direction (PD 27 at [2.4]). This includes an order that, unless a statement of case is verified by a statement of truth, within a prescribed period of time, it should automatically be struck out (PD 22 at [4.2]).

4. Pre-action protocols & PD – Pre-Action Conduct

Pre-action protocols explain the conduct, and set out the steps, that are normally expected before commencing proceedings.

There are 15 pre-action protocols currently in force.

Where no specific pre-action protocol applies, however, as is the case in most claims that are allocated to the small claims track, the parties are expected to comply with the Practice Direction – Pre-Action Conduct ("the Practice Direction") (appendix E).

a. Objectives

The parties must exchange sufficient information before proceedings, so that the following objectives are achieved.

First, to understand each other's position. Secondly, to make decisions about how to proceed. Thirdly, to try to settle the issues without proceedings. Fourthly, to consider a form of alternative dispute resolution to assist with settlement. Fifthly, to support the efficient management of proceedings. Sixthly, to reduce the costs of resolving the dispute.

b. Reasonable & proportionate

Reasonable and proportionate steps should be taken to identify, narrow, and resolve, the legal, factual, or expert, issues.

Costs incurred in complying with the requirements of pre-action conduct should be proportionate. This includes the cost of correspondence, and information, that is exchanged. Proportionate steps before issuing a claim usually include the following.

First, the claimant writing to the defendant, setting out concise details of her claim. Secondly, the defendant responding to the claimant within a reasonable period. Typically, no more than 14 days in a straightforward claim. Thirdly, the parties disclosing key documents that are relevant to the issues in dispute.

c. Non-compliance

The court will take into account non-compliance in *substance* with the terms of the relevant pre-action protocol, or the Practice Direction. The court is not likely to be concerned with *minor* or *technical* infringements (Practice Direction at [13]).

The court will take into account non-compliance when making orders for costs (Practice Direction at [13] and CPR 44.2(5)(a)).

The court may decide that there has been a failure to comply in the following circumstances (Practice Direction at [14]).

First, failing to provide sufficient information to enable the objectives of pre-action conduct to be met. Secondly, failing to act within a relevant time limit, or otherwise within a reasonable period. Thirdly, unreasonably refusing to use a form of alternative dispute resolution, or failing to respond to an invitation to do so.

d. Contempt of court

A person who knowingly makes a false statement in a document prepared in anticipation of legal proceedings may be subject to proceedings for contempt of court (Practice Direction at [2]).

5. Statements of case

Statements of case set out (plead) a party's position. They should enable the other party to know what is alleged against them.

They are *formal* documents. Formalities that must be followed.

Statements of case plead the key law (where it is unusual), the material facts, and what the claim, or the defence, is actually about.

a. Types

A "statement of case" includes the following.

First, claim form. Secondly, particulars of claim (where not in the claim form). Thirdly, defence. Fourthly, counterclaim. Fifthly, additional claim under CPR 20. Sixthly, reply to the defence.

b. Rules & practice directions

CPRs and PDs apply (CPR 27.2(1) and (2)).

There are two reasons to be familiar with their requirements.

First, to ensure that the party who you represent has complied. Secondly, to identify another party's substantial non-compliance.

The following is intended to provide an insight into relevant considerations when drafting statements of case, in the context of a claim following a road traffic collision.

It is not intended to be comprehensive. There are other, excellent professional texts on drafting statements of case. This guide does not seek to compete with, but rather to complement, them.

i. Legible & intelligible

When completing any court form by hand, use capital letters and black ink. This is for two reasons.

First, so that the original is legible. Secondly, if the original is scanned and photocopied, copies will be legible.

Most statements of case are typed. All the necessary elements to establish a claim, or defence, must be pleaded. Facts should be limited to those necessary to understand the claim, or defence.

ii. Heading

A statement of case must have a heading.

In general, the name of the court should be in the top, left-hand corner. It should be capitalised, emboldened, and underlined.

The claim number should be in the top, right-hand corner. It should also be capitalised, emboldened, and underlined.

Underneath, on the left-hand side, '**BETWEEN:**' should appear.

Below this, the names of the parties should be capitalised, centralised, and emboldened.

A party's status should appear in the line underneath their name. This should be underlined, and aligned to the right-hand side.

'And' is used in civil cases. Criminal cases use 'v'.

Following the name of the parties, between horizontal tram lines, the form of the statement of case should be stated, capitalised, centralised, and emboldened.

For example: '**DEFENCE AND COUNTERCLAIM**'.

iii. Numbers & figures

Pages, paragraphs, and lists, should be numbered consecutively.

Numbers and dates must be expressed as figures.

iv. Authority & evidence

Statements of case *may* do any of the following (PD 16 at [13.3]).

First, refer to any point of law on which the claim, or defence, is based. Secondly, give the name of any witness who that party proposes to call. Thirdly, attach a copy of any document that that party considers necessary, or serve it with the statement of case.

v. Particularity

Statements of case are fundamental.

Often, they are too general, or too detailed.

Too general means failure to set out the material details of law and fact that are necessary for a claim, or defence, to succeed. Too detailed, repetitive and encumbered with unnecessary authority, however, and, at best, the court is likely to skim read it.

The art is in finding a balance.

Allegations must be particularised. For example, after a road traffic collision, an allegation of negligence should list the ways in which a party is alleged to have been negligent.

If it is claimed that the defendant was negligent in that she drove too fast for the road conditions, it should be pleaded.

vi. Contributory negligence

Where contributory negligence is alleged, often in a defence, or as an alternative in the particulars of claim, following a road traffic collision, it should be pleaded (PD 16 at [13.3(1)]).

This assists the court to further the overriding objective by actively managing cases. This issue will be identified early on.

There is no need to put a percentage on the alleged negligence.

If relied on in closing submissions, a percentage can be submitted. This will take into account any oral evidence. Usually, one-half, one / two-thirds, or one / two / three-quarters.

vii. Endorsement

If drafted by a legal representative, it should bear her signature.

If drafted by a legal representative as a member or employee of a firm, it should be signed in the name of that firm (PD 5A at [2.1]).

viii. Statement of truth

It must be verified by a statement of truth (CPR 22.1(1)(a)).

Where particulars of claim are not included in the claim form, they must be verified by a statement of truth (PD 16 at [3.4]).

a.1 Form

The form of the statement of truth is prescribed (PD 16 at [3.4]):

> [I believe / The claimant / The defendant believes] that the facts
> stated in [these particulars of claim / this defence (and counter-
> claim) / this reply to the defence and counterclaim] are true. [I
> understand / The claimant / The defendant understands] that
> proceedings for contempt of court may be brought against any-
> one who makes, or causes to be made, a false statement in a docu-
> ment verified by a statement of truth without an honest belief in
> its truth.

When signed by a party, the first sentence begins: 'I believe'. The
second sentence begins: 'I understand'.

When signed by a legal representative, the first sentence begins: 'The
claimant / The defendant believes'. The second sentence begins: 'The
claimant / The defendant understands'.

a.2 Who

It must be signed by one of the following (PD 22 at [3.1]).

First, a party, or her litigation friend. Secondly, the legal representative
of the party or litigation friend.

The full name of the individual who signs must be printed clearly be-
neath her signature (PD 22 at [3.9]).

Entering a name on an online form satisfies the requirement for a statement of truth to be signed (PD 7E at [10]).

a. Legal representative

Where a party is legally represented, the legal representative may sign the statement of truth on her client's behalf.

It will refer to *her client's* belief. She must state the capacity in which she is signing, and the name of her firm (PD 22 at [3.7]).

A legal representative *must* use her own name (PD 22 at [3.10]).

A legal representative's signature will be taken by the court as her confirmation of the following three circumstances (PD 22 at [3.8]).

First, her client has authorised her to do so.

Secondly, before signing, she explained to her client that, in signing the statement of truth, she would be confirming her client's belief that the facts stated are true.

Where necessary, explanation may be through an interpreter.

Thirdly, before signing, she informed her client of the possible consequences to her client if it subsequently appears that her client did not have an honest belief in the truth of those facts.

b. Companies & partnerships

A director, treasurer, secretary, chief executive, manager, or other officer, may sign (PD 22 at [3.5(1)]).

A partner, or a person having control or management of the partnership, may sign (PD 22 at [3.6]).

c. Insurers

An insurer may sign on behalf of a party where the insurer has a financial interest in the result of proceedings brought wholly, or partially, by, or against, that party (PD 22 at [3.6A]).

3. Default

If a party fails to verify her statement of case with a statement of truth, the *court* may act on its own initiative.

First, by striking it out (CPR 22.2(2)). Secondly, by making an unless order (CPR 3.3 and PD 40B at [8.1] and [8.2]). That is, unless the statement of case is verified by a statement of truth before a certain date, it will automatically be struck out.

A *party* may also make an application for the statement of case to be struck out (CPR 22.2(3)), or an unless order (PD 22 at [4.2]).

A party's statement of case *remains effective* until it is struck out, however, that party cannot rely on it as evidence of any of the matters set out within it (CPR 22.2(1) and PD 22 at [4.1]).

In practice, where a statement of case is not verified by a statement of truth, the court will make an unless order.

If the issue arises on the day of the final hearing, however, the court has two options. First, require the party to verify the statement of case before, or during, the hearing. Secondly, strike it out.

6. Claim form

There are two methods for commencing proceedings. In general, it depends on whether there is a *substantial dispute of fact*.

a. Substantial dispute of fact

In general, where there is no substantial dispute of fact, the *alternative* method of commencing proceedings may be used: CPR 8. Form N208 is the claim form.

In principle, there is nothing to stop a CPR 8 claim being allocated to the small claims track. In practice, however, it is uncommon.

Where there is a substantial dispute of fact, CPR 7 usually prescribes the procedure for starting a claim. Form N1 is used. Form N1A provides guidance.

To commence proceedings, a claim form is issued. This is sealed by the court with an official seal.

Unless there is an extension, the claim form must be served within four months of the date of issue (CPR 7.5).

b. Court

The name of the court should be on page one, in the top, right-hand corner. It is automatically completed when using Money Claim Online ("MCOL"). If not, it is 'County Court Money Claims Centre'.

i. Money Claim Online

MCOL is an internet-based service. It purports to be a convenient, simple and secure way of making, or responding to, a money claim.

The 'User Guide for Claimants' (December 2018) is available at https://assets.publishing.service.gov.uk/government/uploads/system/uploads/attachment_data/file/762843/mcol-userguide-eng.pdf.

ii. Online suitability

MCOL is suitable for three types of claim.

First, a fixed sum of money less than £100,000. Secondly, where there is no more than one claimant, and no more than two defendants. Thirdly, where the defendant's address for service is in England or Wales.

To use MCOL, you need the following.

First, a valid credit or debit card to pay court fees. Secondly, an address in the United Kingdom. Thirdly, an email address. Fourthly, regular internet access.

MCOL cannot be used in any of the following circumstances.

First, the claimant is under 18 years old. Secondly, the claimant is eligible for legal aid or help with fees. Thirdly, the claim is for compensation following personal injury.

Fourthly, the claimant has been prevented from making claims by the court because she is a "vexatious litigant". Fifthly, the claimant intends to issue a joint warrant of control against two defendants.

Sixthly, a defendant is a child under 18. Seventhly, a defendant is someone who lacks "mental capacity". Eighthly, a defendant is a government department or agency. Ninthly, a defendant is an individual or company as a result of a tribunal award. Tenthly, the claim relates to the tenancy deposit scheme.

c. Parties

The identity and capacity of the parties must be clear.

i. Individuals

For individuals, title, and full name, must be provided.

For a recent name change, '(formerly …)' should follow.

A protected party should include the name of her litigation friend. For example: 'Ms Sarah Smith (by Mrs Helen Smith, her litigation friend)'.

ii. Companies & partnerships

For a partnership, the name of the partnership, followed by '(a firm)' should be used. For example: 'Smith & Smith (a firm)'.

For sole traders, the title and full name of the individuals, followed by 'trading as …' should be used. For example: 'Ms Sarah Smith, trading as Smith's Bakery'.

Limited companies should include the word 'limited'.

To check whether a company has limited liability, search the website of 'Companies House' (beta.companieshouse.gov.uk). Company number, registered office address, and type (private or public limited company), are publicly available.

iii. Insurers

The European Communities (Rights against Insurers) Regulations 2002 (SI 2002/3061) allows claimants to bring proceedings arising out of road traffic collisions against the insurer of the defendant vehicle. This does not extinguish the right of the claimant to bring an action against the defendant.

d. Address

Postal addresses, including postcodes, must be used.

i. Individuals

For individuals, this is the *residential* address. Even with legal representation, a residential or business address must be provided.

ii. Businesses

For businesses, the *business* address can be used.

The *registered office* address of a limited company must be used. Companies House can be used to identify this.

e. Detail

Concise details of the claim always include the following.

First, the nature of the claim. Secondly, the remedy sought.

For example: 'The claimant claims damages and other losses arising from a road traffic collision on 24 October 2020 caused by the negligent driving of the defendant.'

Issues under the Human Rights Act 1998 are unlikely.

In principle, particulars of claim can be pleaded on page two of the claim form. In practice, they are usually attached as a separate document. If so, the words 'to follow' should be crossed out.

f. Value

There are three sets of rules.

i. Money

If claiming a fixed sum, this should be provided to the right of the box, entitled 'Amount claimed', in the bottom, right-hand corner.

Otherwise, under the heading 'Value', one of the following should be provided. First, 'not more than £10,000'. Secondly, 'more than £10,000 but not more than £25,000'.

When it is not possible to put a value on the claim, 'I cannot say how much I expect to recover' should be pleaded.

This is necessary for allocation. The small claims track is not the "normal" track for a claim with a value of more than £10,000.

ii. Personal injury

In a claim for personal injuries, the following must be provided: 'My claim includes a claim for personal injuries and the amount that I seek to recover as damages for pain, suffering and loss of amenity is'. This should be followed by one of the following.

First, 'not more than £1,000'. Secondly, 'more than £1,000.'

This is for allocation. The small claims track is not the "normal" track where a claim for personal injuries is more than £1,000.

iii. Housing disrepair

In a claim for not more than £5,000 in respect of housing disrepair to residential premises, the following must also be pleaded.

First: 'My claim includes a claim against my landlord for housing disrepair relating to residential premises. The cost of repairs or other work is not estimated to be'. Secondly, 'not more than £1,000', or 'more than £1,000'.

In a claim for unrelated damages, you must also plead: 'I expect to recover as damages'. This is followed by one of the following.

First, 'not more than £1,000'. Secondly, 'more than £1,000'.

This is necessary for allocation. The small claims track is not the "normal" track for a claim by a tenant of residential premises against a landlord where the cost of repairs, or other work, is estimated to be more than £1,000.

g. Interest

Interest must be particularised (CPR 16.4(2) and PD 16 at [3.7]).

Where a claim for interest is pursued at a final hearing, but that claim has not been pleaded, the following submissions are likely.

First, there has been a breach of a CPR, and PD. Secondly, the defendant has not had the opportunity to respond to the claim for interest in the defence. Thirdly, allowing the claim for interest will not further the overriding objective.

The parties are not on an equal footing as the defendant has been ambushed. The case has not been dealt with fairly. The court has not enforced compliance with rules and practice directions.

These factors weigh against an unparticularised claim for interest.

h. Preferred hearing centre

Contact details for county court hearing centres can be found at https://courttribunalfinder.service.gov.uk/search/.

i. Individual

Where the defendant is an individual, and the claim has not been sent to a county court hearing centre, the claim will be sent to the defendant's home court in two circumstances (PD 7E at [12.1]).

First, if the defendant applies to set aside, or vary, judgment. Secondly, if either party makes an application, which cannot be disposed of without a hearing.

ii. Not an individual

Where the defendant is not an individual, and either of the above circumstances apply, the claim will be sent to the county court hearing centre which serves the claimant's address for service.

This should be pleaded on the claim form (PD 7E at [12.2]).

iii. Transfer

If a defence is filed to all, or part of, the claim, and the parties have filed directions questionnaires, the proceedings will be transferred as follows (PD 7E at [12.3]).

Where the defendant is an individual, and the claim is for a specified sum, it will be transferred to the defendant's home court.

If a different preferred court is specified by the claimant or defendant in the respective directions questionnaires, the claim will be transferred to that court.

In the event of a conflict, the judge will decide. Otherwise, the claim will be transferred to the claimant's preferred court.

i. Address for service

The address for service of both parties must be provided.

i. Claimant

Where a claimant is represented, the address for service is that of the legal representative. This must be in the UK. It must include postal address and postcode. DX, fax, and email, may be provided.

Where an individual has conduct of a case for a company that is not represented, the business address of that person should be used. This is so that correspondence is received by that individual.

ii. Defendant

This is where the defendant is (last) known to live, or carry on business. The defendant can provide an address for service. This may be the name of her legal representative.

If the following apply, CPR 6.9 prescribes the rules for service.

First, the defendant is not represented. Secondly, the defendant has not otherwise stated her address for service.

j. Issue fee & costs

The issue fee and legal representative's costs should be inserted into the bottom, right-hand corner.

A legal representative's costs may only be claimed where one has been instructed. Appendix H shows the relevant amounts.

k. Remission

A claimant can apply for help with fees for a court hearing.

This is called "fee remission". Form EX160A provides detailed guidance. In summary, only individuals can apply.

For eligibility, a claimant must satisfy one of the following.

First, no savings, investments, or only a small amount of the same, and in receipt of certain benefits. Secondly, on a low income.

If successful, there will be no fee, or it will be reduced.

l. Issue

If using the County Court Money Claims Centre ("the CCMCC"), the postal address is PO Box 527, Salford M5 0BY.

The following should be posted to the CCMCC.

First, copies of the completed claim form. Secondly, the issue fee.

The number of copies depends on the number of defendants. If there is one defendant, then two copies should be posted. One for the court, and one for the defendant.

A copy of the claim form should be retained. This is so that the claimant has a copy.

There are three methods to pay a court fee.

First, cheque, addressed to 'HM Courts & Tribunals Service'. Secondly, telephone, calling General Public Enquiries on 0300 123 5577, requesting a call back from a member of court staff. Thirdly, for solicitors only, fee account.

The following applies in respect of the latter.

If posting, ensure that the Payment by Account ("PBA") number is clearly marked.

If emailing, ensure that it is marked as 'urgent'. The subject field should be marked 'Urgent – Hearing Fee Payment'. The PBA number should be clearly set out.

When in receipt of the issue fee, the court will "issue" the claim.

The claimant can elect to "serve" proceedings herself, however, generally the court will serve the defendant by First Class post.

m. County Court Money Claims Centre

The CCMCC is not open to the public visiting in person.

It can be contacted by telephone, or email.

For telephone, opening hours are Monday to Friday, 08:30 to 17:00. The telephone number is 0300 123 1372.

For enquiries, the email address is ccmcccustomerenquiries@justice.gov-.uk. For filing and records, the email address is ccmcce-filing@justice.gov.uk.

7. Particulars of claim

Not all statements of case are equal.

If a *defence* is struck out, the claim may still fail. If the *particulars of claim* ("particulars") are struck out, however, the claim cannot succeed. The burden is on the party bringing the claim.

a. Within claim form or separate document

Particulars may be within the claim form or a separate document.

Whether the form is paper or electronic, there is limited space.

There are rules for separate particulars (CPR 7.4(1) and (2)).

First, after service of the claim form, particulars must be served within 14 days. Secondly, they must be served no later than the latest time for serving the claim form. Thirdly, unless already filed, particulars must be filed within seven days of service.

The latter has two exceptions. Both relate to proceedings that have not been transferred, and where the claimant has not been ordered to file particulars (PDs 7C at [5.4(4)] and 7E at [6.4]).

Separate particulars must contain the following (PD 16 at [3.8]).

First, the name of the court in which the claim is proceeding. Secondly, the claim number. Thirdly, the title of proceedings. Fourthly, the claimant's address for service.

If not contained in, or served with, the claim form, the claim form must state that the particulars will follow (CPR 16.2(2)).

b. Contents

Particulars must contain the following (CPR 16.4).

First, a concise statement of the facts on which the claimant relies. Secondly, details of any interest claimed. Thirdly, 'other matters' that are set out in a PD. For example, personal injury claims.

c. Personal injury

The following *must* be pleaded (PD 16 at [4]).

First, the claimant's date of birth. Secondly, brief details of personal injury. Thirdly, that a schedule detailing claimed past and future expenses and losses is attached. Fourthly, where the evidence of a medical practitioner is relied on, it is attached to, or served with, the particulars.

d. Contract

Where based upon an agreement, the following must be pleaded.

i. Written

Written agreements require the following (PD 16 at [7.3]).

First, a copy of the contract, or documents constituting the agreement, should be attached to, or served with, the particulars. Secondly, the original(s) should be available at the hearing. Thirdly, any general conditions of sale incorporated into the contract should be attached. Where bulky, the relevant parts suffice.

ii. Oral

Oral agreements require the following (PD 16 at [7.4]).

First, the contractual words used. Secondly, by whom. Thirdly, to whom. Fourthly, when. Fifthly, where they were spoken.

iii. Conduct

Agreements by conduct require the following (PD 16 at [7.5]).

First, the conduct relied on. Secondly, by whom. Thirdly, when. Fourthly, where the acts constituting the conduct were done.

e. Statement of facts

In a claim following a road traffic collision, where there is no counter-claim, the defendant does not have to prove that the mechanism of the collision is pleaded in the defence.

The burden is for the claimant to prove, on a balance of probabilities, that the collision occurred as pleaded in the particulars.

If a defendant proves that the mechanism of the collision pleaded in the particulars is wrong, the claim should fail.

Accordingly, particulars can be particularly helpful to *defendants*. Especially if the claimant's evidence is inconsistent with what is pleaded in the particulars. Where this is the case, it will form the substance of closing submissions (see chapter 21(c)(iii)(2)).

f. Hire of a replacement vehicle

The following must be pleaded (PD 16 at [6.3]).

First, the need for the replacement vehicle at the relevant time. Secondly, the period (start and end dates) of hire claimed. Thirdly, the rate of hire. Fourthly, the reasonableness of the period, and the rate of hire. Fifthly, impecuniosity if the claim relates to credit hire.

In practice, the latter is usually the main issue in a claim for credit hire. It is often the difference between an award based on the credit hire, or the basic hire, rate.

Addressing impecuniosity in a witness statement is insufficient.

In *Zurich Insurance Plc v Umerji* [2014] EWCA Civ 357, [2014] RTR 23 at [37], Underhill LJ (with whom Robin Jacob and Moses LJJ agreed) said the following (with emphasis added):

> "... The correct analysis would appear to be as follows. A claim for the cost of hire of a replacement vehicle is, strictly, a claim for expenditure incurred in mitigation of the primary loss, namely the loss of use of the damaged vehicle ... *The burden is thus on the claimant to prove (and therefore plead) that such expenditure was reasonably incurred* ... But in this kind of case it is clearly right that a claimant who needs to rely on his impecuniousness in order to justify the amount of his claim should plead and prove it. ..."

g. Considerations following a road traffic collision

Many claims follow a road traffic collision.

Accordingly, potentially relevant considerations when drafting particulars in claims following a road traffic collision follow. Not every consideration will be relevant to every claim; different considerations will be relevant to different claims.

Particulars should plead only those facts that are necessary for the claim to succeed. Written evidence can set out the rest.

i. When, where & who

What was the date, time and location of the collision? Who (or what company) is responsible for each vehicle? Is the claim subrogated? That is, does an insurance company have a right to pursue a third party causing an insurance loss to the insured?

ii. Road layout

What was the name of the road, junction or island? How many lanes were there? Were there traffic lights? Signage? Road markings? Were the lanes on the roundabout clearly separated?

iii. Traffic

Light traffic? Gridlocked? What were the types of vehicles on the road? Personal cars only, heavy goods vehicles, or slow-moving tractors and farm machinery? Was this usual for the time of day?

iv. Weather

What were the weather conditions? Light or dark? Was there any street lighting? If so, was it on? Was it snowing, hailing or raining? Was the road wet? What was the visibility like?

v. Vehicles

What were the makes, models and vehicle registrations of the relevant vehicles? What direction(s) were they traveling in? Southeast, towards Reading, or in different directions?

vi. Speed

What was the speed limit? How fast were the relevant vehicles travelling? Were these speeds appropriate for the traffic, and weather, conditions? Was the claimant's vehicle stationary at the time of the collision? If so, was the engine off, and the handbrake on? If it was a manual transmission, was the gear stick in neutral?

vii. Proximity

Where were the relevant vehicles in relation to each other? Was the claimant's vehicle in front of, level with, or behind, the defendant's vehicle? How many metres behind the claimant's vehicle was the defendant's vehicle? If there were multiple lanes on the approach to a junction, which lane was the claimant in? Which lane was the defendant in?

viii. Perception

When did the claimant first see the defendant's vehicle before the collision (if at all)? When did the defendant first see the claimant's vehicle? Was a visual (hand) or audible (horn) signal used to notify the defendant of the claimant's vehicle?

ix. Objective intention

What were the parties' objective intentions? Were both vehicles indicating right? Was the claimant's vehicle positioned to the left of the lane, broadcasting an intention to turn left? Or, in the centre of the lane, presenting an intention to go straight on? What (if any) mirrors were checked before changing speed, or direction? Was the left blind spot checked for cyclists before turning left?

x. Subjective intention

Where was the claimant's destination? Was it to work? If so, was it a routine journey? Was the claimant familiar with the road layout? What about the traffic conditions for that time of day?

xi. Mechanism

What was the mechanism of collision? Was the claimant's vehicle hit by the defendant's vehicle when the latter was emerging from a side road? Was it a rear-end shunt? Was the claimant's vehicle parked? Was the collision in a car park, on a roundabout, or did it involve vehicles changing lanes? Was it a concertina collision? Did the defendant swerve into the claimant's lane?

xii. Mitigation

Was there time to take defensive action, so as to avoid the collision? Was it possible for the claimant to steer, brake, or sound the horn, so as to avoid the defendant's vehicle entirely, or at least warn the defendant of the claimant's presence? If not, why?

xiii. Damage

Where was the damage to the relevant vehicles? Modest scratch, moderate dent, or heavy impact? Was there damage to the tailgate of the claimant's vehicle, causing the bonnet of the defendant's vehicle to crumple severely? Is there an engineers' report commenting upon the damage? Is there an estimate for repair? Or just an invoice for the repairs? If so, does it particularise the repairs that were in fact undertaken?

h. Interest

The following *must* be pleaded to claim interest (CPR 16.4(2)).

Whether it is under the terms of a contract, another enactment, or on some other basis. If it is under another enactment, the name of it must be pleaded. If it is on some other basis, what is it?

A claim for a specified amount of money requires the following.

First, the percentage rate at which interest is claimed. Secondly, the date from which it is claimed. Thirdly, the date to which it is calculated. This must be no later than the date on which the claim form is issued. Fourthly, the total amount of interest claimed to the date of calculation. Fifthly, after that date, the daily rate that interest accrues.

i. Contractual

An agreed contractual term for interest should be pleaded.

In *Chaplair Ltd v Kumari* [2015] EWCA Civ 798, [2015] HLR 39, it was held that a county court judge could make an award of costs in favour of a landlord in a claim for rent arrears. The terms of the lease allowed recovery of the costs of legal proceedings.

Where a party has a contractual right to costs, she is not restricted to fixed costs. That is, provided that there has been no conduct on behalf of that party disentitling her to the exercise by the court of its discretion in accordance with that entitlement.

The same principle applies to a contractual entitlement to interest.

ii. Statutory

There are two relevant statutory provisions.

A contractually agreed rate of interest is likely to be greater. In a business-to-business contract, a term for interest is implied.

1. County Courts Act 1984

Section 69 of this Act provides the court with a *discretion* whether to make an award. It reflects the fact that a claimant has been denied use of a sum that the court has found due.

The *rate* and *period* that interest accrues is also discretionary. The annual rate of eight percent is often claimed. In practice, two percent is often awarded.

Interest is not recoverable in respect of credit hire charges that have not been paid (*Pattni v First Leicester Buses Ltd* [2011] EWCA Civ 1384, [2012] RTR 17 at [70]).

2. Late Payment of Commercial Debts (Interest) Act 1998

This Act implies three terms into business-to-business contracts.

First, *at least* eight percent interest a year on the price of goods or services. Secondly, a fixed sum is payable. Thirdly, reasonable costs of recovering the debt are payable.

The first implied term is for *simple* interest. It is at a fixed rate. This is set twice a year by adding eight percent to the Bank of England's official base / bank rate.

This can be found at https://www.bankofengland.co.uk/monetary-policy/the-interest-rate-bank-rate.

The rate that was current when interest started to run is claimable. This depends on when the contract was made. Interest ceases on payment of the principal sum.

For a debt below £1,000, the fixed sum is £40. For a debt of at least £1,000, but less than £10,000, the fixed sum is £70. For a debt of £10,000 or more, the fixed sum is £100.

Reasonable costs of recovering a debt are likely to include instructing a legal representative, and pre-action costs.

iii. Personal injury

Where general damages are awarded in claims following personal injury, interest is awarded at two percent from the date of service of the claim form (*Birkett v Hayes* [1982] 1 WLR 816 (CA)).

8. Defence (& counterclaim)

To defend against a claim started using the procedure in CPR 7, a defence *must* be filed and served (CPRs 15.1, 15.2 and 15.6).

The time limit is either, within 14 days of service of the particulars of claim, or 28 days if the defendant has acknowledged service.

a. Response

A defence *must* respond to each allegation in the particulars of claim. There are three responses (CPR 16.5(1)).

First, denied. Secondly, unable to admit or deny, but which the claimant must prove. Thirdly, admitted.

There are two rules relating to denied allegations (CPR 16.5(2)).

First, reasons must be pleaded. Secondly, if a defendant has a different version of events to that set out in the particulars of claim, the defendant's version must be pleaded.

Where a specific allegation has not been dealt with, but the nature of the defence in relation to that allegation has been pleaded, the court will require the claimant to prove the allegation.

The court will take any allegation relating to an amount of money that is claimed to be proved, unless it is expressly admitted.

Subject to this, the court will take any allegation that is not dealt with in a defence to be admitted (CPR 16.5(3), (4) and (5)).

Admitted facts do not need to be proved. Authority and evidence supporting them is irrelevant. The court will not consider them.

b. Address for service

If two conditions are satisfied, the defendant *must* provide an address for service in the defence (PD 16 at [10.4] and [10.5]).

First, the defendant is an individual. Secondly, the claim form does not contain an address at which she resides, carries on business, or contains an incorrect address.

Where the defendant's address for service is not where she resides, or carries on business, an address at which she does in fact reside, or carries on business, *must* still be provided.

c. Individuals

Where a defendant to a claim, or claimant to a counterclaim, is an individual, she must provide her date of birth (if known) in the acknowledgment of service, admission, defence (and counterclaim), reply, or other response (PD 16 at [10.7]).

d. Counterclaim

A counterclaim is a separate claim.

CPRs and PDs for particulars of claim apply (see chapter 7).

Where there is a defence to the claimant's claim, and a counterclaim against the claimant, the statement of case is known as a "defence and counterclaim".

A counterclaim should follow the defence. If the facts pleaded in the defence are relied on in the counterclaim, this can be succinctly stated in a single sentence. In practice, this is usual.

Where a counterclaim is filed with the defence, the court's permission is not required (CPR 20.4(2)(a)).

Issuing a counterclaim will attract an issue fee. This is based on the amount claimed in the counterclaim (see appendix F).

To defend against a counterclaim, the claimant *must* file and serve a defence to the counterclaim (CPRs 15.2, 15.6 and 20.2).

9. Reply to the defence (& counterclaim)

Reply to a defence is optional. Defence to a counterclaim is not.

Where a counterclaim is not defended, the defendant may request that default judgment is entered on the counterclaim.

a. Reply

There are two rules (CPR 15.8).

First, any reply to the defence *must* be filed with the claimant's directions questionnaire. Secondly, it *must* be served on all other parties at the same time.

The deadline is no less than 14 days after service of the provisional allocation notice (CPR 26.3(6)(b)(i)). This is form N149A.

b. Defence

There *must* be a defence to a counterclaim to defend against it.

CPRs and PDs relating to defences apply (see chapter 8).

Where there is a reply to a defence, and a defence to a counterclaim, the statement of case is known as a "reply to the defence and counterclaim".

A party's statements of case must not be incompatible.

For example, particulars of claim that are irreconcilable with a reply to the defence. To this extent, they risk being struck out.

10. Directions questionnaires

The *court* must further the overriding objective by actively managing cases. This includes three considerations (CPR 1.4(2)).

First, appropriately encouraging the parties to use alternative dispute resolution. Secondly, fixing timetables, or otherwise controlling the progress of the case. Thirdly, giving directions to ensure that the final hearing proceeds quickly and efficiently.

The *parties* are under a duty to help the court to further the overriding objective. This includes ensuring that the case is dealt with expeditiously and fairly (CPR 1.1(2)).

This is why directions questionnaires ("questionnaires") are vital.

a. Notice of proposed allocation

If a defence is filed, the court will do two things (CPR 26.3(1)(a)).

First, provisionally decide the track which appears to be most suitable for the claim. Secondly, serve on each party a notice of proposed allocation. This is Form N149A.

This notice will do four things (CPR 26.3(1)(b)).

First, specify any matter to be complied with by the date prescribed in the notice. Secondly, require the parties to file completed questionnaires, and serve copies on all other parties.

Thirdly, state the address of the court office to which the questionnaire must be returned. Fourthly, inform the parties how to obtain the questionnaire.

b. Filing

The questionnaire is Form N180. It will *always* be served by the court on an unrepresented party (CPR 26.3(1B)).

The questionnaire should be returned by the date in the notice of allocation. It cannot be extended by agreement (CPR 26.3(6A)).

The name of the court to which the questionnaire must be returned may be different from that in which the claim was issued.

Ensure that the questionnaire is returned to the correct court.

c. Default

If a party fails to comply with the notice of proposed allocation by the specified date, the court will serve a further notice on that party. They will be required to comply within seven days.

If the party *still* fails to comply, that party's statement of case will be struck out, *without* further order of the court (CPR 26.3(7A)).

If a *claimant* fails to file a questionnaire, the court may strike out her claim. Where the *defendant* is in default, judgment may be entered against her (PD 26 at [2.5(3)]).

A party who was in default will not normally be entitled to an order for the costs of any application to set aside or vary that order, or the costs of attending a case management conference.

Unless the court considers that it is *unjust*, she *will* be ordered to pay any costs caused to any other party (CPR 26.3(10)).

d. Informing the court

The parties *must* let the court know immediately if there is no need for a final hearing. In practice, this will be due to settlement.

Both parties are under the same duty to help the court to allocate an appropriate share of the court's resources to the case, while taking into account the need to allot resources to other cases.

Every effort should be made to settle.

Both parties are under a duty to consider whether the dispute can be settled without a hearing. This can be achieved by the parties having a discussion directly, negotiation between the legal representatives, or mediation.

e. Small Claims Mediation Service

Mediation is a *confidential* process. It gives the *parties* control over any agreement. Settlement may be *facilitated*.

i. Features

A mediator may be able to assist with what the law says in a particular circumstance. This will be from a neutral perspective. It will be dispassionate. She will have no interest in any agreement.

Offers can be made without influencing what will happen if the claim is subsequently disposed of by the court.

This enables the parties to attempt to reach an agreement, *without* compromising their positions, should the claim continue to a final hearing. Positions are reserved in absence of agreement.

If an agreement is reached, reduced to writing, and signed, it is binding like any other contract.

The terms of any agreement may be inserted into a "Tomlin" order. This is enforceable by the court. Remedy exists for breach.

As a mediated settlement is *voluntary*, however, freely agreed terms of settlement are usually honoured. There is seldom a need to enforce a freely-negotiated agreement in the courts.

Accordingly, the confidential, free and voluntary, Small Claims Mediation Service, merits careful consideration. It is one a number of forums that can be explored without prejudice.

It is also *convenient*. A suitable time for both parties is agreed. The process is usually carried out over the telephone in under an hour.

It is also usually quicker than waiting for a final hearing.

This will likely be exacerbated by the COVID-19 pandemic. In person hearings to dispose of claims became the *exception* to the rule from the second quarter of 2020. Remote, telephone and audio-visual, hearings, are in the ascendancy.

The pandemic is also likely to have caused a substantial backlog of cases to be listed for final, in-person hearings.

ii. Procedure

The parties have to agree before the case may be referred. This is why section A1 of the questionnaire is so important.

It asks whether a party agrees to the claim being referred. If all parties agree to mediation, their contact details will be passed on.

The parties will be contacted. A mutually convenient appointment will then be arranged by the Small Claims Mediation Service.

Contact will be made within normal working hours. Monday to Friday, from 09:00 to 17:00. This excludes bank holidays.

f. Stay

Upon request of the parties, the court will "stay" proceedings for one month and notify the parties (CPR 26.4(2)).

The court can extend the stay until such date, or for such specified period, as the court considers appropriate (CPR 26.4(3)).

The *claimant* must inform the court of settlement (CPR 26.4(4)).

Otherwise, if the end of the period of the stay has been reached, the court will give such directions as to the management of the case as the court considers appropriate (CPR 26.4(5)).

g. Track

The questionnaire asks if the small claims track is appropriate.

This is the opportunity to give reasons why it is not, if that is the case. In so far as they apply, the matters that are relevant to allocating a claim to a track should be addressed (see chapter 11(b)).

h. Hearing centre

The hearing centre closest to the party who is completing the questionnaire is likely to be the preferred venue.

Where a party has a registered disability, childcare commitments, or acts as a carer, this is a good reason to justify the claim being heard in the hearing centre that is nearest to that party.

If a claimant files a request for judgment in the county court, which includes an amount of money to be decided by the court in accordance with the procedure for obtaining default judgment, the claim will be sent to the preferred hearing centre (CPR 12.5A(1)).

In certain circumstances, defended cases may be sent from one hearing centre, or court office, to another (CPR 26.1(1)(a1)).

Money claims may be transferred within the court (CPR 26.2A).

i. Experts

In claims following a road traffic collision, there is an increasing number of claims that, although the vehicle has been repaired, there is also diminution in the market value of the vehicle.

The evidence relied on is often in the form of a (main) report, or a number of (subsidiary) reports that are appended to the main report. The main report expresses that there is diminution in value.

Frequently, there is a similar statement to that required for expert reports. That is, the person who is offering her opinion is aware of her duty to the court.

If so, the importance of section D2 of the questionnaire is second only to the notice of allocation.

Where there is no request to rely on expert evidence by a party in her questionnaire, and the court has not given permission, there is a robust argument that expert evidence should not be allowed.

The party has not discharged her duty to help the court to further the overriding objective. This is because the court has been unable to actively case manage. This includes giving directions to ensure that the final hearing proceeds quickly and efficiently.

The allocation questionnaire provides that: 'It will be used to assist the court in the management of the claim.' If it has not been accurately completed, the court has not been assisted.

'The small claims track in the civil courts' (Form EX306) provides:

> If you want to use an expert, you need the court's permission. Because of this, you should say so in the directions questionnaire. You must say what the expert's evidence will deal with and whether you would like the expert to give evidence in a written report, by speaking at the hearing, or both.

This guidance will not have been followed.

Opportunities to further the overriding objective were missed.

First, to consider at an early stage whether the likely benefits of granting permission justify the cost. Secondly, to deal with this on the same occasion as making directions for the final hearing.

The notice of allocation is likely to include the following:

> If a party is aware of a reason why this estimate might be substantially inaccurate, that party must notify the court immediately.
> …
> No party may rely at the hearing on any report from an expert unless express permission has been granted by the court beforehand. Anyone wishing to rely on an expert must write to the court immediately on receipt of this Order and seek permission, giving an explanation why the assistance of an expert is necessary.
> …
> Because this Order has been made without a hearing, the parties have the right to apply to have the Order set aside, varied or stayed. A party making such an application must send or deliver the application to the court (together with any appropriate fee) to arrive within seven days of service of this Order.

All three directions have been breached.

An oral application was not contemplated when the time estimate for the hearing was made. This is a reason that the time estimate might be substantially inaccurate. Yet, that applicant did not notify the court immediately, or in fact at all.

A written application for permission to rely on an expert has not been made, immediately on receipt of the order, or in fact at all.

A written application to set aside or vary the order in relation to expert evidence has not been made within seven days of service of the order, or in fact at all. No application fee has been paid.

Furthering the overriding objective includes enforcing compliance with rules and court orders. In particular: the rule prescribing the duty of the parties to help the court to further the overriding objective; and the court order set out above, so as to ensure that the case is dealt with expeditiously and fairly.

j. Witnesses

How many witnesses will attend the final hearing?

This enables the court to allocate the claim. If oral evidence is likely to take more than a day, it will not normally be allocated to the small claims track.

Having done so, a time estimate for the final hearing can be made. When a witness, or an expert, will be unavailable over the following six months, this should be set out. It may be due to professional, or personal, commitments. For example, a holiday.

k. Interpreters

If a party or a witness requires an interpreter, the relevant box at section D4 should be ticked. The *type* should also be stated.

Otherwise, if the matter proceeds to a final hearing, the witness cannot sufficiently understand English, there is only one witness statement in English, and there is no interpreter, the court is much more likely to strike out that witness' evidence.

In some circumstances, the court will arrange, and meet the cost of, an interpreter. In general, however, cases that do not involve possession of property, or committal, do not qualify for legal aid.

In any event, three conditions must be satisfied.

First, inability to pay for an interpreter. Secondly, ineligibility for legal aid. Thirdly, lack of friends or family who can interpret.

Those who can only follow proceedings with a Welsh interpreter, however, are entitled to one.

If a party *subsequently* becomes aware of the need for an interpreter, the court, and the other party, should both be notified *immediately*. This is likely substantially to affect the time estimate of the final hearing. Usually, there is a direction ordering the parties to notify the court immediately where this is the case.

l. Signature

The questionnaire must be signed by the party, legal representative, or litigation friend.

m. Further information

The court may order a party to provide further information if the court considers that it is appropriate (CPR 27.2(3)).

In practice, this power is typically used where a statement of case is unclear. The court may go further. It may in fact strike it out.

For example, where a statement of case is *so* incoherent that it makes no sense; or, if there *is* a coherent set of facts, *even* where those facts are true, they do not disclose any legally recognisable claim, or defence (PD 3A at [1.4]).

The court will usually be hesitant, however, before deciding to exercise this draconian power. Using it effectively extinguishes a claim, or defence. This should be a last resort.

n. Other directions

A *party* may invite the court to make a direction (PD 27 at [2.4]).

The best place to do so is in the questionnaire.

The *court* also has a general power to make directions (CPR 27.7).

For example, there is no photograph, or sketch plan, of the location of a road traffic collision. The court may then make an order for further information, such as: 'Parties must agree and file a clear and legible plan, together with pictures, of the accident location, at least seven days before the final hearing.'

11. Allocation

In general, a claim will be allocated to a track when all parties have filed their directions questionnaires (CPR 26.5(1)(a)).

This will be with the benefit of the competing statements of case, and the completed directions questionnaires.

Once allocated, the case will be stayed for settlement discussions, mediation, or the court will give directions for the final hearing.

a. Generally suitable

The following are 'generally suitable' (PD 26 at [8.1(1)(c)]).

First, consumer disputes. Secondly, accident claims. Thirdly, disputes about the ownership of goods. Fourthly, most landlord and tenant disputes, other than opposed claims under CPR 56, disputed claims for possession under CPR 55, and demotion claims.

A disputed allegation of dishonesty will usually mean that the case is unsuitable for the small claims track (PD 26 at [8.1(1)(d)]).

b. Relevant matters

In general, the small claims track is the "normal" track for a claim with a value of not more than £10,000 (CPR 26.6(1) and (3)).

To decide whether to allocate to the normal track, the court 'will also have regard to' (CPR 26.7(1)) the following (CPR 26.8(1)).

First, financial value (if any) of the claim. Secondly, nature of the remedy sought. Thirdly, likely complexity of the facts, law or evidence.

Fourthly, number of (likely) parties. Fifthly, value of any counterclaim, or other Part 20 claim, and the complexity of it.

Sixthly, amount of oral evidence which may be required. Seventhly, importance of the claim to non-parties. Eighthly, views expressed by the parties. Ninthly, circumstances of the parties.

This list is not exhaustive. Neither is it hierarchical.

i. Financial value

It is for the *court* to assess the financial value of a claim.

The following will be disregarded (CPR 26.8(2)).

First, any amount not in dispute. Secondly, any claim for interest. Thirdly, costs. Fourthly, allegations of contributory negligence.

1. Amount in dispute

The following are amounts that are *not* in dispute (PD 26 at [7.4]).

First, an amount in respect of which the defendant admits liability. Secondly, a sum in respect of an item forming part of a claim for which judgment has been entered.

Thirdly, a specific sum claimed as a distinct item, and which the defendant admits that she is liable to pay. Fourthly, a sum offered by the defendant, which has been accepted by the claimant, in satisfaction of any item which forms a distinct part of the claim.

A claim with a financial value of more than £10,000 *may* be allocated to the small claims track (PD 26 at [8.1(2)]).

2. Admissions

If an admission is made before allocation, reducing the amount in dispute to a figure of not more than £10,000, the normal track is the small claims track (PD 26 at [7.4(4)]).

a. Unequivocal

In *Pervez Akhtar v Jordan Boland* [2014] EWCA Civ 872, [2015] 1 All ER 644, Sir Stanley Burnton (with whom Gloster and Floyd LJJ agreed) said (with emphasis added) that:

> "[16]   Where an allegation made by one party in proceedings is admitted by the other party in *unqualified* terms, that other party must not, seek to adduce evidence or raise arguments to the effect that that admission is not binding on him. *The court has no jurisdiction to investigate a fact that has been admitted,* unless the party making the admission obtains the permission of the court under CPR 14.1(5) to withdraw the admission and does so.
>
> [17]   This principle applies even more strongly to a judgment for all or part of a claim. Neither party may adduce evidence or make submissions that if accepted would lead to decisions or findings inconsistent with the judgment, unless there is a successful application to set the judgment aside.
>
> [18]   Where a defendant admits part, and not the whole, of an unliquidated damages claim, the claimant is entitled to seek judgment on that admission, and to pursue the proceedings and seek and obtain judgment for the balance. ..."

For example, in a claim for £12,000, the defendant unequivocally admits that the claimant is entitled to judgment for £5,000, so that the only *amount in dispute* is the balance of £7,000.

This may be allocated to the small claims track for three reasons.

First, the amount in dispute is not more than £10,000. Secondly, the court disregards any amount not in dispute (CPR 26.8(2)(a)). Thirdly, in any event, a claim of more than £10,000 may still be allocated to the small claims track (PD 26 at [8.1(2)]).

b. Equivocal

Where an admission is merely *equivocal*, or inconsistent with other allegations, there should be a request for clarification.

In the first instance, a *party* may do so informally, in writing. A party may also invite the court to make a direction (PD 27 at [2.4]).

The *court* may also order a party to provide further information, if the court considers that it is appropriate (CPR 27.2(3)).

3. None

A claim without financial value will be allocated to the 'most suitable' track. The following matters are relevant (CPR 26.7(2)).

ii. Remedy

For example, a claim for personal injuries, where the value of the claim is not more than £10,000, but the value of the claim for damages for personal injuries is more than £1,000, should not be allocated to the small claims track (CPR 26.6(1)(a)(ii)).

The remedy means that small claims is not the normal track.

The court may grant any final remedy that the court could grant if the claim were allocated to the fast track, or the multi-track (CPR 27.3). The court has jurisdiction to grant the following.

First, injunctions. Secondly, declarations. Thirdly, damages and interest of any amount. Fourthly, possession. Fifthly, restitution. Sixthly, specific performance.

iii. Factual, legal or evidential complexity

Complex facts, law or evidence may mean that the fast track is the normal track. The following will be determinative (CPR 26.6(5)).

First, whether the final hearing is likely to last no longer than a day. Secondly, whether oral evidence is limited to one expert per party in relation to any expert field. Thirdly, whether expert evidence is limited to two fields.

If the answers to all of the above are 'yes', the fast track is the normal track. If not, it is the multi-track.

iv. Counterclaim / Part 20 claim

Where the case involves more than one money claim, the court will not generally add the value of the claims together.

There may be a claim, counterclaim, and Part 20 claim. Generally, the largest will determine the financial value (PD 26 at [7.7]).

v. Oral evidence

The court will not normally allocate a claim to the small claims track if it is likely to last more than a day (PD 26 at [8.1(2)]).

vi. Party view

This is 'an important factor'. It is not decisive (PD 26 at [7.5]).

Even if it is not the normal track, the parties may agree that the case should be allocated to the small claims track.

In practice, this is common due to fixed, modest costs.

c. Pre-allocation hearing

Where a hearing takes place before allocation, the court may treat that hearing as an allocation hearing (PD 26 at [2.4(1)]).

For example, an application for summary judgment.

Otherwise, an allocation hearing will only be held on the court's own initiative if it considers that it is *necessary* (PD 26 at [6.1]).

If so, the parties will have at least seven days' notice of the hearing. This will be in Form N153. It will contain a brief explanation of the decision to order an allocation hearing (PD 26 at [6.2]).

Failure to attend may lead to an order that that party pays the costs of the party who did attend.

Failure to pay these costs within the time limit may lead to that party's statement of case being struck out (PD 26 at [6.6(3)]).

d. Challenging

A party who is dissatisfied with an order allocating the claim to a track may challenge it in one of two ways (PD 26 at [11.1(1)]).

First, appeal. Secondly, application for re-allocation.

If made at a hearing, and that party was present, represented, or gave notice that she would not attend, she should appeal.

In any other case, she should apply to re-allocate the claim.

The court may re-allocate after a change of circumstances. This will be pursuant to one of the following (PD 26 at [11.2]).

First, a party's application. Secondly, the court's own initiative.

e. Standard directions

"Standard directions" includes the following (CPR 27.4(3)(a)).

First, 'a direction that each party shall, at least 14 days before the date fixed for the final hearing, file and serve on every other party copies of all documents (including any expert's report) on which he intends to rely at the hearing'.

Secondly, any other standard directions set out in PD 27.

In practice, standard directions are made with two exceptions.

First, where the case has been stayed. Secondly, where the judge specifies other directions.

Standard directions are in PD 27 at Appendix B. See appendix D.

f. Witness statements

The court *must* have regard to five circumstances when deciding whether to order exchange of witness statements (PD 27 at [2.5]).

First, whether either, or both, parties are represented. Secondly, the amount in dispute. Thirdly, the nature of the matters in dispute. Fourthly, whether the need for any party to clarify her case can better be dealt with by an order requiring her to give further information. Fifthly, the need for the parties to have access to justice, without undue formality, cost or delay.

CPR 32 (the rules of evidence) does not apply (CPR 27.2(c)). The sole exception is the rule permitting the court to control evidence.

In other words, the rules prescribing form of, and consequences of failure to serve, witness statements, do not apply.

The separate rule, enabling the court to direct a witness statement that has not been verified by a statement of truth shall not be admissible as evidence, is not disapplied (CPRs 27.2(2) and 22.3).

In practice, where the notice of allocation provides for witness statements, it usually includes the following direction:

> Witness statements must:
>
> a)   Start with the name of the case and the claim number;
> b)   State the full name and address of the witness;
> c)   Set out the witness' evidence clearly in numbered paragraphs on numbered pages;
> d)   End with this paragraph: 'I believe that the facts stated in this witness statement are true. I understand that proceedings for contempt of court may be brought against anyone who makes, or causes to be made, a false statement in a document verified by a statement of truth without an honest belief in its truth.'

g. Experts

An expert may not give evidence at a hearing, whether written or oral, without permission of the court (CPR 27.5).

The court is under a duty to restrict expert evidence to that which is reasonably required to resolve the proceedings (CPR 35.1).

Where required, in practice, the court usually directs that evidence is to be given by a single joint expert (CPR 35.7).

Form, content and duties are *not* prescribed by CPR 35 (the rules relating to experts). There are two exceptions (CPR 27.2(1)(e)).

First, the overriding duty is to the court (CPR 35.3). Secondly, the rules relating to instructions to a single joint expert (CPR 35.8).

The amount that a party may be ordered to pay for experts' fees is a sum not exceeding £750 for each expert (PD 27 at [7.3(2)]).

h. Special directions

"Special directions" means 'directions given in addition to or instead of standard directions' (CPR 27.4(3)(b)).

The information and documentation usually required for certain types of claim in PD 27 at Appendix A is informative.

Special directions are in PD 27 at Appendix C. See appendix D.

No later than 28 days after giving special directions, the court may consider what further directions are to be given (CPR 27.4(1)(c)).

In practice, the court will do one of the following.

First, vary standard directions. Secondly, add special directions, and order a final hearing. Thirdly, order a preliminary hearing.

i. Preliminary hearing

A preliminary hearing may be ordered (CPR 27.6(1)).

When deciding whether or not to hold one, the court *must* have regard to the desirability of limiting the expense to the parties of attending court (CPR 27.6(2)).

The parties must be given at least 14 days' notice (CPR 27.6(3)).

They may only be held in three circumstances (CPR 27.6(1)).

First, special directions are needed to ensure a fair hearing, and it appears necessary for a party to attend a hearing, so as to ensure that she understands what she must do to comply.

Secondly, to dispose of the claim, on the basis that a party has no real prospect of success.

Thirdly, to enable a statement of case, or part thereof, to be struck out, on the basis that it discloses no reasonable grounds for bringing, or defending, the claim.

If all parties agree, it may also be the *final* hearing (CPR 27.6(4)).

Otherwise, at, or after, a preliminary hearing, the court will do the following (CPR 27.6(5)).

First, fix the date of the final hearing (if the court has not done so already), and give the parties at least 21 days' notice of the same, unless they accept less notice. Secondly, inform the parties of the amount of time allowed for the final hearing. Thirdly, give any other appropriate directions.

j. Hearing fee

When a claim is allocated, a hearing / trial fee becomes payable.

Usually, it must be paid 28 days before the hearing.

If the action does not proceed on the *claim*, but merely on the *counter-claim*, the hearing fee is payable by the *defendant*.

See appendix G for hearing fees.

In practice, the notice of allocation usually contains the following:

> Unless the claimant does by 4.00pm on the [**date**] [**month**] [**year**] pay to the court the trial fee of £[amount] or file a properly completed application (i.e. one which provides all the required information in the manner requested) for help with fees, then the claim will be **struck out with effect from [date] [month] [year] without further order and, unless the court orders otherwise, you will also be liable for the costs which the defendant has incurred.**
>
> ...
>
> The trial fee is **non-refundable**. If the parties settle before the trial fee is due, the trial fee will not be payable. If a consent order settling the matter is requested after the trial fee has been paid, the consent order fee will still be payable.
>
> **Please note, unless you apply for help with fees, there will be no further correspondence from the court office regarding payment of the fee or warnings as to the consequences of non-payment.**

k. Disposal without a hearing

The court may dispose of the claim without a hearing. This requires the agreement of all parties (CPR 27.10).

The court may still order a final hearing, however, even when the parties agree to disposal without a hearing.

12. Preparation

Everyone prepares in their own way.

The following are merely suggestions. With experience, rituals of preparation often mature with the consequent benefit of increasing time-efficiency, and effectiveness.

There are some rules, however, to prepare for a final hearing.

First, promptly check that you have all of the documents. Secondly, have a spare, unmarked copy of the documents. Thirdly, consider the relevant information and documentation checklist.

a. Contact

The initial contact is likely to be a professional client contacting a barristers' chambers. They will try to book counsel. The professional client will speak to a "clerk" or "practice manager".

Sometimes, professional clients know who they want. On other occasions, they want a recommendation. If so, practice managers put forward counsel who are able to accept instructions.

If the names are not known to the professional client, an online search will likely follow. A selection will then be made.

This is one reason to keep online, professional profiles up to date, including: areas of practice; recent instructions; publications; training and seminars.

The practice manager will request that the professional client send whatever documents there are, agree a fee, and enter the case into the selected barrister's professional diary.

The documents, often sent by email, may be printed off by the practice manager, and left in the barrister's pigeon-hole.

Increasingly, however, an electronic copy of the documents is forwarded via email by the practice manager to the barrister.

Counsel is notified. She can then scan the papers.

b. Scan

Upon receipt of the documents, scan them. Promptly.

Those instructing should be put on notice of the following.

First, a document appears to be missing, or otherwise unreadable. Secondly, there appears to be a material breach of a CPR, PD or court order. Thirdly, it becomes apparent that an application is necessary or desirable.

Your professional client should then be able to act promptly.

The documents should contain the following.

First, written instructions. Secondly, statements of case. Thirdly, evidence. Fourthly, court orders. Fifthly, relevant correspondence, including pre-action, evidence of filing and service, offers of settlement, and interim payments.

Instructions will state the documents that should be attached. Ensure that they are, in fact, attached.

Often, a joint bundle has not been agreed. If so, the claimant's documents will be separate to those of the defendant.

Ensure that you have both parties' documents.

i. Instructions

It is *always* preferable to have *written* instructions.

Professional clients will often have drafted statements of case, and correspondence with witnesses. They will likely have a view on the issues, merits, and compliance with CPRs, PDs and orders.

Without written instructions, a telephone call should be made to the professional client. Oral instructions can then be taken. These can be confirmed in writing via email to the professional client.

This may begin: 'Further to our telephone conversation this afternoon, just to put in writing your instructions …'.

Written instructions are often in a similar format.

First, enclosed documents. Secondly, name of your professional client, their firm, and the name of the other party's legal representatives (if they are represented). Thirdly, material facts of the case.

Fourthly, issues in dispute. Fifthly, evidence. Sixthly, agreements to extend a time limit. Seventhly, any authority that is relied on, including (ideally) the neutral citation, where it is found in the law reports, and the relevant paragraph(s).

Eighthly, costs claimed. Ninthly, interim payments. Tenthly, name, email address, and telephone number of your professional client.

1. Enclosures

The documents enclosed with your instructions are likely to include a joint bundle for the final hearing (if there is one).

Otherwise, there may be two bundles, or just a collection of documents on which the parties seek to rely.

Although your professional client may have provided you with a pagin-ated bundle of documents, it may not have been filed with the court, and served on the other side. If so, you will not be able to rely on the page numbers in your bundle during the hearing. The court and the other party will not have the same pagination.

Relevant correspondence should also be enclosed. This includes offers, and agreements to extend the time for filing and service.

2. Clients

Instructions should confirm the following.

First, the name of the party who you are representing. Secondly, whether the hearing is preliminary, disposal, or final. Thirdly, the name of the court. Fourthly, the date and time of the listing. Fifthly, the way in which the hearing will take place. For example, in person, telephone, or audio-visual. Sixthly, the time estimate.

The listing time may be differ in your instructions, the notice of alloca-tion, and the listing. The notice of allocation is authoritative.

The notice of hearing should specify whether it is in person, or remote. If remote, it should also state whether it is telephone or audio-visual, and the software. For example, BT MeetMe or CVP.

Final hearing time estimates range from an hour to a day. Most prelim-inary or "disposal" hearings are no longer than half an hour.

If the time estimate appears to be substantially inaccurate, advise your professional client. She can then notify the other party, and the court. It may be necessary or desirable to make an application for relief from sanctions following breach of an unless order.

3. Facts

For example: 'The claim arises out of a road traffic collision which took place on 15 September 2020'.

It should be clear whether or not there is a *counter*claim. In any event, check the defence. If there is a counterclaim, there should also be a defence (and reply) to the counterclaim.

Is liability, quantum, or both in dispute?

In a claim following a road traffic collision, duty of care and breach may be admitted, but causation denied. Or, liability (including causation) may be admitted, but quantum is denied.

Alternatively, one head of loss may be admitted (such as a claim for repairs). Another (such as credit hire) may be disputed.

Quantum may even be agreed, subject to liability. If so, ensure that you have a breakdown of the agreed sums for each head of loss.

How many witnesses will give evidence?

For example, the defendant may not have a witness in a claim for credit hire where liability is admitted. If the claimant has filed and served *two* witness statements, but the directions questionnaire provides that the claimant proposes to rely on *one* witness, the time estimate for the hearing may be substantially inaccurate.

Finally, is interest claimed? If so, at what rate, and for what period?

Eight percent is often claimed on special damages. Two percent is usually awarded (see chapter 7(g)(ii)(1)).

4. Issues

There is often a difference between the issues that are apparent from the competing statements of case, and the issues that you are instructed to cross-examine, or make submissions, on.

This is not only because evidence will have been exchanged.

a. Claim

Often, particulars of claim include heads of loss that are effectively irrecoverable. This may be due to the law, or lack of evidence.

For an example of an irrecoverable head of loss, take the fee of an engineer's report. This is often pleaded. Especially in claims for credit hire. There are three reasons why this is not recoverable.

First, CPR 45.12 prescribes that this is a disbursement. Secondly, CPR 27.14 prescribes the only recoverable disbursements. Thirdly, the (obiter) authority of *Clark v Ardington* [2002] EWCA Civ 510, [2003] QB 36 at [155]-[156].

For these reasons, if pleaded, an engineer's fee is often dropped.

Or, there may be a claim for the cost of repairs, but there is no invoice, or other evidence of the sum claimed, for this head of loss. If so, although a claim for repairs may be pleaded, it is not likely to be pursued at the final hearing because of this lack of evidence.

Further, there may be a claim for interest on special damages that have not been paid. For example, there may be a claim for interest on the cost of repairs. In fact, there is no evidence that the sum claimed for repairs has actually been paid. Accordingly, it is unlikely that this claim for interest will be pursued at a final hearing.

b. Defence

The defence may deny each and every allegation, putting the claimant to proof, and requiring the claimant to provide a repair estimate, evidence of impecuniosity, and a credit hire agreement.

If the claimant provides this evidence, the defendant may admit the cost of repairs, and the sum claimed under the credit hire agreement. If so, these issues will no longer be in dispute.

5. Evidence

If a party indicates in the directions questionnaire that she will rely on a witness, the notice of allocation usually orders any witness statement to be filed and served 14 days before the hearing.

Check whether the evidence has, in fact, been filed and served in accordance with these directions. *Proof* that the evidence on which a party seeks to rely has been filed and served is *invaluable*.

a. Filing & service

Often, the other party, the court, or both, indicate that they do not have any evidence for the party who you represent. This appears to be the case especially for remote hearings. If so, filing and service is likely to form a preliminary issue.

If you are able to submit that you have proof that the evidence was filed and served, this often short-circuits such issues. If not, you can forward this proof to the relevant court actor by email.

Proof of filing and service thereby guard against strike out, summary judgment, and dismissal due to want of evidence.

Proof may take the form of an email, with evidence attached. Or, it may be a cover letter, stating what evidence is enclosed.

The deadline for filing and serving evidence may appear to have been breached. The parties may have agreed to extend the deadline, however, so proof of this agreement would be helpful.

In practice, this would likely consist of an email chain. Your professional client should be able to forward this to you.

Proof of filing and service can also alert you to the fact that, for example, the key evidence (an invoice) in the counterclaim (for the cost of repairs) has not been filed and served at all.

You are then able to advise your professional client to file and serve ahead of the final hearing, and prepare to make submissions as to why that evidence should be admitted.

b. Experts

If a party has provided an expert report, check whether the notice of allocation has granted permission to rely on it. If not, check whether that party has requested permission to rely on expert evidence in her directions questionnaire.

Where permission has not been granted, but there is a request to rely on expert evidence in the directions questionnaire, the court may be more likely to admit an expert report into evidence.

c. Absence

A party may have given notice that she would like the case to be decided in her absence. If so, check whether the requirements for doing so have been met (see chapter 19(c)(i)).

6. Authority

Case law may be included in the documents that you receive.

If so, check that it conforms to PDs governing the citation of authorities (see chapter 13(b)). Has it been subsequently considered or appealed (see chapter 13(g))?

There may be additional authority in the statements of case. If so, find the relevant law report. Does it conform to the PDs governing the citation? Has it been subsequently considered, or appealed?

In any event, conduct a cost / benefit analysis (see chapter 13(f)).

7. Costs

You may be instructed to make an application for costs on the basis that the other party has behaved unreasonably. If so, what is the factual basis?

Is there a witness statement in support? If not, and your view is that one would be of assistance, is there enough time for your professional client to draft one?

In any event, if instructed to make an application for substantial costs, a statement of costs should have been filed and served (see chapter 24(e)). Proof of the same is helpful in case of dispute.

Your instructions may state that numerous requests for an invoice have been made. Yet there has been no response. If so, the requests themselves are invaluable, so as to make submissions.

8. Offers

The offer and any cover letter enclosing it should be provided.

In any event, speak to your professional client to confirm whether an offer has been made. If so, how many? When? What were the terms? Was there any response?

9. Payments

If a payment has been made in respect of a claim, it is either an interim, or a final, payment. Where an interim payment is made, there is no admission as to liability, or quantum. Final payments are made where there is an admission for that amount.

a. Interim

If there was an interim payment, it is likely that it will be acknowledged explicitly as an "interim payment" in the defence. That is, if it was made before the date that the defence was signed.

Ideally, it should also be acknowledged in the particulars of claim. If an interim payment is not credited in a statement of case, the advocate for the party who made the payment may only be able to invite the court to order that credit be given for sums already paid.

Where an interim payment is not acknowledged in a statement of case, and the party who made it successfully defends against the claim, the court may decline jurisdiction to order repayment. This is why it is *crucial* to acknowledge interim payments.

b. Final

Where a final payment has been made in respect of a head of loss that is claimed, liability for that head of loss, and the sum paid towards it, cannot be disputed.

Where a final payment is made before a claim for the same has been issued, the paying party should be able to provide evidence of the date, amount, and recipient.

If so, the court will not order the paying party to pay the same sum again. The paying party will also have a strong argument that the other party has behaved unreasonably, or at least that payable costs should be reduced.

10. Contact details

If your professional client is out of the office for any period of time, this should be stated. Details should be given of a person to contact in her absence. If not, your practice manager may be able to assist.

In practice, when an email is sent to a professional client who is out of the office for a significant period of time, they are likely to have set up an automated "out of office" reply. If so, it will often include the email address of another person who can be contacted.

ii. Statements of case

Statements of case *must* comply with CPRs, PDs, and court orders.

1. Compliant

Check for compliance (see chapters 5-9 and 11).

In particular, that they are verified by a statement of truth.

2. Names

The names of the parties should be correct.

If the claimant has a contract with a limited company, but the name on the claim form and particulars of claim does not end with 'limited', an application to amend should be made.

Ensure that you have written instructions before making an oral application for permission to amend the name on those statements of case, and to dispense with service.

The relevant pages on the website of Companies House can be used to evidence the fact that a company is limited, as well as the company number. The court can take judicial notice of the same.

If you are attending an in-person hearing, copies should be printed for the judge, and the other party. Otherwise, the relevant page(s) of Companies House can be saved as a pdf, ready to be attached and sent via email upon request.

Where the name of a party has been amended, ensure that the order reflects the amendment.

iii. Evidence

Usually, whatever submission you are instructed to make can be made on the evidence that has been filed and served.

Sometimes, however, you may need to weigh up the benefit of relying on an *objective*, *public* document, from a *reputable* source, against the likelihood that the other party, or the judge, will object to adducing it. In any event, speak to your professional client.

Ensure that you act with instructions.

1. In the documents

The enclosed documents may not be arranged in the usual way.

That is, statements of case, evidence, then correspondence. There may be no rhyme or reason as to the ordering.

Ensure that you do not miss a defence to the counterclaim. There may be a reference to it in the documents. If there is a counterclaim, it is likely that there will be a (reply and) defence to it.

The documents may not be paginated. If there are page numbers, they may not be continuous. Or, if there are separate bundles for the claimant and the defendant, a document may appear at page ten of the former, and one of the latter.

If an original document was double-sided, the copy may be single-sided, so that your copy is missing every other page. Photocopies of written, or even typed documents, may be impossible to read, truncated, or cropped. Photographs may be in black and white, so that they are of little assistance.

Not all documents necessarily will be relevant. Especially this holds true with correspondence. Often, all correspondence relating to a case will be included.

Important correspondence includes evidence of filing, service, and offers to settle. Ensure that you have the same before the hearing.

2. Not in the documents

For example, in a claim following a road traffic collision, there may not be any images, or other evidence, of the road layout. Where liability is in dispute, however, the court will likely be assisted by this evidence. The other party is unlikely to resist it provided that you ensure the following.

First, that party and the court are provided with copies before the hearing. Secondly, you explain to the other party, and to the court, what it is, where it is from, and the good reason that it assists. Thirdly, it is from an objective, public, freely available source. For example, Google Maps.

In the unlikely event that evidence can be rebutted using, for example, a printout from the website of Companies House, it is unlikely to be agreed by the other party.

The court, on the other hand, may well allow it to be adduced. The strict rules of evidence do not apply. The court will balance the factors that further the overriding objective.

iv. Orders

Court orders are necessary to confirm whether or not the parties have complied with the directions for the final hearing.

For example, whether the date for filing and service of witness statements has been complied with. If not, why?

Some notice is preferable to no notice.

If the other party has had a day to consider it, they may also have been able to take instructions. The prejudice of excluding it will be weighed against the prejudice of admitting it. That balance is likely to change if there is at least some notice.

v. Correspondence

Correspondence falls under five sub-headings.

First, pre-action. Secondly, evidence of filing and service. Thirdly, agreements. Fourthly, offers of settlement. Fifthly, payments.

1. Pre-action

Pre-action correspondence is relevant for costs.

2. Filing & service

Especially on an unassigned list, or where a claim has been transferred between courts, evidence of filing and service is vital.

All too often, the same is disputed. With evidence, you help the court to further the overriding objective by dealing with filing and service issues expeditiously and fairly.

3. Agreements

The parties may agree to extend a deadline. Or, there may be an agreement that a point will not be taken.

For example, where a witness statement is served after the deadline, the recipient may confirm that it is unnecessary to address the court on service, as this point will not be taken.

Where there is agreement, evidence of that agreement is invaluable. Without it, a submission on whether or not there was an agreement is hollow. It is unlikely to succeed if disputed.

4. Offers

Offers, and any associated replies, are important for two reasons.

First, if an offer remains open for acceptance, there may have been a material change in circumstances since the offer was made. It may now be advisable to accept. For example, a key witness is no longer able to attend the final hearing.

Secondly, offers are relevant when deciding what order for costs (if any) to make (see chapters 23(a)(i)(3) and 24(c)(iv)(3)(a)).

5. Payments

If there has been an interim payment, and it is not acknowledged in a statement of case, you should have evidence of it.

If there is no evidence, and the other party does not accept that there has been an interim payment, then, you can invite the court to add a paragraph in the order, providing that credit is to be given for any sums already paid.

c. Analyse

Having confirmed that you have written instructions, statements of case, and evidence, a careful reading will enable you to confirm for yourself the *relevant* facts, issues, and evidence.

Salient parts of written instructions may be usefully highlighted.

The evidence on which you must cross-examine may also be high-lighted. Marking often assists to recall relevant facts, over and above reading alone. Evidence can be highlighted, underlined, or a vertical line can be drawn down the margin.

i. Agreed facts

Having carefully read your instructions, and the documents, it should be possible to identify material facts that are *not* in dispute.

In a claim for an unpaid parking charge, for example, it may be possible to make a note that the following are *agreed* facts.

First, the defendant parked on the relevant land. Secondly, she did so for the time alleged by the claimant. Thirdly, the defendant was obliged to pay. Fourthly, the claimant was responsible for the management of the relevant land.

Agreed facts are important.

They are the *anchor* from which the judge can build a picture as to what happened. From this, you must construct your client's case, using the evidence that *is* in dispute, so as to persuade the court that the claimant has (not) discharged the burden of proof.

ii. Disputed facts

Having noted the facts that are *not* in dispute, it should be possible to identify the facts that *are* in dispute, relevant, and therefore assist, or undermine, one of the competing cases.

For example, in that claim for an unpaid parking charge.

First, the sign notifying the defendant that payment was required was clear / confusing. Secondly, there was / was not a way to make the payment because the machine was / was not working. Thirdly, in these circumstances, the sum claimed is / is not excessive.

If the likelihood of each of the conflicting cases are finely balanced, then, the burden of proof can effectively be deployed. A defendant can use it successfully to argue that the claim should be dismissed.

If there is a claim, and a counterclaim, following the same incident, however, the burden of proof is of less assistance. The *claimant* has the burden of proving the *claim*. The *defendant* has the burden of proving the *counter*claim. Both parties have a burden.

iii. Issues

It should be possible to identify the *real* issues in the case.

These are often more discrete than the statements of case suggest.

Once an issue has been identified, the opposing positions taken on that issue in the statements of case can be identified. Then, the disputed evidence going to that issue can be considered.

This informs cross-examination. There is no need to ask questions going to issues that are not in dispute.

d. Checklist of information & documents

Depending on the type of case, the court usually needs certain information and documentation (PD 27 at Appendix A).

i. Road traffic

First, witness statements (including statements from the parties themselves). Secondly, invoices and estimates for repairs. Thirdly, agreements and invoices for the cost of any car hire.

Fourthly, the police accident report. Fifthly, a sketch plan, which should, wherever possible, be agreed. Sixthly, photographs of the scene of the accident, and photographs of the damage.

ii. Building, repairs, goods sold & contract

First, any written contract. Secondly, photographs. Thirdly, any plans. Fourthly, a list of works complained of. Fifthly, a list of any outstanding works.

Sixthly, any relevant estimate, invoice, or receipt, including any relating to repairs to each of the defects. Seventhly, invoices for work done or goods supplied. Eighthly, estimates for work to be completed. Ninthly, a valuation of work done to date.

iii. Landlord & tenant

First, a calculation of the amount of any rent alleged to be owing, showing amounts received, preferably in the form of a schedule. Secondly, details of breaches of an agreement which are said to justify withholding any deposit itemised, showing how the total is made up, with invoices and estimates in support.

iv. Breach of duty

First, what it is said by the claimant that is alleged to have been done negligently by the defendant. Secondly, why it is said that this negligence is the fault of the defendant. Thirdly, what damage is said to have been caused.

Fourthly, what injury, or losses, have been suffered, and how any (and each) sum that is claimed has been calculated. Fifthly, the response of the defendant to each of the above.

e. Telephone

If a document appears to be missing, evidence appears not to have conformed to CPRs, PDs or court directions, or you just wish to touch base before the hearing, speak to your professional client.

There may be important context that has not made its way into your written instructions. Perhaps, due to time constraints.

Your professional client may feel at ease with confirmation that her chosen counsel has received the documents, understands the instructions, and is grateful for them.

f. Spare copies

Ensure that you have unmarked, colour copies of the documents.

All too often, evidence is filed and served, but the court and the other side do not have it before a hearing.

13. Authority

In *Parr v Keystone Healthcare Ltd & Ors* [2019] EWCA Civ 1246, [2019] 4 WLR 99 at [26], Lewison LJ opined that "it is a matter of considerable regret that the practice direction on the citation of authorities … has been almost wholly ignored."

Even in an appellate court, then, authorities are relied upon other than in accordance with the guidance that the court has given.

Whether you are in the Court of Appeal, or the county court, the parties are under an obligation to help the court to further the overriding objective when relying on authority.

a. Legal principle

In *Kaur & Anor v Secretary of State for the Home Department* [2019] EWCA Civ 1101, [2019] 4 WLR 94 at [48], Floyd LJ endorsed a warning from over one hundred years ago:

> "Cases, so far as regards the law, are most useful, but when they are applied to particular facts, they, as a rule, are of little service. Each case depends on its own particular facts, and the facts of almost every case differ …".

The lesson is that, as a general rule, authority should be relied on for a statement of *legal principle*. A previous case is unlikely to be so factually similar that it can be relied on to resolve a claim.

Most claims are decided on the facts. This is usually with the benefit of oral evidence. So, it is unlikely that an authority is capable of identification in advance of a final hearing.

b. Practice directions

There are four PDs prescribing when authority may (and may not) be cited, and the procedure for doing so.

i. Citation of Authorities [2012] 1 WLR 780

In 2012, the then Lord Chief Justice issued the above PD.

The preamble provides that it was "issued in order to clarify the practice and procedure governing the citation of authorities and applies throughout the … county courts".

Under the heading 'Citation of authority', it prescribes that: "When authority is cited, whether in written or oral submissions, the following practice should be followed."

1. Official Law Reports

Where a judgment is reported in any of the four, *official* Law Reports ("the Law Reports"), *that* report *must* be cited.

They are as follows: Appeal Cases ("AC"); Queen's Bench ("QB"); Chancery ("Ch"); and Family ("Fam").

This is for two reasons.

First, these are the most authoritative. Secondly, they contain a summary of the arguments.

2. Weekly Law Reports & All England Law Reports

Until a case is reported in the Law Reports, if it is reported in the Weekly Law Reports ("WLR"), or the All England Law Reports ("All ER"), the WLR or the All ER should be cited.

There is no hierarchy. Either may be used.

3. Specialist series

If three conditions are satisfied, a specialist report may be cited.

First, the case is not reported in the Law Reports, WLR, or All ER. Secondly, it contains a headnote. Thirdly, it was made by individuals holding a Senior Courts qualification.

4. Other reports

When not reported in any of the above, other reports may be cited.

5. Transcripts

Only when a case has not been reported may the official transcript be used. This may be found on the website of the British and Irish Legal Information Institute: www.bailii.org.

It should not usually be cited, "unless it contains a relevant statement of legal principle not found in reported authority."

6. Format

Authority must be in one of two formats.

First, a photocopy of the published report. Secondly, a copy of a reproduction of the case in electronic form, which has been authorised by the publisher of the relevant reports.

In any event, it must be easily legible, ideally with a 12-point font.

ii. Citation of Authorities [2001] 1 WLR 1001

With the substantial growth in the number of cases that are available, reported in a number of different law reports, and transcripts that are freely available online, the court has limited the *nature,* and the *amount,* of authority, that may be relied upon.

Increasing efficiency and proportionality of litigation, so as to reduce cost, must be balanced against the interests of justice.

It is in conformity with the overriding objective to deal with cases justly and at proportionate cost.

Accordingly, the then Lord Chief Justice issued the above PD prescribing three rules governing the use of authority.

1. Relevant & useful

The overriding objective will be compromised if the court is burdened with a weight of inappropriate, unnecessary authority, and advocates are uncertain as to when it is necessary to use authority.

Accordingly, this PD limits citation of authority to cases that are both *relevant,* and *useful to the court.*

The latter is a reference to the duty to cite adverse authority.

2. Adverse authority

The duty of an advocate to draw the court's attention to adverse authority applies if two conditions are satisfied.

First, it undermines the case that she is advancing. Secondly, it has not been cited by the other party.

In the context of a claim for credit hire, for example, where enforceability is in dispute, this may include *Irving v Morgan Sindall Plc* [2018] EWHC 1147 (QB), [2018] RTR 23.

In this case, it was held that the claimant, who had been assured by a credit hire company that she would never be personally responsible for hire charges, had a *contingent* liability to the hire company. She was not getting a free hire car. The defendant was liable to pay these charges.

3. County court authority

It may *not* be cited unless one of the following is satisfied.

First, it clearly indicates that it purports to establish a new principle. Secondly, it clearly indicates that it purports to extend the present law.

It *must* be in the form of an *express statement* to that effect.

There are two exceptions.

First, to illustrate the conventional measure of damages in a personal injury case. Secondly, to demonstrate current, county court authority, on an issue where there is no higher-level authority.

In practice, then, before relying on county court authority, you should be able positively to submit that there is no binding (High Court, Court of Appeal, or Supreme Court) authority on the point.

iii. Judgments: Form and Citation [2001] 1 WLR 194

In 2001, the arrangements for the preparation, distribution and citation of judgments were modernised.

A PD prescribed rules for the formatting of judgments, including the requirement for numbered paragraphs.

The main reason was to facilitate the publication of judgments on the internet. It was hoped that it would also assist those searching for judgments on electronic databases.

The neutral citation is the "official number attributed to the judgment". It "must always be used on at least one occasion when the judgment is cited in a later judgment."

After EWCA, 'Civ' is the reference used for 'Civil Division'. The reference for 'Criminal Division' is 'Crim'.

The tenth Civil Division case of the year, for example, has the same official number as the tenth case of the Criminal Division. So, it is important to include the reference 'Civ'.

When a judgment is reported, the neutral citation "will appear in front of the familiar citation from the law report series."

The paragraph number of a judgment should remain consistent, whichever report of the case is used.

If more than one paragraph of a judgment is cited, each numbered paragraph should be enclosed with a square bracket.

iv. Judgments: Form and Citation [2002] 1 WLR 1346

In 2002, the practice of neutral citation was extended to all judgments handed down by the High Court in London. Ever since, a unique number has been given to these judgments.

After 'EWHC' and the unique number, High Court judgments have the following descriptive words: (Ch) Chancery Division; (Pat) Patents Court; (QB) Queen's Bench Division; (Admin) Administrative Court; (Comm) Commercial Court; (Admlty) Admiralty Court; (TCC) Technology and Construction Court; and (Fam) Family Court.

Unlike Court of Appeal judgments, however, it is unnecessary to include the descriptive words when citing the paragraph number of a High Court judgment. This is because each High Court judgment has a *unique* number. Court of Appeal judgments do not.

c. Citation

When a case is cited, the full case name should be used.

When written, *italics* should be used for the names of the parties.

This should be followed by the neutral citation (if there is one), and a comma, followed by where it is cited in the law reports.

By convention, if two conditions are satisfied, the name of the court should appear in brackets after the first page of the report.

First, no neutral citation. Secondly, decided after 1865.

The most frequently used references include: (HL) House of Lords; (CA) Court of Appeal; and (QB) Queen's Bench Division.

When a particular paragraph is cited, the number can be encompassed within square brackets. For example: *Barton v Wright Hassal LLP* [2018] UKSC 12, [2018] 3 All ER 487 at [18].

d. Marked

The relevant paragraph(s) can be marked.

When marking a hard copy, black pen should be used. Then, where the authority is scanned, or photocopied, it remains legible.

A vertical, straight line can be drawn down the side of the page encompassing the relevant paragraph(s).

e. Copies

At an in person hearing, ensure that you have hard copies of any authority that you rely on. For the court, and the other party.

After signing in with the usher, a copy of any authority should be handed to that usher. She will pass it on to the judge. Any authority handed to an usher must also be handed to the other party.

This should be as soon as practicable. The other party should have as much time as possible to consider it. Both the legal principle that decided the case, and the relevant paragraph(s), should be communicated to the other party.

At a remote hearing, ensure that you have an electronic copy. You may be requested to email it to the court, and the other party.

f. Cost / benefit

Claims are usually determined by findings of fact. The relevant legal principles are usually trite.

Accordingly, authority should be the exception. Not the norm.

If you are aware that the other side is not represented, balance the benefit of relying on an authority, against the perception that you are intimidating a litigant in person.

In any event, beware not to court the ire of the judge. She may not wish to read a lengthy, appellate analysis, discussing trite law.

g. Context

Using a professional legal database, check for three material circumstances before deciding to rely on an authority.

First, whether it has been positively considered in later cases. Secondly, whether it has been successfully appealed. Thirdly, whether it is subject to a pending appeal.

If the answer to any of these questions is "yes", it *must* be communicated to the other *party*, and to the *court*.

i. Subsequent consideration

If the legal principle that decided a case has been *applied* to *decide* a later case, this is likely to indicate that it is *good* law.

Especially if the latter is an *appellate* court, the paragraph that you rely on is cited *word-for-word*, or the reasoning behind that principle is approved by *express* words.

It may also indicate, however, that the legal principle is trite. This will call into question whether it is necessary to cite authority.

If a case has been negatively considered, criticised, or confined to its facts, this weakens any general authority that it may have.

Especially if this was by a higher court.

These facts would need to be communicated to the court, and to the other party. It follows that, on balance, an authority of questionable weight may not be worth relying on.

ii. Determined appeal

Check for the following.

First, whether the appeal was successful. Secondly, whether the legal principle on which you rely was endorsed. Thirdly, whether the reasoning applying that principle was endorsed.

For example, in *Stevens v Equity Syndicate Management Ltd* [2014] EWHC 689 (QB), [2014] RTR 34 at [21], Burnett J (as he then was) held that the court was entitled to find a lack of impecuniosity:

> "It is striking that the bank statements showed very little activity at all. In other words, the money passing through the bank account could not conceivably reflect the totality of economic activity of a man, still less a family man. ..."

On appeal ([2015] EWCA Civ 93, [2015] 4 All ER 458 at [7]), Kitchin LJ (as he then was, with whom Floyd and Jackson LJJ agreed) said that: "Burnett J upheld the Recorder's findings on impecuniosity and there is no further appeal against that decision".

Accordingly, the judgment of Burnett J was appealed. His judgment on *impecuniosity*, however, was not.

Burnett's J reasoning on impecuniosity remains good law.

It was not expressly endorsed by the Court of Appeal. As High Court authority binds a (deputy) district judge, recorder, and circuit judge, however, this is of no consequence.

iii. Pending appeal

If there is an *application* for permission to appeal, or permission to appeal has been *granted*, this is a relevant fact that should be communicated to the other party, and to the court.

In principle, these circumstances *weaken* the authority upon which you intend to rely. There is a prospect of the following.

First, the judgment will be *reversed*. Secondly, the legal principle upon which you intend to rely will be *criticised*. Thirdly, *different* reasoning surrounding the principle will be endorsed.

The benefit of this authority should therefore be considered.

14. Skeleton arguments

The purpose of a skeleton argument 'is to assist the court by setting out as concisely as practicable the arguments upon which a party intends to rely' (PD 52A at [5.1(1)]).

a. Assist the court

Skeleton arguments are usually unnecessary. Often, the applicable law is trite. The issues, facts and evidence are straightforward.

Judgment usually turns on oral evidence.

When instructed to make an application to strike out a statement of case because it is an abuse of process, however, a skeleton argument is likely to assist the court.

It will set out the key facts, relevant legal principles on misuse of the court's procedure, and submissions as to why allowing proceedings to continue would be manifestly unfair, or otherwise bring the administration of justice into disrepute.

Skeleton arguments also provide an opportunity to get the judge on-board with your submissions before the hearing.

b. Requirements

A skeleton argument has six requirements (PD 52A at [5.1(2)]).

First, concision. Secondly, define and confine areas of controversy. Thirdly, numbered paragraphs and pages. Fourthly, cross-reference relevant documents. Fifthly, be self-contained. Sixthly, omit extensive quotations.

i. Concision

Words, sentences and paragraphs should be *short*.

Headings, sub-headings, and lists, can all be used for ease of navigation, organising content, and reducing word count.

Skeleton arguments before substantive appeals in the Court of Appeal should be less than 25 pages. Accordingly, there should be a *very* good reason to go beyond ten pages.

1. Headings & sub-headings

Typical headings may include facts, issues and submissions.

Sub-headings can also be used to make arguments.

When resisting an application for relief from sanctions, for example, under the heading 'submissions', the sub-headings may be as follows: breach is serious and significant; no good reason; and all the circumstances weigh in favour of refusing relief.

2. Lists & punctuation

Lists enable brevity. They reduce the number of necessary words.

Punctuation can aid pithiness.

For example: appropriate use of the Oxford comma; semi-colons to separate two, closely related, but independent sentences; and full colons before a list, or where a semi-colon will not do.

Paragraphs should be *short*.

3. Layout

Concision does *not* mean that the font, size of font, and space in between each line, should be reduced.

The objective is *not* to cram content onto each page.

Content should be well-spaced, so that it is clear. Free space can then be used for notes in the margins, and in between sentences.

Times New Roman, font size 12, and 1.5-line spacing, is often used.

ii. Define & confine areas of controversy

Identify the issues that are in dispute, and the issues that are not in dispute. The scope of each should be set out.

In a claim for credit hire, for example: 'Liability is admitted. Quantum is disputed. There are three heads of loss: repairs are admitted in the sum of £2,000; and credit hire and the engineer's fee are denied. The credit hire issues are need, period and rate.'

iii. Numbering

Pages and paragraphs should be numbered, for ease of navigation.

There are advantages to single-sided skeleton arguments.

First, blank pages, so that lengthy, handwritten notes may be written on these pages, where there is insufficient space in the margin, or in-between lines. Secondly, should the skeleton argument need to be photocopied, or scanned, there is a greater prospect that all of the pages will, in fact, be photocopied, or scanned.

iv. Cross-referencing

Where there is an admission in a statement of case, the name of the document, and the paragraph, should be precisely identified.

Often, a paginated bundle does not exist.

If so, for example, 'paragraph 7 of the Defence', or 'page 2 of the claimant's engineers' report', provide a workaround.

Authority should conform to the PDs (see chapter 13(b)).

When an authority is cited, set out the following.

First, the legal principle for which it is authority. Secondly, the paragraph(s) of the authority where it is found. Thirdly, if more than one authority is relied on to establish this principle, the reason.

For example:

1 When a claim is issued, a claimant must bring forward her whole case. She cannot subsequently open the same litigation in respect of matters which ought to have been brought forward, but, in fact, were not.

2 This is "Henderson abuse". It has been well-established law since Wigram V-C set out the rule in the case of *Henderson v Henderson* [1843-60] All ER Rep 378 at 381, in these terms:

> "… where a given matter becomes the subject of litigation in, and of adjudication by, a court of competent jurisdiction, the court requires the parties to that litigation to bring forward their whole case, and will not (except under special circumstances) permit the same parties to open the same subject of litigation in respect of matter which might have been brought forward as part of the subject in contest, but which was not brought forward only because they have,

> from negligence, inadvertence, or even accident, omitted part of their case. ..."

State the consistent shorthand used for pages and paragraphs.

For example: 'References in square brackets are to paragraph numbers.' If so, don't also use square brackets for page numbers.

v. Self-contained

Key submissions should be set out.

For example, an argument that is *not* self-contained may state that: 'The first submission is in paragraph four of the Defence'; and 'the second submission is in paragraph twelve of the Defence'.

Footnotes should be unnecessary.

vi. Quotations

As a general rule, only the *key* sentence should be quoted.

Occasionally, there will be more than one key sentence. There should be a *good* reason to quote more than a paragraph.

Do not quote out of any material context.

c. Content

Few strict rules exist. There is flexibility to find your own style.

i. Headings

The header should be similar to a statement of case.

The sole exception is, of course, the *title* of the document.

This should also be within tramlines, capitalised, and emboldened. In contrast to a statement of case, it should start with the status of the party, followed by the name of the document.

The name of an application can be used. For example: '**DEFENDANT'S SKELETON ARGUMENT RE ABUSE OF PROCESS**'.

ii. Reading time

How long will it take to read? This should follow the heading.

It enables the court to gauge how long it will take to consider. This in turn permits the court to actively manage the case.

It is likely to take no more than ten minutes.

iii. Invitation

What is the court being asked to do? A sentence should suffice.

For example, 'strike out this claim as an abuse of process under CPR 3.4(2)(b) because there is a binding settlement.'

Cite the relevant CPR, PD, or court order.

Specify the power that you are inviting the court to exercise.

iv. Facts

Set out only the *necessary* facts.

In the above example, the salient facts may be as follows:

1   This claim arises out of a road traffic collision, which occurred on 10 July 2020.

2   Liability is not in dispute.

3   On 12 August 2020, the claimant submitted a Claim Notification Form ("CNF") under the MOJ Portal.

4   Section E of the CNF was completed relating to provision of an alternative vehicle. The claimant indicated that she required an alternative vehicle, but also that she had not been provided with one. No details of hire were provided.

5   No request was made to the defendant insurer to provide an alternative vehicle.

6   From 5-20 August 2020, the claimant hired a vehicle on credit hire terms.

7   On 29 October 2020, the claimant submitted the Stage 2 Settlement Pack, claiming personal injury, and physiotherapy charges.

8   On 12 November 2020, the defendant made a final offer of £3,500. On 3 December 2020, this was accepted.

9   On 4 February 2021, proceedings were issued against the defendant to recover the following:

    9.a credit hire in the sum of £4,545.53; and
    9.b repairs, in the sum of £4,210.12.

10 This was two months after settlement.

v. Costs

Are costs sought because a party has behaved unreasonably?

For example:

> If the court strikes out this claim as an abuse of process, it follows that the claimant has behaved unreasonably in bringing this claim for the purposes of CPR 27.14(2)(g).

> Accordingly, the defendant invites the court to award the reasonable costs of defending the claim. This is set out in the Defendant's Statement of Costs.

vi. Sign & date

The name of the legal representative, who has drafted the skeleton argument, should appear at the bottom.

By convention, it is capitalised, emboldened, and aligned to the right-hand side of the page. This is followed by the date.

These are the last words before the back sheet.

vii. Back sheet

Skeleton arguments should have a back sheet.

The heading is identical to the first page. The text is on the right-hand side of the page only. The left-hand side is blank.

The name, professional address, and status of the legal representative who has drafted the skeleton argument, should be stated. For example, 'counsel for the defendant'.

The name, professional address, and status of the legal representative who is instructing counsel, should also be stated. For example, 'solicitor for the defendant'.

If printed off and stapled, the *back* sheet should face the *back*.

When the skeleton argument is picked up, you should be able to see the front page. When you turn it over, you should be able to see the back sheet. This is for ease of reference.

viii. Spelling, grammar & punctuation

This may indicate that the necessary time has not been invested in researching, drafting and proofreading.

If so, the ability to persuade will diminish.

The judge is likely to have formed a negative view of you, or your client's case, before you have even opened your mouth.

d. Form

Substance is important. So is *form*.

A skeleton argument should look aesthetically pleasing.

This demonstrates that time has been invested in proofreading.

Font, size, and spacing, is consistent. Shorthand is consistent.

For example: 'paragraph 4', 'para. 4', or '[4]'; and 'Particulars of Claim', 'PoC', or 'particulars of claim'.

Define abbreviations.

In practice, brackets and quotation marks are used: ("…").

e. Notice

If there is a need for a skeleton argument, there is likely to be factual, legal, or evidential, complexity.

Accordingly, the judge, and the other party, should have sufficient notice of it. This provides them with an opportunity to read, process, and conduct their own research into the relevant complexity.

If a party has sufficient notice of your submissions, and remains unable to counter them effectively, they become more powerful.

The court will then be more likely to exercise a draconian power of case management. This includes early termination. For example: striking out a claim; or granting summary judgment.

i. File & serve

A notice of trial date may include a direction as to how and when.

If so, follow this direction. If there is no such direction, skeleton arguments should be filed and served no less than three days before a hearing. Some notice, however, is better than no notice.

The afternoon before a hearing is preferable to on the day.

Ensure that you have evidence that the skeleton argument has been filed and served. There may be a dispute.

This may be emails with attachments, or cover letters.

ii. Springboard

Skeleton arguments are not statements of case, or evidence.

If it has not been filed and served, the *court* may not use it.

If so, *you* may still decide to use it. The judge may be inclined to find a reason to give judgment against your client if you read it word-for-word. It should not be used as a script.

Use it as a springboard into the law, facts and evidence.

15. Arrival

On arrival, sign in with the usher.

Have a conference with your client and any witnesses for the party who you represent. Then, have a discussion with the other party.

a. Sign in

There are three reasons for signing in.

First, the hearing will not proceed without you. Secondly, if you have any witnesses, when they sign in, the usher will be able to inform them that you are at court, so that you can have a conference. Thirdly, when the other party signs in, the usher will be able to inform them that you are at court, so that you can speak.

b. Note

Note the courtroom that the matter will be heard in. This is because a transcript may be requested in the case of an appeal.

Note the title, and surname, of the judge. For example: 'Deputy District Judge Smith'.

Note the title, and surname, of any other legal representative.

c. Listing

Many claims are listed at 10:00, or 14:00.

This does not mean that your case will be called before, or even at, this time. It is the time before which you must have signed in.

You may be waiting an hour, morning, or even a day, before your case is adjourned due to lack of judicial time. If this is a realistic prospect, ensure that any witnesses are made aware.

Your case may not have an assigned listing. This means that there may not be a fixed courtroom in which the matter will be heard, judge who will hear it, or time before the matter will be called on.

If so, it is on an "unassigned" or "floating" list.

i. Managing expectations

Often, lay clients equate listing with a professional appointment. They may need to make childcare arrangements, renew their parking, or otherwise make additional arrangements.

ii. Spare copies

When the claim is on a floating list, the prospects that the court will have all of the documents, and that a witness bundle has made its way to the correct court, are often drastically reduced.

This is a good reason to take at least one spare, unmarked, hard copy of the documents to any in person hearing. Evidence of filing and service is invaluable in case of dispute.

iii. County Court at Central London

When you sign in, you will be asked for your name, and often your mobile telephone number.

When a courtroom, and a judge, becomes available, the parties will be notified. This may be via text message.

The parties will often be released for the luncheon adjournment by the same means. If you wish to speak to the other side, you can request that a text message is sent, inviting them to return to the reception area, so as to facilitate a discussion.

iv. Alternative dispute resolution

You may be waiting for some time.

The duty to assist the court to further the overriding objective requires you to attempt to narrow, if not in fact settle, the issues.

If you do not have authority to do so, telephone your professional client. Request it.

You may have to explain why it is a good use of time. It will save the expense of further counsel' fees in the event that the matter is adjourned.

The Small Claims Mediation Service may also be available.

In practice, if both sides have legal representation, and have instructed counsel, authority to use this service may not be given. If this is the case, the parties should at least be able to narrow the issues to only those which are properly arguable.

The phrase "let's let the judge decide" is often the sign of weakness. It usually reveals that counsel does not think that the point will succeed. Yet she feels obliged to raise it on instructions.

This likely demonstrates that authority, or evidence, is against it.

Never agree that a point is doomed to fail. If it is, drop it.

It is useful to hear what the other party says about their case before the hearing. You will often learn the following.

First, how the other party will pitch their case. Secondly, perceived strengths. Thirdly, perceived weaknesses.

v. Subsequent listing

If adjourned, request a *fixed* listing on the return date.

It is likely to be granted. If you do not ask, you may not get.

d. Non-attendance of witnesses

If it appears as though a witness is not going to attend, telephone your professional client. Failing that, send an email.

There may be a good reason that they have not attended.

For example, they may have had to attend an accident and emergency department of a hospital.

Instructions from your professional client, confirming the same, will often secure an adjournment.

They will also go some way to defending an application for costs of the adjournment (see chapter 24(c)(ii)(3)(b)).

Especially where the matter has been transferred from one court to another, a witness may have gone to the wrong court.

Act *promptly.* Do not wait until the last minute.

e. Late attendance of legal representative

If you are likely to be late, act *promptly.*

First, send an email to your professional client. Copy in your practice manager. Relay that you are likely to be late, the reason, and your estimated time of arrival.

Your professional client may email the other party to convey the same. Especially if she is represented.

Secondly, invite your practice manager to email the court. The email should relay that you are likely to be late, the reason, and your estimated time of arrival. Ask to be copied in.

Other claims may be able to be called on before you arrive.

Parties and witnesses will be grateful to be kept informed. Court can be stressful enough without the prospect that their legal representative will apparently abandon them in their hour of need.

This is also a professional courtesy.

Public transport is often delayed. It may even be cancelled.

Prompt communication with court actors is key.

f. Conference

If the issues in dispute do not require oral evidence, you may not have a witness. If so, a conference is unnecessary.

Especially where liability is in dispute, however, you will likely need a conference. This will be with the party who you represent, and any of her witnesses (see chapter 16(c)).

g. Speak to the other party

There are five reasons to speak to the other party.

First, to confirm that the parties have the relevant documents. Secondly, to agree the issues in dispute. Thirdly, to attempt to agree quantum, subject to liability. Fourthly, to exchange authority. Fifthly, to agree costs and witness expenses, subject to liability.

i. Papers

If a legal representative has not got a copy of a document that you seek to rely upon, you should be able to provide them with a copy.

If they say that they have not seen the document before, or dispute that they have been served with a copy of it, speak to your professional client. Request evidence of service via email.

It is also worth requesting evidence that the document has been filed with the court. If the other party does not have a document, it is likely that the court will be in the same position.

Evidence of filing and service can be shown to the other party, so that these potential issues can be resolved before the hearing.

ii. Issues

In a credit hire claim, if evidence of impecuniosity has been served, the defendant may decide not to dispute it.

This means that one significant issue will no longer be in dispute.

The need to cross-examine a claimant on her wage slips, current bank and credit card statements, therefore falls away.

The claimant will likely be reassured to hear this.

It will also enable the parties to state the issues that are in dispute at the outset of the hearing, so as to focus evidence, and then submissions, on the real issues. These are likely to be different, or at least narrower, than the statements of case suggest.

iii. Quantum

If there is an invoice, subject to liability, it may be possible to agree the head of loss to which it relates. This saves court time.

For a claimant, it can be reassuring to agree quantum subject to liability. If she succeeds on liability, a known amount will follow. There is no uncertainty that the court will award a different sum.

The estimated length of the hearing may also reduce. In an unassigned list, your case is then more likely to be called on.

If quantum can be agreed, subject to liability, in principle, so can interest, and the period for payment. For example, within 21 days.

In absence of agreement, the normal order is within 14 days.

iv. Authority

Authority that is relied upon should be provided to the other side.

This includes rules of the *Highway Code*.

Do not assume that the other party is familiar with an authority.

The *legal principle* for which it is authority, and the *paragraph* at which it is found, should both be clearly communicated.

This is especially important where a party is unrepresented.

v. Costs, disbursements & witness expenses

These can usually be agreed, subject to liability (see chapter 23).

Where witness expenses appear to be unreasonably high, the paying party may request to cross-examine. This will usually take place after judgment. If so, ensure that you do not agree to a witness being released before she is cross-examined on expenses.

h. Case management form

Some courts have a case management form which must be completed before a hearing. They often differ.

Having had a conference, and confirmed the issues in dispute, you should be in a position to complete it.

This is likely to request the following details.

First, the time estimate for the hearing. Secondly, whether there are any applications. Thirdly, whether liability, quantum, or both are in dispute.

16. Conference

Where liability is in dispute, a conference is often necessary.

Even where only quantum is in dispute, a witness may be needed to give evidence. For example, in a claim for credit hire, where the defendant wishes to cross-examine on the need to hire.

In these circumstances, a conference is useful for three reasons.

First, to build rapport. Secondly, to outline procedure. Thirdly, to confirm whether the witness statement requires amendment.

a. Venue

If the hearing is in person, the conference will usually be in person.

If remote, it will often take place over the telephone.

i. In person

Instructions usually request counsel to attend court up to an hour before the time that the hearing is listed. This is for a conference.

If not, do not assume that any witnesses will attend court before the hearing is listed. Contact your professional client. Request that any witnesses attend court before the hearing for a conference.

ii. Remote

Instructions may request counsel to telephone a witness before the time that the hearing is listed. This is for a conference.

In any event, you may email your professional client during working hours the day before the hearing to confirm the following.

First, any witnesses giving evidence. Secondly, their telephone numbers. Thirdly, that they have a copy of the documents. Fourthly, the time that you intend to start a conference. Fifthly, that they have a separate electronic device, connected to the internet, and access to email.

A witness may not have been told that there will be a conference. She may not have the relevant documents. She may intend on participating in the hearing, and being taken to the documents in oral evidence, using one electronic device. Often, a mobile telephone.

She may need to receive additional documents on the day.

b. Build rapport

To fill in gaps in the evidence, you need rapidly to build rapport.

The witness is then more likely to have trust and confidence in you. Answers will be given to the questions that have been asked.

You will then be in a position to advise, take instructions, and to represent the best interests of your client during the hearing.

It is often easier to build rapport during in-person conferences.

i. Greeting

This varies depending on the form of the conference.

Briefly introducing yourself often puts a witness at ease.

1. In person

A genuine smile, appropriate eye contact, and a sincere greeting, all assist to build rapport. Open body language can also help.

Stating that you have told the usher that you are here, and that you will try to find a private room, will both put a witness at ease.

Finding a private conference room is often easier if you arrive early. In many courts, there are a limited number. If you find one, let the usher, and the other side, know which room you are in.

If possible, sit next to the witness. Not opposite.

The latter can appear adversarial, as though you are interviewing them. Sitting next to a witness, however, so that you can both look at a document, is often perceived as *collaborative*, thereby assisting to put a witness at ease.

A cup of water can also help.

2. Remote

The majority of communication is non-verbal. Gestures, facial expressions, posture, and eye contact. This is lost using a telephone.

Importance of the *actual words* used is therefore likely to increase.

ii. Break the ice

Some small talk is often preferable before questioning.

Once the ice is broken, and a level of trust and confidence has been established, you can progress to outline the procedure.

iii. Note

You may wish to briefly explain that you will be taking a note.

First, so that, if your lay client has any questions about what was said, there is a contemporaneous note. Secondly, so that your lay client's legal representative can read what was discussed. Thirdly, if necessary, to advise on prospects of appeal.

It can be helpful to relay that the note is confidential. It will not be shown to the other party, or to the court.

c. Outline the procedure

What is the agenda for the conference? What will happen in court?

i. Before

The agenda for the conference will likely be as follows.

First, outline the procedure that the court is likely to adopt. Secondly, questioning, so that you understand your lay client's version of events, and to fill in any gaps in the evidence. Thirdly, advice on prospects, if necessary.

ii. During

Imagine that you have not been to court before.

Who sits where? Who speaks first? How do you address the judge?

The hearing will be recorded by the court. The hearing must not be recorded by anyone else. It is a criminal offence to do so.

1. In person

Wait for the usher to announce the case.

It is etiquette to bow when entering and exiting the courtroom.

This is more than merely a nod, but less than a full bow.

If the judge greets the parties, respond appropriately. It is unusual to speak to the judge first. If the judge greets the parties with "good morning", it is appropriate to repeat that greeting.

As one faces the judge, usually the claimant sits on the left. The defendant sits on the right.

There is no need to stand.

2. Remote

No person, other than a court actor, may take part in the hearing without the permission of the judge. Parties, legal representatives, witnesses, interpreters, and the judge, are court actors.

Before joining, you should be in a private and quiet area. Another person should not be able to hear you. Reduce background noise.

Treat the hearing as though you were going to court.

If uncertain about how to join the hearing, or what to do if there is a technical problem, check the notice of hearing.

a. Telephone

Usually, the court will call the telephone numbers that have been provided. Often, this is five minutes before the hearing starts.

The call may be from an unknown number.

On answering, you will usually be invited to join a conference call.

You will be asked to press 'star' and '1' to join.

You will be asked to give your full name. You may also be asked to press the 'hash key' afterwards.

Upon joining, press 'star' and then '6' to mute. Repeat to unmute.

b. Audio-visual

Dress as if it was an in person hearing.

Often, audio-visual hearings are via Cloud Video Platform ("CVP").

If there is a problem using CVP, the court may be contacted.

Details will be provided in the notice of hearing.

Joining using a computer and Google Chrome is recommended.

Close all browsers and tabs. Open a new window. Maximise it.

Copy the address from the email arranging the hearing. Paste it into the address bar of your browser. Click: 'Enter'.

Type your full name into the box, entitled: 'Your name'. This should be followed by your role. For example: 'Defendant'.

Click the downward arrow on the bottom right. Click the top option. Click: 'Connect'.

Check that 'Microphone' and 'Camera' are set to 'Default'. Test and adjust your video and sound. Click: 'Start'.

Enter the 'PIN'. This is usually in the email arranging the hearing. If not, check the notice of hearing. Click: 'Connect'.

If you do not have a PIN, click: 'Guest' then 'Connect'.

You will enter a digital waiting room. Mute your microphone and turn off your camera. The buttons are in the bottom of the window.

The 'chat room' should be used to report technical issues. For example, inability to hear, or see, another court actor.

To leave the hearing, click the red telephone button.

3. Giving evidence

When giving evidence, the following guidance may assist.

First, speak clearly, loudly, and slowly. The judge, and any legal representative, will be taking a note.

Secondly, answer the question. If the question misses an important detail, answer the question, *then* add that detail.

Thirdly, if possible, answer "yes" or "no". A *short* answer is usually more persuasive than a long one.

Fourthly, if the question is not understood, ask for it to be repeated. If it remains unclear, ask for it to be put in other words.

Fifthly, it is not a memory test. For example, if a relevant date is in your statement, you can look at it. If you cannot remember the answer to a question, just say so.

4. Submissions & judgment

The advocate for the claimant does not usually open a case, unless requested to do so by the judge. Claims are usually straightforward. It is unusual to have complex issues of law, fact or evidence.

The court will often be assisted by the claimant outlining the documents, the issues in dispute, and who is in the hearing.

Salient parts of the evidence that assist, or undermine, the competing cases, may be briefly summarised before judgment.

The claim will likely be allowed, or dismissed, in an oral judgment.

iii. After

After the hearing, you will have a brief conference with your *lay* client, so as to explain the result, and outline any next steps.

You will also speak to your professional client, outline the order, and email your attendance note to your *professional* client.

d. Questioning

What evidence relates to the issues in dispute?

Fill in gaps. Clarify any material ambiguities.

You should then be in a position to provide summary advice on prospects, and go on to represent your client's best interests.

i. Ethics

When questioning, be careful not to lead, or otherwise suggest, answers, to questions on issues that are in dispute.

This includes verbal, and non-verbal, communication.

Confirming, and filling in gaps, in your instructions, are different skills to cross-examination. You are not determining liability. You are advising on what the court is likely to find on the evidence.

ii. Active listening

Often, people feel more comfortable relaying their version of events, in the way that they wish to do so. Then, once they are happy that they have been understood, they are usually comfortable answering questions.

Often, the quicker that you build rapport using active listening skills, the quicker you are able to progress to collecting full instructions effectively, and time-efficiently.

iii. English

If the statement of a witness is in English, that witness *must* be able to understand *written* and *spoken* English.

The exception is where an interpreter is present.

Witnesses *must* be able to answer questions in English under cross-examination.

If it becomes apparent that the witness is unable to do so, or you are otherwise not able to take full instructions in conference, call your professional client *promptly*.

Check whether an interpreter has been booked. If not, was there any indication that an interpreter was needed in the directions questionnaire? If not, an application to adjourn will be difficult.

It will be even more difficult, however, where you have not confirmed the need for an adjournment before the hearing.

First, you can explain the need for an adjournment to the other party. This provides an opportunity to make a *joint* submission that the matter ought to be adjourned.

Secondly, an application to adjourn is more likely to succeed if it is *voluntarily* made *before* a hearing, so that you are on the front foot, as opposed to being *forced* to make it *during* a hearing, when it is clear that a witness cannot sufficiently understand English.

Thirdly, as there is a real risk that the evidence of that witness will be struck out, and therefore the party who you represent will be unsuccessful, put your *professional* client on notice of these risks.

Fourthly, if you are unable to take instructions in conference, this will become clear during the hearing. You might also be reprimanded by the court for failing promptly to flag up this problem.

iv. Confirm written evidence

A witness should have an opportunity to read her statement.

This should be an unmarked copy of the same document that has been filed, served, and in the bundle (if there is one).

Having read the statement, invite a response as to whether or not there is anything to be amended.

If so, take a *word-for-word* note as to which *paragraph* is to be amended, and the *words* to be substituted.

Repeat this to the witness to confirm that your note is accurate.

If there is no request to amend, enquire whether the statement is accurate. It is helpful to record this in your attendance note.

This is so that, if under cross-examination, the witness agrees that her statement is inaccurate, or has otherwise changed her evidence, you have a contemporaneous note of the above.

Ask *open* questions on issues that are likely to be in dispute.

Even if the witness is giving evidence against the case theory of the party who has called her, or the bulk of the evidence, you have an ethical duty not to coach, or otherwise to train, a witness.

Routine witness preparation, however, is ethical.

v. Fill in gaps

If a head of loss is not evidenced in a party's statement, or otherwise evidenced in the documentation that has been filed and served, ask *open* questions to find out about it.

For example, where 'miscellaneous expenses' are claimed, but they are not evidenced in the documents, there may be evidence in the form of receipts that that party has brought to the hearing.

Or, the witness may be able to state *what* those expenses were, *when* they were incurred, and *why* they were necessary.

If permitted, you could ask a couple of open questions in examination-in-chief. This evidence would then be taken into account.

vi. Loss of earnings & expenses

Loss of earnings and expenses can be claimed, should the party for whom a witness gives evidence succeed (see chapter 23(d)).

They should be noted.

Ideally, they will be agreed with the other party before the hearing. If not, you will be able swiftly to relay them at the relevant time (see chapter 15(g)(v)).

e. Advising

If required to advise, you should now be in a position to do so.

If an issue is not properly arguable, this should be stated. The reason should be briefly explained. Both should be understood.

Counsel must not let her professional discretion be fettered.

Of course, there is a *qualitative* distinction between a point that is not *properly arguable*, and one that is *merely weak*.

The former is a *legal* question. It is *binary*. It involves *professional* ethics. The latter is often grounded in the facts and evidence.

f. Time management

Usually, you will have up to half an hour if you have one witness.

With multiple witnesses, you will have to manage your time carefully. Ensure that you have full instructions before the hearing.

17. Applications

The court may act on the application of a party, or under the court's general powers of case management (CPR 3).

In general, applications should be made by issuing an application notice. The procedure is prescribed in CPR 23.

Form N244 should be used. This is an "application notice".

Applications for early termination should be made before, or when filing, directions questionnaires (PD 26 at [5.3(1)]).

In any event, any application should be made as soon as it becomes *apparent* that it is *necessary* or *desirable* (PD 23A at [2.7]).

It may only become apparent that an application should be made on the day of the hearing. If so, speak to your professional client. Explain the need for the application. Get instructions to make it.

Some judges will refuse to hear an application unless an application notice has been filed and served. To guard against this possibility, you can take the following instructions.

Your professional client undertakes to file and serve an application notice promptly. In any event, within three working days.

These instructions should be in writing. They may be in the form of an email: 'Further to our conversation, I instruct you to …'.

In receipt of these instructions you have two options.

First, invite the court to exercise the court's general powers of case management. Secondly, if the court refuses to act on its own motion, you can make an application on instructions.

Counsel should never undertake to file and serve an application, or to pay court fees. *Professional clients* give undertakings.

a. Default judgment

"Default judgment" means judgment without a hearing.

Where a defendant in a claim, or a claimant in a counterclaim, fails to file and serve a defence before the relevant date, default judgment may be entered.

It is in accordance with the overriding objective to deal with an undefended claim, or counterclaim, for two reasons.

First, it is *just* because it is undefended. Secondly, as there is no need for directions, full investigation, or a final hearing, early termination disposes of the matter at *proportionate cost*.

It is also in accordance with the court's duty of active case management for two reasons.

First, it is an example of promptly deciding which issues need full investigation, followed by a final hearing, and disposing summarily of those that do not. Secondly, it considers whether the likely benefits of allowing the case to continue justify the cost.

i. Administrative

A party merely has to file a *request* for judgment to be entered.

Administrative staff can enter judgment. It does not need to be a judge. There is no consideration of the merits of the claim.

ii. Excluded claims

Judgment cannot be entered in the following types of claim.

First, for the delivery of goods, subject to an agreement regulated by the Consumer Credit Act 1974 (CPR 12.2(a)). Secondly, Part 8 claims (CPR 12.2(b)). Thirdly, where the defendant has applied for strike out, or summary judgment, and that application has not been disposed of (CPR 12.3(3)(a)).

Fourthly, where the defendant has satisfied the whole claim, including any claim for costs, on which the claimant is seeking judgment (CPR 12.3(3)(b)). Fifthly, the claimant is seeking judgment on a claim for money, and the defendant has filed, or served, an admission of liability to pay all of the money, together with a request for time to pay (CPR 12.3(3)(c)).

iii. Default of acknowledgement of service

To obtain judgment in default of an acknowledgment of service, the following conditions must be satisfied (CPR 12.3(1)).

First, the defendant has not filed an acknowledgment of service, or defence to any part of the claim. Secondly, the relevant time period has expired.

iv. Default of defence

To obtain judgment in default of a defence, the following conditions must be satisfied (CPR 12.3(2)).

First, an acknowledgment of service has been filed, but not a defence; and, in a counterclaim, a defence to that counterclaim has not been filed. Secondly, the relevant time limit has expired.

v. Procedure

In general, default judgment is obtained by making a request using the relevant form in the following claims (CPR 12.4(1)).

First, a specified amount of money. Secondly, an amount of money to be decided by the court. Thirdly, delivery of goods, where the claim form gives the defendant the alternative of paying their value. Fourthly, any combination of these remedies.

There are forms for specified, unspecified, and non-money, claims.

vi. Set aside

There are two rules. One is mandatory. The other is discretionary.

1. Must

Default judgment wrongly entered *must* be set aside (CPR 13.2).

There are three grounds.

First, in case of a judgment in default of an acknowledgement of service, there has not in fact been such default. Secondly, in case of a judgment in default of a defence, there has not in fact been such default. Thirdly, the whole of the claim was satisfied before judgment was entered.

2. May

There are two grounds on which a court *may* exercise its *discretion* to set aside default judgment (CPR 13.3).

First, the defendant has a *real prospect of successfully defending* the claim. Secondly, it appears to the court that there is *some other good reason* why the judgment should be set aside, varied, or the defendant should be allowed to defend the claim.

There is no *right* to set aside. Even where a ground is satisfied.

The court will take into account whether or not the party seeking to set aside made the application *promptly* (CPR 13.3(2)).

An application must be supported by *evidence* (CPR 13.4(3)).

Default judgment may be set aside on an application by a party, or the court acting on the court's own motion.

b. Transfer

An application can be made, to the court in which the case is being heard, for it to be transferred to another court.

There should be a *good* reason in support. For example: distance to the court; disability; or childcare commitments.

This should have been set out in the directions questionnaire, however, before the case was initially transferred. Accordingly, the good reason is likely to be consequent upon a *change in circumstances* since the directions questionnaire was completed.

c. Consent

Where the parties agree an order, or a judgment, it may be entered and sealed (CPR 40.6).

Where the parties have written to the court, consenting to the making of an order that has been filed in draft form, they must ensure that they provide the court with any material that is needed to satisfy the court that it is appropriate to make the order.

In general, a letter will be acceptable.

The draft order must: be in the agreed terms; be expressed to be 'by consent'; and be signed by the parties (CPR 40.6(7)).

Legal representatives may sign on behalf of the parties.

Where a hearing date has been fixed, the parties must inform the court immediately (PD 23A at [10.5]).

d. Summary judgment

The jurisdiction is closely related to strike out (PD 3A at [1.7]).

There is a wider scope, however, for dismissing a claim, or a defence (*Monsanto Plc v Tilly* [2000] Env LR 313 (CA) at [19]).

It is a procedure by which the court may decide a claim, or a particular issue, without a final hearing (CPR 24.1).

Summary judgment may be granted on an application by a party, or the courts own motion (PD 26 at [5.2]).

i. When

Any application should be made before, or when filing, the applicant's directions questionnaire (PD 26 at [5.3(1)]).

Where an application is made, the court will not normally allocate the claim before hearing the application.

Where a party files a directions questionnaire, stating that she *intends* to make such an application but has *not* yet done so, the court will usually list an allocation hearing.

ii. Allocation hearing

An application may be heard at the allocation hearing, if the application notice has been issued, and served, in sufficient time.

If summary judgment is granted before allocation, the general rule is that the successful party can apply for costs.

These are not necessarily limited to those that are otherwise available on the small claims track (CPRs 46.11(2) and 46.13(3)).

iii. Grounds

Two grounds must be satisfied (CPR 24.2).

First, *no real prospect of succeeding* on the claim, defence, or issue. This means that it must carry some *degree of conviction*. In other words, it is not *merely fanciful*. It is more than merely arguable.

The standard is therefore *not* on a balance of probabilities.

Secondly, there is no other *compelling* reason why the case, or issue, should be disposed of at a final hearing.

The burden of proof is on the applicant.

e. Strike out

The jurisdiction is related to summary judgment (PD 3A at [1.7]).

In general, where properly arguable, an application should apply for strike out *and* summary judgment.

The court may treat an application for strike out as one for summary judgment. This is to dispose of issues, claims, or defences, that do not deserve full investigation, and a final hearing (*Three Rivers District Council & Ors v Governor & Company of the Bank of England (No 3)* [2001] UKHL 16, [2003] 2 AC 1 at [88]).

i. When

If an application is not made before directions questionnaires must be filed, the intention to make an application should be included in the applicant's directions questionnaire.

This is likely to help the court because it is relevant to allocation and case management (PD 26 at [2.2(1)] and [(3)(a)]).

Where a statement of case is not verified by a statement of truth, a party may apply to the court for an order that, *unless* it is verified by the service of a statement of truth, within such *period* as the court specifies, it will *automatically* be struck out (PD 22 at [4.2]).

ii. Grounds

The court may strike out a statement of case, or any part thereof, if one of the following conditions are satisfied (CPR 3.4(2)).

First, it discloses *no reasonable grounds* for bringing, or defending, the claim. Secondly, it is an *abuse* of the court's process, or otherwise *likely to obstruct the just disposal* of proceedings. Thirdly, there has been a *failure to comply* with a CPR, PD, or court order.

The court has a *separate* power to strike out a statement of case that is not verified by a statement of truth (CPR 22.2(2)).

1. No reasonable grounds

Where a statement of case satisfies one of the following, it discloses no reasonable grounds.

First, it does not set out a *clear* statement of facts. Secondly, it is *incoherent*. Thirdly, even if correct, it does not amount to a cause of action, or defence, that is *recognised in law*.

Upon application, it may be amended with permission of the court if it would further the overriding objective.

2. Abuse of process & obstructing just disposal

In *Hunter v Chief Constable of the West Midlands Police & Ors* [1982] AC 529 (HL) at 536, Lord Diplock (with whom Lords Russell, Keith, Roskill and Brandon agreed) defined an "abuse of process" in these terms (with emphasis added):

> "It concerns the inherent power which any court of justice must possess to prevent misuse of its procedure in a way which, although not inconsistent with the literal application of its procedural rules, would nevertheless be *manifestly unfair to a party* to litigation before it, or would otherwise *bring the administration of justice into disrepute* among right-thinking people."

a. Unlawful conduct

Unlawful conduct is not a necessary condition.

In *JSC VTB Bank v Skurikhin & Ors* [2020] EWCA Civ 1337 at [51], Phillips LJ (with whom Sir Keith Lindblom and Lewison LJ agreed) said (with emphasis added) that:

> "… proceedings can be struck down as an abuse of process where there has been no unlawful conduct, no breach of relevant

procedural rules, no collateral attack on a previous decision and no dishonesty or other reprehensible conduct. Indeed, *the power exists precisely to prevent the court's process being abused through the lawful and literal application of the rules*, and most likely would not be needed or engaged where a party was acting unlawfully or in breach of procedural rules, where established rules of law or procedural sanctions would usually suffice to protect the court process. …"

b. Forms

The most common forms of abuse are as follows.

First, a *collateral* attack on a factual issue *decided* in another court of competent jurisdiction.

Secondly, *res judicata*. That is, where there has already been a *final* decision, on the *same* cause of action, between the *same* parties, in which the issue in dispute in the earlier decided claim, and the latter undecided claim, are *identical.*

Thirdly, where a later claim *could*, and *should*, have been made in *previous* proceedings (*Henderson v Henderson* [1843-60] All ER Rep 378 at 381).

Fourthly, where the claim has already been settled, or compromised. For example, through a binding settlement agreement.

c. Fact-sensitive

In *Yearwood v Yearwood (Antigua and Barbuda)* [2020] UKPC 26 at [31], Lady Black reflected on previous authority from the House of Lords: "This makes clear that a broad, merits-based judgment, taking into account all of the circumstances, is involved in determining whether there has been an abuse of the court's process."

3. Default

Material default frequently takes the following forms.

First, failure to verify a statement of case, or a witness statement, with a statement of truth. Secondly, failure to comply with an unless order. Thirdly, where a party, who is unable to read or sign a statement of truth, purports to do so.

a. Statement of truth

The consequences of failure to verify a statement of case, or a witness statement, are often different. Both may be serious.

i. Statement of case

There are two consequences following failure to verify a statement of case with a statement of truth (PD 22 at [4.1]).

First, it remains effective, unless it is struck out. Secondly, a party may not rely on its contents until it has been verified.

ii. Witness statement

There will usually be two reasons that witness statements need to be verified with a statement of truth.

First, the *rule* prescribing that witness statements *must* be verified by a statement of truth (CPRs 27.2(2) and 22.1(1)(c)). The consequence in default is that 'the court may direct that it shall not be admissible as evidence' (CPR 22.3).

Secondly, the *court order* directing the form that witness statements must take (see chapter 17(e)(ii)(3)(a)(ii)).

It will likely prescribe that 'the court may decide not to take [it] into account'. This will usually be in the notice of allocation. It often takes the following form:

> Witness statements must:
>
> …
>
> d)   End with this paragraph: 'I believe that the facts stated in this witness statement are true. I understand that proceedings for contempt of court may be brought against anyone who makes, or causes to be made, a false statement in a document verified by a statement of truth without an honest belief in its truth.'
>
> …
>
> The court may decide not to take into account a document or the evidence of a witness if these directions have not been complied with.

In practice, whether the rule and / or the court order bites, it is unlikely that there will be any material distinction in consequence.

Both provide the court with a *discretion.*

Where a witness statement is not taken into account, it will likely mean that the party who she is giving evidence for has no evidence. That party's case may therefore be struck out.

b. Unless order

Failure to comply with an unless order will mean that the sanction in that order will take effect. The exception is where the party in default applied for, and in fact obtains, relief (CPR 3.8(1)).

The application must be supported by evidence (CPR 3.9(2)).

Take the following example.

The court directs a claimant to fully particularise the allegations in the particulars of claim. This must be done within a certain period of time. The sanction for default is specified in the order: the statement of case is automatically struck out.

c. Inability to read or sign

A court order or PD usually prescribes what must be done where a person cannot read or sign a document that must be verified by a statement of truth.

i. Court order

The notice of allocation will usually include this direction:

> If a witness is unable to read the statement in the form produced to the court, the statement must include a certificate that it has been read or interpreted to the witness by a suitably qualified person. If a witness who has made a statement is to give evidence or be cross-examined and is unable to do so in spoken English (or Welsh if the hearing is in Wales), the party relying on that witness must ensure that a suitable independent interpreter is available.

> The judge may refuse to hear the evidence or consider any statement of any witness whose statement has not been prepared and copied to the other party and the court in accordance with the paragraphs above.

Where the direction for a certificate, or suitable independent interpreter, is applicable, but has not been complied with, the judge may refuse to take into account the relevant evidence.

ii. Practice direction

The PD prescribes that, where the inability is *other than by reason of language alone,* the document must contain a certificate made by an "authorised person" (PD 22 at [3A.1]).

An authorised person is a person able to administer oaths, and take affidavits. She need not be independent of the parties, or independent of their representatives.

She must certify the following (PD 22 at [3A.3]).

First, the document has been read to the person signing it. Secondly, that person appeared to understand it, and approved its content as accurate. Thirdly, the declaration of truth has been read to that person.

Fourthly, that person appeared to understand the declaration, and the consequences of making a false declaration. Fifthly, that person signed, or made her mark, in the presence of the authorised person.

The form of the certificate is prescribed (PD 22 at Annex 1):

> I certify that I [name and address of authorised person] have read over the contents of this document and the declaration of truth to the person signing the document [if there are exhibits, add 'and explained the nature and effect of the exhibits referred to in it'] who appeared to understand (a) the document and approved its content as accurate and (b) the declaration of truth and the consequences of making a false declaration, and made his mark in my presence.

Failure to follow these requirements will mean that the document is not verified by a statement of truth.

f. Adjourn

Contact the other side to see whether the parties can agree, subject to the court making the order.

If the other side is not contacted before a formal application is made, which is not resisted, the court will be unlikely to award the cost of it. It will have been unnecessary.

In absence of agreement, a formal application must be made.

This will need a *good* reason (PD 27 at [6.2]).

The court may adjourn a hearing (CPR 3.1(2)(b)).

When exercising this power, the court will discharge its duty.

First, to give effect to the overriding objective (CPR 1.2(a)). Secondly, actively managing cases to do so (CPR 1.4).

Accordingly, the court is often persuaded whether or not to grant an adjournment on the basis of the factors and considerations set out below. They can be used to structure submissions.

i. Overriding objective

The overriding objective includes the following (CPR 1.1(2)).

First, saving expense. Secondly, dealing with the case in a way which is proportionate to the: amount of money involved; importance of the case; and financial position of each party. Thirdly, ensuring that the case is dealt with expeditiously and fairly.

Fourthly, allotting an appropriate share of the court's resources to the case, while taking into account the need to allot resources to other cases.

ii. Court's duty to manage cases

Active case management includes the following (CPR 1.4(2)).

First, deciding which issues need full investigation and a final hearing, and accordingly disposing summarily of others. Secondly, fixing timetables, or otherwise controlling the progress of the case. Thirdly, considering whether the likely benefits of taking a particular step justify the cost of taking it.

Fourthly, dealing with as many aspects of the case as it can on the same occasion. Fifthly, giving directions to ensure that the final hearing proceeds quickly and efficiently.

iii. Health

Success will likely depend on the following.

1. Material difference

Where a witness cannot attend, but the evidence that she would be able to give would make no material difference to the outcome of the case, the court should refuse an adjournment.

Where the witness is *key,* her evidence is likely to be *material.*

In a claim where liability is in dispute, and both witness accounts are wholly inconsistent, the court will seek to place the parties on an equal footing. To do so, an adjournment may be granted.

Where a key witness can show *genuine* ill-health, the court will usually grant (at least) a *first* adjournment.

2. Evidence

To establish genuine ill-health, medical evidence may be expected.

Ideally, this will satisfy the following criteria in *General Medical Council v Hayat* [2018] EWCA Civ 2796 at [38].

First, the medical professional should be identified. Secondly, she should give details as to her familiarity with the party's medical condition. This includes detailing recent consultations.

Thirdly, the party's medical condition should be identified, with the features of that condition, which, in the medical professional's opinion, prevent that party attending the final hearing. Fourthly, there should be a reasoned prognosis. That is, likely course of the medical condition.

The court is *not* bound to accept medical evidence.

If it is rejected, however, there should be a *good* reason.

3. Directions

Notwithstanding the above, if a party, or other witness, is *needed for the case to be dealt with justly*, but is unable to be present *through no fault of her own*, the court will usually grant an adjournment, however disproportionate that may appear.

The obvious example is where a party has been abruptly admitted to an accident and emergency department of a hospital.

If the court has reservations, it may give directions (CPR 27.7).

For example, that (further) medical evidence is filed and served before a specified time and date.

In default, the issue of costs may be specified, or reserved.

g. In-person / remote hearing

In the exceptional circumstances of the COVID-19 public health emergency, the court may decide that a case is suitable for disposal by way of remote, telephone or audio-visual, hearing.

i. Court order

If so, this will be set out in the notice of trial date.

Usually, it will contain the following direction:

> If any party considers that the hearing cannot proceed by way of [Cloud Video Platform] they must **within 48 hours** of receipt of this Order send to the Court office by email to … and send to the other party a full explanation of why they say that a hearing by [Cloud Video Platform] should not take place. Such written communication will be treated as an application to adjourn the [Cloud Video Platform] hearing and will be placed before the Judge on the papers for decision and any further directions.

If a party considers that a remote hearing would not further the overriding objective, they must follow the prescribed procedure.

ii. Rules

No *right* exists to in-person, or remote, hearings, for three reasons.

First, factors of the overriding objective. Secondly, the court's active case management considerations. Thirdly, authority.

Relevant factors to the overriding objective include the following.

First, saving expense. Secondly, dealing with the case in ways that are proportionate to the importance of the case. Thirdly, ensuring that it is dealt with expeditiously and fairly. Fourthly, allowing to it an appropriate share of the court's resources, while taking into account the need to allot resources to other cases.

Active case management includes the following considerations.

First, whether the likely benefits of taking a particular step justify the cost. Secondly, dealing with the case without the parties needing to attend court. Thirdly, making use of technology. Fourthly, giving directions to ensure that the final hearing proceeds quickly and efficiently.

iii. Authority

There are three recent authorities.

1. *Lucas v Gatward*

In *Lucas v Gatward* [2020] 10 WLUK 205, the High Court refused an application to vacate a trial. The reason for the application was the vulnerability of the applicant and other witnesses, and therefore inability to attend, during the COVID-19 pandemic.

Those who are unable to attend are able to give evidence in a *remote* hearing. Unless there was certainty as to when the hearing would take place, there was a risk that witnesses would not be available. Adjournment would lead to further costs.

2. *Muncipio de Mariana*

In *Muncipio de Mariana v BHP Group Plc (formerly BHP Billiton)* [2020] EWHC 928 (TCC), [2020] BLR 421 at [16]-[17] and [24], the court gave guidance on applications for adjournment during the COVID-19 pandemic.

The starting point is the overriding objective. The court must also take into account the impact of the pandemic so far as it is compatible with the proper administration of justice (PD 51 ZA at [4]).

HHJ Eyre QC gave the following guidance at paragraph 24:

"In the light of those authorities and the material referred to therein I have concluded that the following principles govern the question of whether a particular hearing should be adjourned if the case cannot be heard face to face or whether instead there should be a remote hearing.

i) Regard must be had to the importance of the continued administration of justice. Justice delayed is justice denied even when the delay results from a response to the currently prevailing circumstances.

ii) There is to be a recognition of the extent to which disputes can in fact be resolved fairly by way of remote hearings.

iii) The courts must be prepared to hold remote hearings in circumstances where such a move would have been inconceivable only a matter of weeks ago.

iv) There is to be rigorous examination of the possibility of a remote hearing and of the ways in which such a hearing could be achieved consistent with justice before the court should accept that a just determination cannot be achieved in such a hearing.

v) Inevitably the question of whether there can be a fair resolution is possible by way of a remote hearing will be case-specific. A multiplicity of factors will come into play and the issue of whether and if so to what extent live evidence and cross-examination will be necessary is likely to be important in many cases. There will be cases where the court cannot be satisfied that a fair resolution can be achieved by way of a remote hearing."

3. *A Local Authority*

In *A Local Authority v A Mother* [2020] EWHC 1086 (Fam) at [23]-[29], it was held that, in care proceedings concerning a four-year-old boy whose parents were accused of causing fatal injuries to his infant sister, the hearing should be remote.

Lieven J drew the following conclusions (with emphasis added):

> "[27]   … Having considered the matter closely, my own view is that is not possible to say as a generality whether it is easier to tell whether a witness is telling the truth in court rather than remotely. It is clear from [*Re A (Children) (Remote Hearing: Care and Placement Orders)* [2020] EWCA Civ 583, [2020] 4 FLR 297] that the Court of Appeal is not saying that all fact finding cases should be adjourned because fact finding is an exercise which it is not appropriate to undertake remotely. *I agree with Leggatt LJ that demeanour will often not be a good guide to truthfulness. Some people are much better at lying than others and that will be no different whether they do so remotely or in court.* …
>
> [28]   I was concerned that a witness might be more likely to tell the truth if they are in the witness box and feel the pressure of the courtroom, but … I do now accept that this could work the other way round. *Some witnesses may feel less defensive and be more inclined to tell the truth in a remote hearing* than when feeling somewhat intimidated in the court room setting. …
>
> [29]   For these reasons *I do not think that it is possible to say as a generality that a remote hearing is less good at getting to the truth than one in a courtroom.* …"

h. Set aside

A party may apply for an order that judgment is set aside, and that the claim is reheard, provided the following (CPR 27.11(1)).

First, she was neither present, nor represented, at the hearing. Secondly, she did not give written notice to the court, requesting that the claim be decided in her absence.

The application must be made not more than 14 days after the day on which notice of the judgment was served on her.

It may only be granted in these circumstances (CPR 27.11(3)).

First, the applicant had a *good* reason for not attending, being represented at the hearing, or giving written notice to the court. Secondly, she has a *reasonable prospect of success*.

An application cannot be made where the parties agreed to deal with the claim without a hearing (CPR 27.11(5)).

If the application is successful, the court must fix a new date for hearing the claim. This may take place *immediately*. It may be dealt with by the *same* judge who set aside judgment (CPR 27.11(4)).

i. Relief from sanctions

Where there has been a failure to comply with a CPR, PD, or court order, any sanction has effect. That is, unless the defaulting party applies for, and in fact obtains, relief (CPR 3.8(1)).

i. Need

Before making a formal application, check whether the CPR, PD, or court order, *specifies* a sanction.

If not, and there is *no* automatic sanction, then there is *no* need to apply for relief. This is because no sanction has taken effect.

1. Discretion

Directions in the notice of allocation usually include that the judge 'may refuse to hear' evidence that has not been prepared, filed and served, in accordance with the directions for the final hearing.

There is a material difference between *may refuse to hear*, and, for example, failure to comply with an *unless* order.

The former provides the court with a *discretion* as to whether or not to *impose* a sanction. An unless order, however, *specifies a sanction.* For example, 'shall stand automatically struck out'.

The latter therefore requires an application for relief from a sanction *that has taken effect*. This is an important distinction.

2. Court order

Often, the application for relief is in respect of an unless order.

In credit hire claims, for example, the following direction is usual:

Because the claim includes a claim for hire of a replacement vehicle:

10.a the Claimant shall be debarred from relying upon the fact of impecuniosity for the purposes of determining the appropriate rate of hire unless the documents to be served by the Claimant includes the following documents which are in his control:

i) copies of the Claimant's wage slips or equivalent documentation evidencing the approximate level of available income to the Claimant for the period of three months pre-accident and covering the period of hire; and

ii) copy bank and credit card statements for a period of three months pre-accident and covering the period of hire.

This unless order requires the claimant to serve the relevant documents that are in her control. The specified sanction in default is that she is debarred from relying on a plea of impecuniosity.

The following is also usually included in the notice of allocation:

Warning: You must comply with the terms imposed upon you by this order; otherwise your case is liable to be struck out or some other sanction imposed. If you cannot comply you are expected to make formal application to the Court before any deadline imposed upon you.

Absent formal application, the following may be submitted.

First, the court order requires a written application to be filed, and served. Secondly, it must be issued before the relevant deadline.

Both court orders have been breached.

The notice of allocation will also include the following direction:

> Because this Order has been made without a hearing, the parties have the right to apply to have the Order set aside, varied or stayed. A party making such an application must send or deliver the application to the court (together with any appropriate fee) to arrive within seven days of service of this Order.

If the application for relief is in respect of an unless order in the notice of allocation, the following submissions may be made.

First, if unable to comply, the court order required a written application to set aside, vary, or stay, the unless order. Secondly, it had to be made within seven days of service of the order.

Both court orders have been breached.

In absence of a *good* reason, a claimant who has failed to make a formal application before the relevant deadline is in difficulty.

ii. Evidence

Applications should follow the procedure in CPR 23 (CPR 3.9(1)).

They *must* be supported by evidence (CPR 3.9(2)).

Often, by a witness statement signed by a professional client.

When resisting an application for relief, the first submission is often that no formal application has been made. The second is that there is no evidence in support. Both breach CPRs.

Counsel cannot give evidence. Submissions are not evidence.

In any event, it is unlikely that counsel is able to give submissions on the detail that is required to address the three-stage test.

iii. Three-stage test

The court will apply the following test when deciding whether or not to grant relief from sanctions (*Denton & Ors v TH White Ltd & Ors* [2014] EWCA Civ 906, [2014] 1 WLR 3926 ("*Denton*") at [24]):

> "… The first stage is to identify and assess the seriousness and significance of the 'failure to comply with any rule, practice direction or court order' which engages rule 3.9(1). If the breach is neither serious nor significant, the court is unlikely to need to spend much time on the second and third stages. The second stage is to consider why the default occurred. The third stage is to evaluate 'all the circumstances of the case, so as to enable [the court] to deal justly with the application including [the factors in CPR 3.9(1)]'. …"

1. Seriousness & significance

Previous breaches are irrelevant ("*Denton*" at [27]):

> "The assessment of the seriousness or significance of the breach should not, initially at least, involve a consideration of other unrelated failures that may have occurred in the past. At the first stage, the court should concentrate on an assessment of the seriousness and significance of the very breach in respect of which relief from sanctions is sought. …"

If neither serious, nor significant, the court should grant relief.

2. Good reason

The question is not whether there is *a* reason.

It is whether there is a *good* reason.

Authority provides that "good reasons are likely to arise from circumstances outside the control of the party in default" (*Andrew Mitchell MP v News Group Newspapers Ltd* [2013] EWCA Civ 1537, [2014] 1 WLR 795 ("*Mitchell*") at [43]; and *Denton* at [30]).

A legal representative's failure will rarely amount to a good reason (*Mitchell* at [41]; and *Denton* at [12]):

"… Solicitors cannot take on too much work and expect to be able to persuade a court that this is a good reason for their failure to meet deadlines. They should either delegate the work to others in their firm or, if they are unable to do this, they should not take on the work at all. …"

One of the following is usually necessary, but not sufficient.

First, failure to consult. Secondly, lack of authority.

The leading authority is Peter Gibson LJ in *Training in Compliance Ltd (t/a Matthew Reed) v Dewse (t/a Data Research Co)* [2001] CP Rep 46 (CA) ("*Training*") at [66] (with emphasis added):

"… It seems to me that, in general, *the action or inaction of a party's legal representatives must be treated under the Civil Procedure Rules as the action or inaction of the party himself.* So far as the other party is concerned, it matters not what input that party himself has made into what the legal representatives have done or have not done. The other party is affected in the same way; and dealing with a case justly involves dealing with the other party justly. It would not in general be desirable that the time of the court should be taken up in considering separately the conduct of the legal representatives from that which the party himself must be treated as knowing, encouraging, or permitting. …"

Training was applied in *Gladwin v Bogescu* [2017] EWHC 1287 (QB) at [30]. In the next paragraph, Turner J said that:

"... since the introduction of the Jackson reforms, the general approach of the courts is likely to be less rather than more indulgent of legal advisors as a justification for granting forbearance to the litigants themselves. ..."

Training was followed by Julian Knowles J in *Deutsche Leasing (UK) Ltd v Zaskin College Ltd* [2018] EWHC 1977 (QB) at [73].

3. All the circumstances

An application following a serious, or significant, breach, for which there is no good reason, is *not* doomed to fail.

Where submissions on the first two stages are not properly arguable, concede them. You will gain credibility with the court. You will also be able to invest more time in the third stage of the test.

This is virtually always properly arguable.

The court will have regard to *all* the circumstances of the case.

The factors in CPR 3.9(1), however, are "of particular importance and should be given particular weight" (*Denton* at [35]).

First, that litigation is conducted efficiently, and at proportionate cost. Secondly, to enforce compliance with CPRs, PDs, and court orders.

Often, applications do not *explicitly* address these factors.

If so, it is often worth emphasising the *particular importance,* and *particular weight,* that must be placed on them.

a. Proportionality

Is the sanction proportionate to the breach?

Take the following example.

The sanction means that the defendant has no evidence. The claim is for £10,000. The defence is fully particularised, and properly arguable. The sanction effectively extinguishes the defence.

On these facts, proportionality may weigh in favour of relief.

b. Compliance

This is where previous breaches are added to the scales.

Multiple breaches can be an especially weighty circumstance.

The court "must always bear in mind the need for compliance ... because the old lax culture of non-compliance is no longer tolerated" (*Denton* at [34]).

c. Promptness

This may be *critical.*

If an application for relief is prompt, the other party may be under an obligation to consent to it, so as to discourage opportunism.

On the other hand, in *Oak Cash & Carry Ltd v British Gas Trading Ltd* [2016] EWCA Civ 153, [2016] 4 All ER 129 at [61], Jackson LJ (with whom King and Lindblom LJJ agreed) said that:

> "In my view the defendant's lack of promptness in applying for relief is the critical factor. When that delay is added to all the other factors, it can be seen that the defendant's default has substantially disrupted the progress of the action. Bearing in mind factors (a) and (b) in rule 3.9 (which under *Denton* must be given particular weight) there is really only one answer to the question which arises at stage 3. The court must refuse the application for relief."

d. Opportunism

Resisting an application that must succeed breaches the duty to help the court to further the overriding objective (*Denton* at [43]):

> "… It is as unacceptable for a party to try to take advantage of a minor inadvertent error, as it is for rules, orders and practice directions to be breached in the first place. Heavy costs sanctions should, therefore, be imposed on parties who behave unreasonably in refusing to agree extensions of time or unreasonably oppose applications for relief from sanctions. …"

Unreasonable opposition should form the basis of a submission that the *manner* in which that party has conducted her case demonstrates that she has behaved unreasonably (see chapter 24(c)(iv)(7)). Accordingly, she should pay the associated costs.

18. Final hearing

This chapter covers the procedure of the final hearing.

First, the judge. Secondly, representation. Thirdly, the general rule that hearings are recorded, and in public. Fourthly, evidence is not usually on oath. Fifthly, cross-examination may be limited. Sixthly, the line between judicial intervention, and "entering the arena".

a. Judge

Generally, judicial functions are carried out by a district judge.

They may be carried out by a circuit judge (PD 27 at [1]). This requires her consent (PD 2B at [11.2(1)]). In practice, this is rare.

b. Representation

A party may be represented by a lawyer. Counsel or solicitor.

i. Lay

They may also be represented by a lay representative, provided that that party is present throughout the hearing (PD 27 at [3.2]).

On the basis of article 3 of the Lay Representatives (Right of Audience) Order 1999 (SI 1999/1225), the court's permission is required where a party wishes to be represented by a lay representative in three circumstances (PD 27 at [3.2(2)]).

First, her client does not attend the hearing. Secondly, at any stage after judgment. Thirdly, on any appeal brought against any decision made by a district judge.

ii. Corporate

Officers, or employees, may represent companies (PD 27 at [3.2]).

iii. Unruly manner

Section 11 of the Courts and Legal Services Act 1990 prescribes that, where the court is of the opinion that a person, who would otherwise have a right of audience, is behaving in an *unruly manner* in any proceedings, the court may refuse to hear her.

If so, the court must specify the conduct that warranted refusal.

iv. Intentionally misled the court

Where the court has reason to believe that a person *intentionally has misled the court,* or otherwise demonstrates that she is unsuitable to exercise a right of audience, in the instant, or any other, proceedings, the court may order that person's *disqualification* from exercising any right of audience. Reasons must be given.

Appeal lies to the Court of Appeal. Any such order may be revoked, however, at any time, by any county court judge.

c. Public

In general, cases *must* be heard in public.

i. Right

If there is any doubt as to whether or not it is a well-established, *common law* right, it is certainly a well-established, *statutory* right.

This follows from article 6 of the European Convention on Human Rights. A court is a public authority. It must act compatibly with Convention rights pursuant to section 6 of the Human Rights Act 1998.

ii. COVID-19

PD 51Y came into force on 25 March 2020.

It provides for audio and video hearings. It will cease to have effect on the date that the Coronavirus Act 2020 ceases to have effect.

The relevant paragraphs are self-explanatory:

> [2]   … where the court directs that proceedings are to be conducted wholly as video or audio proceedings and it is not practicable for the hearing to be broadcast in a court building, the court may direct that the hearing must take place in private where it is necessary to do so to secure the proper administration of justice.

> [3]   Where a media representative is able to access proceedings remotely while they are taking place, they will be public proceedings. …

> [4]   Any hearing held in private under paragraph 2 must be recorded, where that is practicable, in a manner directed by the court. …

d. Recording

Recording may be official, or unofficial.

i. Official

Hearings *will* be tape recorded (PD 27 at [5.1]).

A party may obtain a transcript by paying a fee to the transcriber.

In any event, "there is generally no right for either a party or a non-party to listen to the recording" (*Cape Intermediate Holdings Ltd v Dring* [2019] UKSC 38, [2020] AC 629 at [25]).

ii. Unofficial

Attention is drawn to section 9 of the Contempt of Court Act 1981, and *Practice Direction (Tape Recorders)* [1981] 1 WLR 1526, which relate to unofficial recordings (PD 27 at [5.2]).

1. Contempt of Court Act 1981

Section 9(1) of this Act provides that:

> … it is a contempt of court—
>
> (a) to use in court, or bring into court for use, any tape recorder or other instrument for recording sound, except with the leave of the court;
>
> (b) to publish a recording of legal proceedings made by means of any such instrument, or any recording derived directly or indirectly from it, by playing it in the hearing of the public or any section of the public, or to dispose of it or any recording so derived, with a view to such publication;
>
> (c) to use any such recording in contravention of any conditions of leave granted under paragraph (a).

2. Practice Direction (Tape Recorders) [1981] 1 WLR 1526

The PD provides guidance as to the *discretion* of the court to grant, withhold, or withdraw, leave to use tape recorders, or to impose *conditions* as to the use of the recording.

The discretion is unlimited.

The following three factors *may* be relevant.

First, any reasonable *need* for the recording. Whether a litigant, a person connected with the press, or broadcasting.

Secondly, the risk that the recording would be used to brief witnesses out of court, where a direction has been made to exclude one or more witnesses from court.

Thirdly, the possibility that proceedings will be *disturbed*, participants would be *distracted*, or otherwise *worried*.

Consideration should be given to whether or not *conditions* should be imposed. The *identity* of the person applying to use a tape recorder, and her role in the proceedings, may be relevant.

Tape recorders are *not* intended to replace official transcripts.

3. Consequences

The consequences can be serious, regardless of status.

a. Party or witness

In *Attorney General v Scarth* [2013] EWHC 194 (Admin), an 87-year-old man was sentenced to 28 days' imprisonment for each contempt of court, suspended for 12 months. In particular, making video or audio recordings, and publishing them on the internet.

b. Legal representative

In *Gubarev & Anor v Orbis Business Intelligence Ltd & Anor* [2020] EWHC 2167 (QB), [2020] 4 WLR 122, a trial was streamed outside the jurisdiction for three days without the court's permission.

The President of the Queen's Bench Division said that:

> "During this pandemic, there have been temporary changes … Nonetheless, whether a court hearing is a remote hearing … or a conventional face to face hearing, it must be conducted in a way that is as close as possible to the pre-pandemic norm."

Breach of express prohibitions in court orders, or prohibitions on broadcasting, "will be treated with the utmost seriousness." It may result in the papers being sent to the regulator (SRA / BSB), or the Attorney General with a view to considering whether proceedings should be brought for contempt of court.

e. Evidence

The court need *not* take evidence on oath (CPR 27.8(4)).

i. In person

In practice, evidence is not on oath.

One reason is that cases involving a disputed allegation of dishonesty will not usually be suitable for, and therefore allocated to, the small claims track (PD 26 at [8.1(1)(d)]).

ii. Remote

It is more common in remote, telephone and audio-visual, hearings, that a witness is required to give evidence on oath.

This may reflect the difficulty in maintaining the integrity of proceedings when a witness is giving evidence. As the President of the Queen's Bench Division said in *Orbis* (see above) at [51]:

> "In normal circumstances a judge can see and hear everything that is going on in court. … The judge can see whether someone is attempting to influence, coach or intimidate a witness whilst they are giving evidence. … That a judge can see and hear everything that happens in court enables the judge to maintain order, discipline and control over what is done in court, and thus to maintain the dignity and the integrity of the proceedings as a whole. …"

f. Cross-examination

The court may adopt *any* fair method of proceeding (CPR 27.8(1)).

This includes the following (PD 27 at [4.3]).

First, to ask questions of any witness before allowing any other person to do so. Secondly, to ask questions of all, or any of, the witnesses before allowing another to do so.

Thirdly, to refuse to allow cross-examination of any witness, until every witness has given evidence in chief. Fourthly, to limit cross-examination of a witness to a fixed time frame, subject or issue.

This does *not* allow the court to prevent *any* cross-examination.

In *Al Rawi & Ors v The Security Service & Ors* [2011] UKSC 34, [2012] 1 AC 531, Lord Dyson said that:

> "[10]   There are certain features of a common law trial which are fundamental to our system of justice …

[11]   The open justice principle is not a mere procedural rule. It is a fundamental common law principle. …

[13]   Another aspect of the principle of natural justice is that the parties should be given the opportunity to call their own witnesses and to cross-examine the opposing witnesses. …"

g. Judicial intervention v entering the arena

There is a distinction between *judicial intervention*, which is sanctioned by the CPR, and "entering the arena", which is not.

Authority provides guidance as to when a party has a legitimate grievance, that the overriding objective has not been achieved, because the parties were not on an equal footing.

i. Judicial intervention

When contrasted to claims that have been allocated to the fast track, or to the multi-track, the procedure can appear much more *inquisitorial.* That is, as opposed to *adversarial.*

Judges should be cautious, however, not to enter the arena.

Especially when *both* parties are legally represented.

ii. Entering the arena

Serafin v Malkiewicz & Ors [2020] UKSC 23, [2020] 1 WLR 2455 is the leading authority on entering the arena, bias and unfairness.

1. Bias

There is a distinction between *bias,* and *unfairness.*

At paragraphs 38 and 39, Lord Wilson (with whom Lords Reed, Briggs, Kitchen and Lady Arden agreed) *assumed,* but did not decide, that bias means "a prejudice against one party or its case for reasons unconnected with the legal or factual merits of the case."

2. Unfairness

At paragraph 40, Lord Wilson said that the "leading authority on inquiry into the unfairness of a trial remains" *Jones v National Coal Board* [1957] 2 QB 55 (CA) at 65, in which Denning LJ said that:

> "… interventions should be as infrequent as possible when the witness is under cross-examination. It is only by cross-examination that a witness's evidence can be properly tested, and it loses much of its effectiveness in counsel's hands if the witness is given time to think out the answer to awkward questions; the very gist of cross-examination lies in the unbroken sequence of question and answer. Further than this, cross-examining counsel is at a grave disadvantage if he is prevented from following a preconceived line of inquiry which is, in his view, most likely to elicit admissions from the witness or qualifications of the evidence which he has given in chief. Excessive judicial interruption inevitably weakens the effectiveness of cross-examination in relation to both aspects that we have mentioned, for at one and the same time it gives a witness valuable time for thought before answering a difficult question, and diverts cross-examining counsel from the course which he had intended to pursue, and to which it is by no means easy sometimes to return."

3. Litigants in person

At paragraph 46, Lord Wilson said that:

> "… Every judge will have experienced difficulty at trial in divining the line between helping the litigant in person to the extent necessary for the adequate articulation of his case, on the one hand, and becoming his advocate, on the other. … Training and

experience will generally have equipped the professional advocate to withstand a degree of judicial pressure and, undaunted, to continue within reason to put the case. The judge must not forget that the litigant in person is likely to have no such equipment and that, if the trial is to be fair, he must temper his conduct accordingly."

At paragraph 48, Lord Wilson concluded as follows:

"… when one considers the barrage of hostility towards the claimant's case, and towards the claimant himself acting in person, fired by the judge in immoderate, ill-tempered and at times offensive language at many different points during the long hearing, one is driven, with profound regret, to [the] conclusion that he did not allow the claim to be properly presented; that therefore he could not fairly appraise it; and, that, in short, the trial was unfair. Instead of making allowance for the claimant's appearance in person, the judge harassed and intimidated him in ways which surely would never have occurred if the claimant had been represented."

For these reasons, a full retrial was ordered.

4. Practical guidance

The following should suffice.

First, keep your cool. If there is a sense on the transcript of proceedings that you are discourteous, argumentative, or otherwise dramatising, it will make any appeal more difficult.

Secondly, do not make an application for recusal, unless the unfairness is *absolutely* clear.

Thirdly, if it is clear, do not wait till the end of the hearing. Make the application promptly.

Fourthly, if you know of the reason for the *real*, or *potential* partiality, you may be held to have waived any right to raise it if you do not say something early on.

For example, in *Locabail (UK) Ltd v Bayfield Properties Ltd & Anor* [2000] QB 451 (CA) at [25], personal friendship, or animosity, between the judge and any member of the public involved in the case constitute "a real danger of bias".

Fifthly, if you identify any obvious unfairness, find a courteous, professional way to convey your concern.

Sixthly, your professional, ethical duty, requires you to put your client's interest first. Not your career. You protect the latter through keeping *calm*, strict adherence to professional *ethics*, and reasoned *judgement*.

Seventhly, speak to other members of chambers, who may know the judge. Seek *their* counsel.

19. Witness evidence

This includes witness statements and oral evidence.

It is usually an essential ingredient of a party's case.

To the extent that the evidence of a witness chimes with *agreed* or *known* facts, a judge is likely to follow it when giving judgment.

Where it is incompatible, however, the credibility of that witness will *diminish*. The ability to give evidence that assists the party who called her will therefore also *diminish*.

a. Contemporaneous

After a road traffic collision, a witness may complete a *questionnaire*. Often, on the same day, or shortly thereafter.

This will likely state the location, registration number of the relevant vehicles, and mechanism of collision.

There may also be a *sketch plan* indicating the following.

First, the lane that a vehicle was in. Secondly, whether the claimant's vehicle was in front of, or behind, the defendant's vehicle. Thirdly, the part of the respective vehicles where the impact occurred. Fourthly, who was at fault. Fifthly, the reason why.

i. Weight

Is it signed and dated?

Is it contemporaneous to the collision?

If so, it is likely to pre-date a witness statement by many days, months, or even *years*. If it is consistent with a witness' statement or oral evidence, this can be particularly persuasive.

Weight usually increases where the author of the questionnaire is not a party, but an *independent* witness. She would therefore not have known either party (see chapter 20(a)).

ii. Cross-examination

Where inconsistent with a witness statement, or oral evidence, it is likely to be good evidence on which to cross-examine.

A concession in cross-examination, that there is no good reason why a witness has changed her account, can undermine that witness as a reliable historian of events. The later account may be in the form of a witness statement, or answers in cross-examination.

In *Onassis v Vergottis* [1968] 2 Lloyd's Rep 403 (HL) at 431, Lord Pearce famously said that: "With every day that passes memory becomes fainter and the imagination becomes more active".

iii. Filed & served

Has it been filed and served?

If in doubt, speak to your professional client. If it has not been filed and served in accordance with directions for the final hearing, the judge may refuse to admit it.

If you provide copies to the court and the other party, it may go into evidence without resistance.

Where the court or the other party do not agree, however, an oral application can be made to the judge, requesting permission, where it is in accordance with the overriding objective.

b. Statements

A witness statement is a written statement of a witness. It has a signed statement of truth by that witness. It contains the evidence that that witness would be allowed to give orally.

At a final hearing, where a witness is called to give oral evidence, her witness statement will usually stand as her evidence in chief.

The witness will usually be cross-examined.

Answers in examination-in-chief, cross-examination, and any re-examination, constitute a witness' oral evidence.

Witness statement and oral evidence is the evidence of a witness.

i. Formalities

The CPR prescribing the form of witness statements is expressly disapplied (CPRs 27.2(1)(c) and 32.8).

They should, however, aspire to follow the same formalities.

ii. Form

The notice of allocation often prescribes form (see chapter 11(f)).

First, start with the name of the case and claim number. Secondly, state the full name and address of the witness. Thirdly, set out the witness' evidence clearly in numbered paragraphs, on numbered pages. Fourthly, end with a statement of truth. Fifthly, be signed by the witness and dated.

Additionally, it should have a header with the name of the court that the matter will be heard in, be in a legible font, and the text should be sized so that it can be read easily.

iii. Statement of truth

Witness statements must be verified by a statement of truth.

There are usually two sources of this obligation.

First, the notice of allocation (see chapter 11(f)). Secondly, PD 22.

The rule requiring witness statements to be verified by a statement of truth is not disapplied (CPRs 27.2(2) and 22.1(1)(c)).

The form of a statement of truth is as follows (PD 22 at [2.2]):

> I believe that the facts stated in this witness statement are true. I understand that proceedings for contempt of court may be brought against anyone who makes, or causes to be made, a false statement in a document verified by a statement of truth without an honest belief in its truth.

Legal representatives are *not* permitted to sign witness statements on behalf of clients. A witness statement *must* be signed by the *witness* who confirms the truth of it (PD 22 at [3.2]).

Without a statement of truth, there are usually two reasons why a court may direct that it shall not be admissible as evidence.

First, a court order. Secondly, CPR 22.3.

The notice of allocation usually directs that:

> The Judge may refuse to hear the evidence or consider any statement of any witness whose statement has not been prepared and copied to the other party and the court in accordance with the paragraphs above [prescribing that a witness statement must have a statement of truth].

CPR 22.3 prescribes that: 'If the maker of a witness statement fails to verify the witness statement by a statement of truth the court may direct that it shall not be admissible as evidence.'

iv. Inability to read or sign

Where a person is unable to read or sign a statement, *other than by reason of language alone,* it must contain a certificate made by an authorised person (PD 22 at [3A.1]).

This is a person able to administer oaths, and take affidavits. She need not be independent of the parties, or their representatives.

She must certify the following (PD 22 at [3A.3]).

First, that the document has been read to the person signing it. Secondly, that person appeared to understand it, and approved its content as accurate. Thirdly, the declaration of truth has been read to that person.

Fourthly, that person appeared to understand the declaration, and the consequences of making a false declaration. Fifthly, that person signed, or made her mark, in her presence.

The form of the certificate is prescribed (in PD 22 at Annex 1):

> I certify that I [name and address of authorised person] have read over the contents of this document and the declaration of truth to the person signing the document [if there are exhibits, add and 'explained the nature and effect of the exhibits referred to in it'] who appeared to understand (a) the document and approved its content as accurate and (b) the declaration of truth and the consequences of making a false declaration, and made his mark in my presence.

v. Contemporaneous

When was the statement dated?

In the context of a road traffic collision, for example, it may have been signed months, or, in many cases, *years* after the collision.

Drawing the court's attention to how *long* after the collision can reduce the weight of it.

The number of days between the date of the collision, and the date that the statement was signed, can be precisely calculated. Where the number is high, a submission may be made that little weight should be attached to the statement.

Alternatively, the statement may be dated *shortly* after the collision. In oral evidence, the witness contradicts a key fact that is confirmed to be true within her statement. Her recollection is likely to have been *greater* when her statement was signed, compared to the *later* date that oral evidence is given.

Where *later,* oral evidence, is inconsistent with *earlier,* written evidence, the *latter* will likely be given more weight.

vi. Detail

Witness statements should be *detailed*.

For example, in a claim for repairs and credit hire following a road traffic collision, a few paragraphs in the claimant's statement are unlikely to convey the necessary detail.

During cross-examination, at least one "important" detail will often emerge that has been omitted from a witness statement. This is one purpose of cross-examination. To elicit evidence which assists one party's case, and undermines that of another.

Quality, but also *quantity,* is important.

If a *single* important fact has been omitted, it may *severely* undermine a witness' credibility. Where *several,* less important, facts, are left out of a statement, however, this may be *understandable.* It is therefore less likely to substantially undermine credibility.

In a road traffic collision, the location, and the mechanism of the collision, should both be set out. Clearly. In detail.

In a claim for credit hire, the need to hire should be set out in reasonable detail. 'Social, domestic and pleasure' is insufficient. This is legal jargon. People do not usually use this phrase in everyday life. They are likely to be the words of a legal representative.

'I needed a vehicle to drop off my two young children to school in the morning, and to take my eldest child to judo on Tuesday and Thursday evenings' is approaching the particularity required.

vii. Hearsay notice

If a witness is unable to attend a hearing, there is no need for a hearsay notice. Nevertheless, one is often provided by a party who has legal representation. This is because it is necessary for cases allocated to the fast track, and to the multi-track.

It is also good practice, and courteous, promptly to inform another party of the reason that a witness will not attend. Otherwise, there is a legitimate expectation that a witness, who *has* written a statement, *will* attend to give oral evidence.

Without the benefit of cross-examination, the court may give that witness' evidence *little* weight. It may even be given *no* weight.

For example, there is a claim after a road traffic collision. Liability is in dispute. It is unlikely that a claimant whose witness failed to attend will be able to discharge the burden of proving that the defendant's driving fell below a reasonable standard.

Likewise, a defendant whose witness did not attend will likely be found liable where a claimant gives oral evidence that the defendant's driving caused a collision.

viii. Non-attendance

The *strict* rules of evidence do *not* apply.

Nevertheless, the Civil Evidence Act 1995 is a useful resource.

Section 4 prescribes that, when attributing weight to hearsay evidence, the court 'shall have regard to any circumstances from which any inference can reasonably be drawn as to the reliability or otherwise of the evidence'.

1. Factors

Hearsay evidence does not necessarily attract *any* weight.

The following non-exhaustive considerations are relevant.

First, whether it would have been reasonable, and practicable, for the party by whom the evidence was adduced to have produced the maker of the original statement as a witness. Secondly, whether the original statement was made contemporaneously with the occurrence, or existence, of the matters stated. Thirdly, whether the evidence involves multiple hearsay.

Fourthly, whether any person involved had any motive to conceal, or to misrepresent matters. Fifthly, whether the original statement was an edited account, made in collaboration with another person, or for a particular purpose. Sixthly, whether the circumstances in which the evidence is adduced as hearsay are such as to suggest an attempt to prevent proper evaluation of its weight.

2. Practice

In practice, the fourth and sixth are likely to be decisive.

Even if there was not a *deliberate attempt* to prevent proper evaluation of the weight of a witness' evidence, if that witness does not undergo cross-examination, the *practical effect* is that a proper evaluation has, in fact, been prevented.

The first consideration is often answered by promptly informing the parties and the court of the good reason for non-attendance.

c. Oral

A party wishing to rely on a witness in relation to an issue of fact to be decided at a final hearing *must* file and serve a witness statement, written by that witness, and verified by a statement of truth.

If a party has filed and served a witness statement, and she wishes to rely on that statement at a final hearing, she should call that witness to give oral evidence.

Where a party knows that a witness is unable to attend, notice should be given to the other party, and the court, of the good reason that that witness is unable to attend. It should be *prompt*.

Where a party is unable to attend a final hearing, she should give written notice, in accordance with CPR 27.9. If a party fails to do so, the court may strike out the claim, defence, or counterclaim.

If it appears as though a witness for the other party has not attended, and that party is legally represented, politely enquire whether that witness will attend the hearing. Dishonestly stating that a witness has attended, when an advocate knows that they have not, or knows that they will not attend, is unethical.

If you know that a witness has not attended, this will strengthen your lay client's negotiating position in relation to settlement.

i. Application to decide in absence

Where three conditions are met, if a party does not attend a hearing, the court *must* take into account that party's statement of case, and any other documents that she has filed and served, when the claim is decided (CPR 27.9).

First, written notice that the party will not attend has been given to the court, and to the other party, at least seven days before the final hearing.

Secondly, at least seven days before the final hearing, any other documents which she has filed with the court are served on the other party.

Thirdly, in the written notice, a request is made that the court decides the claim in her absence, and compliance with the first and second conditions are confirmed.

Where these conditions are satisfied, there is "written notice".

The judge will then provide written reasons for her judgment.

A copy will be sent to each party (PD 27 at [5.4]).

ii. Claimant

If a claimant does not attend the final hearing, and does not give written notice, the court may strike out the claim.

The claimant must then apply for the order striking out the claim to be set aside, so that the claim can be heard (CPR 27.11).

iii. Defendant

The court may decide the claim on the basis of the claimant's evidence alone in the following circumstances (CPR 27.9(3)).

First, the *defendant* does not attend the final hearing, or give written notice. Secondly, the *claimant* attends, or gives written notice.

Where the defence has been struck out, the defendant must apply for the order striking out the defence to be set aside, so that the claim can be heard (CPR 27.11).

iv. Claimant & defendant

If neither party attends, or gives written notice, the court may strike out the claim, defence, and counterclaim (CPR 27.9(4)).

20. Independent & objective evidence

Directions in a claim following a road traffic collision usually order that documents and information sent to the court, and to each party, should, where possible, include plans, maps, photographs of the scene, and photographs of the damage.

If possible, they should be agreed.

A police accident report is also likely to assist the court.

In principle, original documents must be available at the hearing.

In practice, copies suffice. Recourse is only had to originals where a copy is illegible.

a. Witnesses

An independent witness is likely to tip the balance where liability is in dispute arising from a road traffic collision. She must usually write a witness statement, attend court to give oral evidence, and thereby undergo cross-examination.

Either party may call an independent witness.

What matters is that she is not previously known to either party, expresses an opinion on fault, and provides cogent reasons.

b. Photographs

For example, photographs were taken immediately after a road traffic collision. They show that the vehicles are touching. The defendant's vehicle is in the claimant's lane.

This can be persuasive evidence that the defendant veered into the claimant's lane.

Ideally, photographs should be exhibited to a witness statement, identifying *when* they were taken, by *whom*, and *what* they show.

As the formal rules of evidence do not apply, however, a witness may confirm the same in oral evidence.

i. Clear

Photographs should be in colour.

Black and white photographs are often of poor quality. This is especially the case where they have been copied.

It may be that the electronic version is in colour. The printer was set to black and white, however, when printed.

In any event, enquire with your professional client whether colour photographs exist. If so, they can be promptly filed, served, and relied on at the hearing.

ii. Location

In a claim following a road traffic collision, if there are no colour photographs of the location of the collision, consider Google Maps.

Pictures can usually be found.

If the party who you represent states that the pictures show the location of the collision, speak to the other side. The parties may agree that the pictures show the location of the collision.

If so, the other party will usually be grateful to accept a colour copy. The court is also likely to be grateful.

If the other side does not agree that these pictures show the location of the collision, however, you will need to ask permission from the court to rely on them.

This is likely to be granted. Evidence of the *alleged* location of the collision is likely to assist the court with the road layout.

iii. Road layout

The number of lanes on a road, whether there were traffic lights, signs, and road markings, should all be apparent.

There may also be an indication of the speed limit.

For example, street lights generally indicate 30 miles per hour (rule 124 of *The Highway Code*).

iv. Damage

Where liability is in dispute following a road traffic collision, colour photographs may show the extent of any damage.

For example, whether the damage to the claimant's vehicle is a scratch, perhaps showing that the vehicles were moving at the point of impact. Or a large dent, perhaps showing that the collision could not properly be described as "low velocity".

It may be possible to deduce the direction of impact from photographs of the damaged vehicles. This may chime with an engineer's report depicting the direction of impact.

c. Sketch plans

They may be of central importance depending on the following.

First, they are contemporaneous. Secondly, they are detailed. Thirdly, they are consistent with a party's statement of case. Fourthly, they are consistent with known, or agreed, facts. Fifthly, they are consistent with independent, or objective, evidence. Sixthly, they are consistent with a party's written and oral evidence.

Where there is a material inconsistency with a statement of case, known or agreed facts, independent or objective evidence, or a party's evidence, however, this can be put in cross-examination.

Demonstrating the *extent* of inconsistency often correlates with the *weight* that is given to the sketch plan.

Either way, it will usually either assist, or undermine, a case.

Sketch plans often assist with the following.

First, the direction along the road that the relevant vehicles were travelling. Secondly, the lane that a vehicle was in. Thirdly, the location of the collision. Fourthly, the mechanism of collision. Fifthly, the point of impact.

Ideally, sketch plans should be exhibited to a witness statement.

They should identify *when* they were taken, by *whom*, and *what* they show. As the formal rules of evidence do not apply, however, a witness can relay the same in oral evidence.

d. Engineers' reports

The court usually needs an engineer's report in claims following a road traffic collision (PD 27 at Appendix A).

The report should also contain a statement identifying who commissioned it, that the engineer understands her overriding duty to the court, and that she has in fact complied with that duty.

An engineer's report usually contains the following evidence.

i. Collision

If the *date* of the collision is inconsistent to that pleaded in a statement of case, the written or oral evidence of a witness, it is either an error, or the report relates to damage that is unrelated to the index incident. Either way, this is an important inconsistency in a party's case, or evidence. It requires an explanation.

ii. Impact

If air bags were fitted, and in fact deployed, this suggests that the impact was considerable. In a claim for personal injury, it makes it more likely that an occupant of that vehicle suffered injury.

iii. Damage

On the location of any damage, the report may evidence 'moderate accidental damage to the right-hand side'.

If this is incompatible with the pleadings, or the written or oral evidence of a witness, it is either an error, or the report relates to damage that is unrelated to the index collision.

Either way, this is an important inconsistency in a party's case or evidence, requiring an explanation from that party.

The report is likely to indicate the results of a vehicle history check. Is there a record of any adverse history? For example, isolated dents and scratches, and the effect on the pre-accident value.

iv. Value

What is the pre-accident value?

It is likely to be based upon the following.

First, when the vehicle was first registered. Secondly, the adjusted retail value for type and age. Thirdly, trade value.

What is the cost of repair? This should include the time involved in conducting repairs using Glass' Repair Estimate, and the reasonable labour charge. The rate per hour should be stated.

Where the damage is extensive, these are more likely to be higher.

The collision is more likely to have been significant.

Any applicable VAT should be set out.

The repair schedule will usually include the following.

First, new parts. Secondly, parts that only require repainting. Thirdly, specialist and sundry charges, such as corrosion protection materials. Fourthly, parts that require removal, and refitting.

v. Write-off

Does the value mean that it is uneconomical to repair?

If so, what is the salvage value? This is the value of parts that can be removed, and sold, where the cost of repair exceeds the pre-accident value. So as to mitigate their loss, claimants are expected to offset this sum when claiming for repairs.

vi. Roadworthy

Is the vehicle roadworthy?

A typical sentence may read: 'In our opinion this vehicle was not road-worthy at the time of our inspection as a result of the damage sustained due to suspension damage'.

In this circumstance, if towing and storage charges for a reasonable period are claimed, they are likely to be agreed, or allowed.

Are temporary repairs practical to make the vehicle roadworthy?

If so, it undermines the need for a hire vehicle. If temporary repairs are impractical, it supports the need to hire.

vii. Pictures

Pictures of the vehicle are likely to be attached.

The registration should match the vehicle registration set out in the report. Many pictures will be irrelevant. Some will show the relevant damage. In any event, they should be in colour.

e. The Highway Code

The Highway Code is often essential, for a final hearing following a road traffic collision, where liability is in dispute.

It is the starting point for the standard of care of a reasonable driver. Section 38(7) of the Road Traffic Act 1988 provides that:

A failure on the part of a person to observe a provision of the Highway Code … may in any proceedings … be relied upon by any party to the proceedings as tending to establish or negative any liability …

It can be highly persuasive. It is not determinative. Whether or not a breach is evidence of negligence depends on the circumstances.

In *Goad v Butcher & Anor* [2011] EWCA Civ 158 at [9], Moore-Bick LJ (with whom Mummery LJ agreed) said that:

> "One can well understand the temptation in a case of this kind to place some emphasis on a breach of the Highway Code when it can be so clearly established, but in my view it was little more than an unfortunate red herring. A failure to observe the Code may be evidence of negligence, but whether it is will depend very much on the circumstances in which the act in question was committed and who is the claimant. …"

At paragraph 20, Jackson LJ dissented in these terms:

> "A breach of the Highway Code does not give rise to a presumption of negligence … It is, however, a relevant circumstance, which the court should take into account when determining whether the driver was negligent: see *Powell v Phillips* [1972] 3 All ER 864."

In *Powell v Phillips* [1972] 3 All ER 864 (CA) at [868D], Stephenson LJ (with whom Davies and Buckley LJJ agreed) said that:

> "It is, however, clear that a breach [of *The Highway Code*] creates no presumption of negligence calling for an explanation, still less a presumption of negligence making a real contribution to causing an accident or injury. The breach is just one of the circumstances on which one party is entitled to rely in establishing the negligence of the other and its contribution to causing the accident or injury."

f. Judicial College Guidelines

In claims for personal injury, the *Judicial College Guidelines for the Assessment of General Damages in Personal Injury Cases* (15th edn, OUP 2019) is essential (see chapter 27(h)).

It achieves the following.

First, a clear and logical framework for the assessment of general damages in personal injury cases. Secondly, takes into account inflation since the previous edition. Thirdly, reflects the decisions of the higher courts on quantum.

Chapter 13, 'Minor Injuries' is likely to be the relevant chapter.

21. Submissions

It is unusual to give *opening* submissions.

There are frequently *preliminary* submissions.

In any event, *closing* submissions are often the only opportunity for a party to invite the court to find in accordance with her case.

a. Preliminary

Preliminary submissions are made before the evidence is heard.

In practice, there are three common examples.

All relate either to identifying the issues at an early stage, or otherwise deciding promptly which issues need a final hearing, and disposing summarily of others.

First, an application for early termination. For example, to strike out a statement of case on the basis that it is an abuse of process.

Secondly, an application for relief from sanctions following failure to comply with an unless order. For example, following failure to file and serve evidence, of impecuniosity in a claim for credit hire, in accordance with the directions in the notice of allocation.

Thirdly, an application for an adjournment. For example, a key witness has indicated on the morning of a final hearing that she will not attend. The court needs to determine this application before hearing the evidence and giving judgment on the claim.

b. Opening

There is usually no need for opening submissions. This is because there are not often complicated issues of fact, law or evidence.

i. Issues

In practice, if the parties are represented, the court will invite the advocates to outline the issues.

Claimants state whether liability, quantum or both are in dispute.

In a credit hire claim, the defendant usually outlines the issues related to this head of loss. They often include the following.

First, need to hire. Secondly, enforceability. Thirdly, need to hire a vehicle of the type hired. Fourthly, period of hire. Fifthly, impecuniosity. Sixthly, rate of hire. Seventhly, additional extras, such as delivery and collection.

ii. Agreement

If quantum is agreed subject to liability, this should be flagged.

If any head of loss is agreed, this should also be flagged. A head of loss, and the amount for that head of loss, may be agreed in a statement of case, later correspondence, or on the day of the hearing.

c. Closing

The court may adopt any fair method of proceeding (CPR 27.8(1)).

Submissions may not be invited from a party at the conclusion of a hearing. This often indicates that the *other* party has not yet persuaded the court of her case. It would not normally be just to dismiss a party's case without hearing her submissions.

Submissions should be clear, concise, and consistent with the statement of case and evidence of the party who you represent.

i. Order

The claimant usually has the last word. It is *her* case.

Where the burden of proof is on the defendant, the court still usually allows the claimant to have the last word.

For example, in a claim for credit hire, where the defendant has the burden of proving that there is a difference in hire rates.

In this case, once you have made submissions, you can invite the judge to hear any reply to points raised by the claimant that you have not yet addressed. Although the court is not obliged, in practice, if you ask for a right to reply, it is often granted.

The defendant is often asked to give closing submissions first.

If so, the claimant may benefit from the following.

First, a careful note of the defendant's submissions can be taken, and responses to those submissions can be incorporated into the claimant's submissions. Secondly, there is not usually an opportunity for the defendant to reply to the claimant's submissions.

ii. Approach to fact-finding

To use Stewart's J words in *Kimathi & Ors v The Foreign & Commonwealth Office* [2018] EWHC 2066 (QB) ("*Kimathi*") at [95], there are three judgments that have "helpfully crystallised and advanced learning in respect of the approach to evidence."

First, *Gestmin SGPS SA v Credit Suisse (UK) Ltd & Anor* [2013] EWHC 3560 (Comm). Secondly, *Lachaux v Lachaux* [2017] EWHC 385 (Fam), [2017] 4 WLR 57. Thirdly, *Carmarthenshire County Council v Y* [2017] EWFC 36, [2017] 4 WLR 136.

Stewart J summarised the key principles in *Kimathi* at [96]:

"i) *Gestmin:*

- We believe memories to be more faithful than they are. Two common errors are to suppose (1) that the stronger and more vivid the recollection, the more likely it is to be accurate; (2) the more confident another person is in their recollection, the more likely it is to be accurate.

- Memories are fluid and malleable, being constantly rewritten whenever they are retrieved. This is even true of 'flash bulb' memories (a misleading term), i.e. memories of experiencing or learning of a particularly shocking or traumatic event.

- Events can come to be recalled as memories which did not happen at all or which happened to somebody else.

- The process of civil litigation itself subjects the memories of witnesses to powerful biases.

- Considerable interference with memory is introduced in civil litigation by the procedure of preparing for trial. Statements are often taken a long time after relevant events and drafted by a lawyer who is conscious of the significance for the issues in the case of what the witness does or does not say.

- The best approach from a judge is to base factual findings on inferences drawn from documentary evidence and known or probable facts. 'This does not mean that oral testimony serves no useful purpose... But its value lies largely... in the opportunity which cross-examination affords to subject the documentary record to critical scrutiny and to gauge the personality, motivations and working practices of a witness, rather than in testimony of what the witness recalls of particular conversations and events. Above all, it is important to avoid the fallacy of supposing that, because a witness has confidence in his or her recollection and is honest, evidence based on that recollection provides any reliable guide to the truth'.

ii) *Lachaux:*

- Mostyn J cited extensively from *Gestmin* and referred to two passages in earlier authorities. I extract from those citations, and from Mostyn J's judgment, the following:

- 'Witnesses, especially those who are emotional, who think they are morally in the right, tend very easily and unconsciously to conjure up a legal right that did not exist. It is a truism, often used in accident cases, that with every day that passes the memory becomes fainter and the imagination becomes more active. For that reason, a witness, however honest, rarely persuades a judge that his present recollection is preferable to that which was taken down in writing immediately after the incident occurred. Therefore, contemporary documents are always of the utmost importance…'

- '…I have found it essential in cases of fraud, when considering the credibility of witnesses, always to test their veracity by reference to the objective fact proved independently of their testimony, in particular by reference to the documents in the case, and also to pay particular regard to their motives and to the overall probabilities…'

- Mostyn J said of the latter quotation, 'these wise words are surely of general application and are not confined to fraud cases… it is certainly often difficult to tell whether a witness is telling the truth and I agree with the view of Bingham J that the demeanour of a witness is not a reliable pointer to his or her honesty.'

iii) *Carmarthenshire County Council:*

- The general rule is that oral evidence given under cross-examination is the gold standard because it reflects the long-established common law consensus that the best way of assessing the reliability of evidence is by confronting the witness.

- However, oral evidence under cross-examination is far from the be all and end all of forensic proof. Referring to paragraph 22 of *Gestmin*, Mostyn J said:

    '…this approach applies equally to all fact-finding exercises, especially where the facts in issue are in the distant past. This approach does not dilute the importance that the law places on cross-examination as a vital component of due process, but it does place it in its correct context.'"

iii. Credibility

In *Kimathi* at [98], Stewart J endorsed the late Lord Bingham's approach to witness credibility. There are "three main tests which in general give a useful pointer as to where the truth lies, although their relative importance will vary from case to case".

First, consistency with agreed facts. Secondly, internal consistency. Thirdly, consistency with what has previously been asserted.

1. Agreed facts

Agreed facts provide an *anchor* from which the court can build a picture as to what happened.

A witness giving evidence that is disputed, but consistent with *agreed* or *known* facts, will likely be given significant weight.

Where her account is *in*consistent, however, it is unlikely to be given much weight. Her credibility is therefore likely to diminish.

Submissions can be made as follows.

First, to what extent a party's evidence is *consistent* with agreed, and known, facts. Secondly, how *near* to the safe, judicial ground of agreed, and known, facts, that party's case is. Thirdly, how *far* it is from this safe ground to the other party's case.

2. Internal inconsistency

Why is a case inconsistent with its statement of case and evidence?

For example, a party's statement of case pleads X. That party's written and oral evidence confirms the truth of Y. X and Y are inconsistent. That party's case appears to be internally inconsistent.

If this party is the claimant, who has the burden of proving that what is pleaded in her statement of case is more likely than not, the court may cite this submission as a reason to dismiss the claim.

For example, the particulars of claim plead that the mechanism of collision was a rear-end shunt. The claimant's statement confirms that the impact was to the left, passenger-side of her vehicle.

The objective evidence supports the claimant's statement. An engineer's report confirms that the damage to the claimant's vehicle is to the left, passenger-side. Supporting photographs are attached. The claimant's answers in cross-examination evidence that the damage was to the left, passenger-side of her vehicle.

The pleaded mechanism of collision is incompatible with the claimant's written and oral evidence, and the objective evidence.

The claimant's case is internally inconsistent.

As the claimant has the burden of proving, on a balance of probabilities, that the collision occurred in accordance with her statement of case, if she has failed to do so, her case will be dismissed.

3. Consistent previous statements

In *Painter v Hutchison & Anor* [2007] EWHC 758 (Ch) at [3], Lewison J (as he then was) discussed unsatisfactory witness evidence.

In doing so, he set out eight indicators. Where applicable, it may also indicate that a witness has been inconsistent. Where none apply, it may indicate that a witness has been consistent.

In either case, the following can be used in closing submissions as a powerful pointer to (in)consistency.

First, evasive and argumentative answers. Secondly, tangential speeches, avoiding the question. Thirdly, blaming legal advisers for documentation, such as statements of case, and witness statements. Fourthly, self-contradiction. Fifthly, internal inconsistency. Sixthly, shifting case. Seventhly, introducing new evidence.

If none of these indicators apply to your witness, it may be helpful to *show* it. Likewise, if one or more of these indicators apply to the other party's witness, it may also be worth *demonstrating*.

Show the contradiction between *earlier* and *later* oral evidence.

This is usually more persuasive than merely stating the fact that there has been a contradiction. This is because the court is able to come to the same conclusion of its own accord.

An accurate note of the hearing is invaluable. This will enable you to quote the witness. Paraphrasing invites dispute and caution.

You are also able to *show* that the witness said X at the beginning of cross-examination. She said Y at the close of it.

X and Y are incompatible.

Therefore, she changed her position in oral evidence.

Y is in accordance with your client's case.

The words should chime with the court's note for full impact.

This should give the court confidence to place little weight on the evidence of the witness who has been inconsistent.

iv. Inherent unlikelihood

Even if a party's case is consistent with agreed or known facts, and internally consistent, it may be *unlikely*.

What is pleaded in a statement of case? What is stated in a witness statement? What is asserted in oral evidence?

Is it more likely than not? If not, then it is *inherently unlikely*.

This is often the least persuasive submission, however, so prioritise time on agreed and known facts, internal consistency, and consistent previous statements. If there is time, go on to demonstrate the inherent unlikelihood of the other party's case.

22. Orders & judgment

An "order" may be made without a judgment.

A "judgment" is usually followed by an order.

Confusingly, "judgment" and "order" are used in the CPRs interchangeably. At other times, they are used in conjunction.

a. Orders

Judgments and orders are usually drafted by the court.

The parties can draw up draft orders, however, including those that are attached to applications, proposed consent orders before judgment, and draft minutes of order following judgment.

i. Carriage

The court usually draws up an order after disposing of a claim, or deciding an application.

A party may also be ordered to do so (CPR 40.3(1)(a)).

If so, the party bringing the claim, or making the application, will have "carriage" of the order. If only one of the parties is represented, however, that party will be directed to draw up the order.

In principle, where an order is drawn up by a party, it must be filed no later than seven days after the date on which the court so ordered (CPR 40.3(3)(a)). In practice, orders should be drawn up on the day. In any event, no later than 24 hours after the hearing.

If requested to draw up the order, ensure that you don't leave the hearing without the relevant email address. Usually, the judge will provide her judicial email address.

If your hearing is in person, you can ask the usher for the relevant email address. Stating that you have been directed to draft the order by the court following a hearing often allays any concerns.

Remote hearings are usually also public. For this reason, the judge may not wish to state her email address in open court. If so, you can give your email address, so that she can reply.

ii. Consent

Where the parties have settled a claim, or an application has been agreed, before the court has given a decision on the same, the parties should draw up a "consent" order.

For an unrepresented party, judicial approval is always necessary (CPR 40.6(2)(b)).

There are three requirements (CPR 40.6(7) and PD 40B at [3.4]).

First, it must be drawn up in the terms that have been agreed. Secondly, it must be expressed as being "by consent". Thirdly, it must be signed by the legal representatives acting for the parties. If a party is not represented, it must be signed by that party.

iii. Tomlin

Parties who have settled their dispute may wish to set out the terms that have been agreed, otherwise than in an order itself.

As court orders are public documents, a "Tomlin" order is useful.

It enables the parties to keep the terms of their agreement confidential. It also stays all further proceedings on the agreed terms.

There are two main ways to record these terms.

First, in a schedule following the order. Secondly, in a settlement agreement, attached to the order.

In any event, the parties may apply to the court for enforcement.

The Tomlin order itself should provide for costs. Not the schedule, or the settlement agreement.

In practice, one of the following is often used.

First, payment and assessment of costs. Secondly, no order.

There are three benefits to including the agreement for payment and assessment of costs in the Tomlin order itself.

First, there is a judgment for costs. Secondly, interest will accrue. Thirdly, the right to a detailed assessment.

The court is reluctant to go behind what the parties have agreed.

iv. Unless

An "unless" order *usually* specifies three details.

First, what action must be taken. Secondly, the time within which that act must be performed. Thirdly, the consequence of default.

It *must* specify the time within which the act must be performed.

The following, suitably adapted, wording *must* be used where possible (PD 40B at [8.2(1)]):

Unless the [claimant / defendant] [files and serves] [an amended, fully particularised particulars of claim / defence / counterclaim] by 4.00pm on [Friday, 20 November 2020] his [claim / defence / counterclaim] will be struck out and judgment entered for the [defendant / claimant].

The key point is that a *fixed* date is given. It does not depend on an *event*. If the event does not take place, uncertainty does not arise.

b. Judgment

In general, "judgment" is a final, reasoned decision of the court. It determines whether a claim is allowed, or dismissed. Judgment takes effect when it is made. That is, when declared, or announced.

i. Default

"Default judgment" is the determination of a claim following failure to file an acknowledgment of service, defence, or defence to counterclaim, within the relevant time limit (see chapter 17(a)).

ii. After final hearing

Judgment *may* be given after the date of a final hearing.

1. Ex tempore

Judgment is usually given orally. Often, immediately after the hearing. This is known as an "ex tempore" judgment.

Take a careful note for the following reasons.

First, you may be directed to draw up a draft minute of order. Secondly, to identify grounds of appeal. Thirdly, to advise on prospects of appeal. Fourthly, so that both your professional client, and your lay client, are able to reflect on the reasoning of the judgment. Fifthly, transcripts are unnecessary to appeal.

2. Reserved

Occasionally, judgment will be "reserved".

This may be the case where there is an exceptionally large amount of evidence, authority that the court wishes to consider in her own time, or where there is insufficient time.

Reserved judgments may be given at a later hearing, or in writing.

iii. Slip rule

Once judgment has been entered, the decision cannot be reconsidered. The sole exception is to correct an accidental slip, or omission, under the "slip rule" (CPR 40.12(1)).

A party may apply for an error in a judgment, or an order, to be corrected (PD 40B at [4.1]). It may be without notice.

The application notice should achieve the following.

First, describe the error. Secondly, state the required correction.

This may be by means of an informal document, such as a letter.

In any event, applications may be considered without a hearing in three circumstances.

First, the application so requests. Secondly, with the consent of the parties. Thirdly, where the court does not consider that a hearing would be appropriate.

If the slip is *obvious*, the court may deal with the application without notice, or direct that notice is served on the other party.

If the application is opposed, it should, if practicable, be listed for a hearing before the judge who gave judgment, or made the order.

The court has an inherent power to vary its orders, so as to make the *meaning*, and the *intention,* of the court clear (PD 40B at [4.5]).

iv. Reasons

The court *must* give reasons for its decision (CPR 27.8(6)).

1. Duty

The court owes a *general duty* to give reasons.

In *Flannery & Anor v Halifax Estate Agencies Ltd* [2000] 1 WLR 377 (CA) at 381G-382C, Henry LJ handed down judgment on behalf of Laws LJJ and Hidden J:

> "(1)   The duty is a function of due process, and therefore of justice. Its rationale has two principal aspects. The first is that fairness surely requires that the parties especially the losing party should be left in no doubt why they have won or lost. This is especially so since without reasons the losing party will not know … whether the court has misdirected itself, and thus whether he may have an available appeal on the substance of the case. The second is that a requirement to give reasons concentrates the mind; if it is fulfilled, the resulting decision is much more likely to be soundly based on the evidence than if it is not.
>
> (2)   The first of these aspects implies that want of reasons may be a good self-standing ground of appeal. Where

because no reasons are given it is impossible to tell whether the judge has gone wrong on the law or the facts, the losing party would be altogether deprived of his chance of an appeal unless the court entertains an appeal based on the lack of reasons itself.

(3)   The extent of the duty, or rather the reach of what is required to fulfil it, depends on the subject matter. Where there is a straightforward factual dispute whose resolution depends simply on which witness is telling the truth about events which he claims to recall, it is likely to be enough for the judge (having, no doubt, summarised the evidence) to indicate simply that he believes X rather than Y; indeed there may be nothing else to say. But where the dispute involves something in the nature of an intellectual exchange, with reasons and analysis advanced on either side, the judge must enter into the issues canvassed before him and explain why he prefers one case over the other. This is likely to apply particularly in litigation whereas here there is disputed expert evidence; but it is not necessarily limited to such cases.

(4)   This is not to suggest that there is one rule for cases concerning the witnesses truthfulness or recall of events, and another for cases where the issue depends on reasoning or analysis (with experts or otherwise). The rule is the same: the judge must explain *why* he has reached his decision. The question is always, what is required of the judge to do so; and that will differ from case to case. Transparency should be the watchword."

Without *reasons,* a judgment is not *transparent.*

The appeal court cannot determine whether or not the judge had adequate *reasons* for the *conclusions.*

Reasons may be as brief, and simple, as the nature of the case allows. They will usually be given at the end of a hearing. The court may give them at another hearing, or in writing (PD 27 at [5.3]).

2. Note

A judge will prepare a note of the reasons for judgment, which will then be sent to each party, in two situations (PD 27 at [5.4]).

First, the case was decided without a hearing. Secondly, a party did not attend a hearing, but gave written notice (CPR 27.9(1)).

3. Failure

Where permission to appeal due to lack of reasons is made out immediately after judgment, *English v Emery Reimbold & Strick Ltd* [2002] EWCA Civ 605, [2002] 3 All ER 385 at [25] prescribes the proper procedure (with emphasis added):

> "… the Judge should consider whether his judgment is defective for lack of reasons, adjourning for that purpose should he find this necessary. If he concludes that it is, *he should set out to remedy the defect by the provision of additional reasons refusing permission to appeal on the basis that he has adopted that course.* If he concludes that he has given adequate reasons, he will no doubt refuse permission to appeal. If an application for permission to appeal on the ground of lack of reasons is made to the appellate court and it appears to the appellate court that the application is well founded, it should consider adjourning the application and remitting the case to the trial Judge with an invitation to provide additional reasons for his decision or, where appropriate, his reasons for a specific finding or findings. Where the appellate court is in doubt as to whether the reasons are adequate, it may be appropriate to direct that the application be adjourned to an oral hearing, on notice to the respondent."

v. Reconsideration

An application for permission to appeal may be well-founded where there are any of the following failures.

First, to identify the elements of the claim or defence. Secondly, to analyse contemporary documents. Thirdly, to deal with the thrust of expert evidence. Fourthly, to take a balanced approach to assessing the credibility of witnesses of fact.

In *Simetra Global Assets Ltd & Anor v Ikon Finance Ltd & Ors* [2019] EWCA Civ 1413, [2019] 4 WLR 112 at [46], Males LJ (with whom Peter Jackson and McCombe LJJ agreed) gave the following guidance (with emphasis added):

> "First, succinctness is as desirable in a judgment as it is in counsel's submissions, but *short judgments must be careful judgments*. Second, it is not necessary to deal expressly with every point, but a judge must say enough to show that care has been taken and that the evidence as a whole has been properly considered. Which points need to be dealt with and which can be omitted itself requires an exercise of judgment. Third, the best way to demonstrate the exercise of the necessary care is to make use of 'the building blocks of the reasoned judicial process' by identifying the issues which need to be decided, marshalling (however briefly and without needing to recite every point) the evidence which bears on those issues, and giving reasons why the principally relevant evidence is either accepted or rejected as unreliable. Fourth, and in particular, fairness requires that a judge should deal with apparently compelling evidence, where it exists, which is contrary to the conclusion which he proposes to reach and explain why he does not accept it."

In the next paragraph, Males LJ said that failure to follow this guidance does not *necessarily* mean that a judgment is inadequately reasoned. Nevertheless, "the judgment will need to be particularly cogent if it is to satisfy the demands of justice."

This is because of the risk that an appellate court will conclude that the judge has plainly failed to take the evidence into account.

vi. Appeals

Section 80 of the County Courts Act 1984 applies (PD 27 at [5.5]).

1. Note

A party may request a judge to note the following.

First, any question of law raised at the hearing. Secondly, the facts in evidence in relation to any such question. Thirdly, her decision on any such question, and of her determination of the proceedings.

2. Signed copy

The judge must provide a signed copy of this note where the following two conditions are satisfied.

First, a party has made an application. Secondly, the relevant fee has been paid. It is *irrelevant* whether a notice of appeal has been served. This note must be used at the hearing of the appeal.

c. Time limits for compliance

The general rule is that the time limit for complying with a judgment, or an order, is within 14 days (CPR 40.11).

The court may order otherwise. For example, during the COVID-19 pandemic, requests for 21 days have usually been successful.

The date must be expressed as a calendar date. It must also include the time of day by which the act must be done (CPR 2.9(1)).

23. Costs, disbursements & witness expenses

The general rule is that there are no substantial costs.

The exception is where the court finds that a party has behaved unreasonably (see chapter 24(a)).

Usually, recoverable costs and disbursements from a defendant after a successful claim can be determined in advance of issue.

a. General discretion

As night follows day, costs do *not* always follow the event.

It is correct that, *if* the court decides to make an order about costs, the *general* rule is that the unsuccessful party will be ordered to pay the costs of the successful party.

The court may make a different order (CPRs 27.2(2) and 44.2(2)).

The court has a *general* discretion. This can be broken down into the following three *particular* discretions (CPR 44.2(1)).

First, *whether* costs are payable by one party to another. Secondly, the *amount.* Thirdly, *when* they are to be paid.

i. Payable

The rule in CPR 27.14(2) does *not* fetter this general discretion:

> The court may not order a party to pay to another party in respect of that other party's costs, fees and expenses …

It does *not* prescribe that the court *will* make an order.

A defendant who has been unsuccessful after a final hearing *may* still argue that the court should not make an order for costs.

To do so, the court should be invited to have regard to all the circumstances. In particular, the following (CPR 44.2(4)).

First, the *conduct* of the parties. Secondly, whether a party has succeeded on *part* of its case, even if that party has not been wholly successful. Thirdly, any admissible *offer* to settle made by a party, which is drawn to the court's attention.

1. Conduct

Conduct includes the following circumstances (CPR 44.2(5)).

First, conduct *before*, as well as *during*, proceedings. In particular, the *extent* to which the parties followed the Practice Direction – Pre-Action Conduct, or any relevant pre-action protocol.

Secondly, whether it was reasonable for a party to *raise*, *pursue*, or *contest*, a particular allegation, or issue.

Thirdly, the *manner* in which a party has pursued, or defended, its case, or a particular allegation, or issue.

Fourthly, whether a claimant who has succeeded, in whole or in part, *exaggerated* the claim.

In the alternative to the submission that a party has behaved unreasonably, the same factors can be used to argue that the conduct is such that the court should make no order (see chapter 23(a)(i)).

2. Limited success

For example, there is a claim for £8,000 in respect of three heads of loss. The court dismisses two heads of loss. One is allowed in the sum of £3,000. There has been "limited success".

In principle, there is an argument that there should be no order as to costs. The reason is that there has been *such* limited success.

In practice, the court is likely to make an order of costs in favour of the claimant. The real question is the *amount*.

3. Offers

Rejection is not a necessary or sufficient condition (CPR 27.14(3)):

> A party's rejection of an offer in settlement will not of itself constitute unreasonable behaviour ... but the court may take it into consideration ...

It may found a submission that there should be no order for costs.

Relevant circumstances include the following.

First, whether it was before the issue fee was paid. Secondly, whether it was before the hearing fee was paid. Thirdly, whether it was for a significantly greater sum than the judgment sum.

If an offer for more than the judgment sum was made *after* the issue fee was paid, it is difficult to resist an order to pay the issue fee. The offer did not mean that the issue fee was unnecessary. It was not possible to accept the offer and avoid paying the issue fee.

Where the offer was made *before* the issue fee was payable, however, the submission is that, if the offer was accepted, the issue fee would not have been incurred. The issue fee was unnecessary.

ii. Amount

If the costs are payable, that is *not* the end of the matter.

The court still has a discretion as to the *amount* of those costs.

1. Issue fee

If there has been limited success, the submission is that the amount of the issue fee should be proportionate to the amount of the judgment sum. Not the claimed sum that was exaggerated.

This submission has even greater force where there is an offer.

For example, the *claimed* sum is £8,000. The *judgment* sum is £3,000. If issued online, the issue fee for the former is £410. The issue fee for the latter is £105. About four times less.

The submission is that the proportionate amount is £105.

This deals with the issue fee in accordance with the overriding object-ive. This requires the court to deal with costs justly and at proportion-ate cost. It means dealing with costs in a way that is proportionate to the amount of money involved.

2. Hearing fee

The same arguments apply in relation to the hearing fee.

For example, the *claimed* sum is £8,000. The *judgment* sum is £3,000. The hearing fee for the former is £335. The hearing fee for the latter is £170. About half.

3. Legal representative's costs

The same arguments apply for the legal representative's costs.

For example, the *claimed* sum is £8,000. The *judgment* sum is £3,000. Where the claim form is served by the court, the legal representative's costs for the former is £100. The legal representative's costs for the latter is £80. One-fifth less.

iii. When

The court has a discretion as to when costs are to be paid.

The general rule is that, unless the court orders otherwise, the time limit for payment of costs is within 14 days (CPR 40.11).

In the COVID-19 pandemic, the court has routinely ordered costs to be payable within 21 days, or later. Usually, the paying party makes the request. It is uncommon for this to be resisted.

b. Fees

Issue, hearing, and application, fees, are payable by the party who starts a claim, requires a final hearing, or makes an application.

They are prescribed in the Civil Proceedings Order 2008 (SI 2008/1053), Schedule 1, paragraph 1 at [1.1]-[1.2], [2.1], and [2.3]-[2.5]. They are also in Form EX50 (3 August 2020).

A party is entitled to apply for help with fees where they have limited means, or on a low income.

i. Issue

To start a claim, a claim form, or counterclaim, must be "issued".

This can either be done online, or by using paper copies. The former is cheaper, however, if you do not know the exact amount that you are claiming, it cannot be issued online.

The issue fee is based on the "amount claimed" including interest.

The issue fee can be found in the bottom, right-hand corner of the first page of the claim form.

See appendix F for issue fees correct as of 1 November 2020.

ii. Hearing

On the court fixing a final hearing, an unless order will be made to pay a hearing fee. This will be in the notice of allocation.

The hearing fee is often called the "trial" fee.

See appendix G for hearing fees correct as of 1 November 2020.

iii. Application

In practice, there are three common types of application.

1. On notice

This means the other side has been notified of the application.

Where no other fee is specified, it is £255.

To set aside judgment, the fee is also £255.

2. Consent

Where an application is made by consent, and no other fee is specified, the fee is £100. For example, to vacate, or adjourn, a hearing.

There is no fee for an application by consent to adjourn, if it is received by the court, at least 14 days before the date of the hearing.

3. Permission to appeal

On filing an appellant's, or respondent's, notice, the fee is £120.

iv. Remission

A party can apply for help with fees (see chapter 6(k)).

c. Legal representatives

Claimants may recover the following costs that are attributable to issuing the claim (CPR 27.14(2)(a)).

First, those that are payable under CPR 45. Secondly, those that would be payable under CPR 45 if it applied.

These are "fixed commencement costs".

CPR 45 is concerned with amounts that are allowable in respect of *legal representatives'* charges (CPR 45.1(1)).

i. Specified sum

Fixed commencement costs are prescribed in CPR 45.2 at Table 1.

See appendix H for these costs correct as of 1 November 2020.

ii. Unspecified sum

Fixed costs will be calculated by reference to the judgment sum awarded after a final hearing. See appendix H.

iii. Counterclaim

There are no fixed costs.

iv. Injunction / specific performance

A party may be ordered to pay a sum not exceeding £260 for legal advice and assistance (CPR 27.14(2)(b) and PD 27 at [7.2]).

d. Party or witness expenses

The court may award the following to either party.

First, loss of earnings, or loss of leave. Secondly, travel expenses.

These can usually be agreed, subject to liability.

i. Loss of earnings or leave

The court may award a sum not exceeding £95 per person per day.

There are two grounds (CPR 27.14(2)(e) and PD 27 at [7.3]).

First, due to attending a hearing. Secondly, due to staying away from home for the same purpose.

1. Employed

When the final hearing is listed and disposed of in the morning, loss of earnings based on an hourly rate can be calculated.

When on a floating list, however, and the matter goes into the afternoon, the daily rate will be appropriate. The court is also able to compensate a witness who has taken leave to attend a hearing.

2. Self-employed

Was there a requirement to work during the hearing?

Was an opportunity to work lost? If so, it is claimable.

Take the following examples.

First, a beautician who lost an appointment.

Secondly, a driver with set hours.

Where the driver is able to work at any time, however, she may not have lost earnings *due to attending a hearing*. There was no *requirement* to work at the time.

3. Other

For example, the cost of a carer to look after an elderly dependent.

ii. Travel expenses

These must be *reasonably incurred* for the *purpose of attending a hearing*. This includes the following (CPR 27.14(2)(d)).

First, travelling to, and from, a hearing. Secondly, staying away from home.

Take the following examples.

First, use of a private car. Secondly, parking.

For an in-person hearing, a witness may travel from her home address to court. The postcode of her address will usually be in her statement. The mileage to and from court can be easily calculated.

Search online for directions from that postcode to court.

If the witness is going to drive home, the mileage is doubled. By convention, it is multiplied by 0.45 to work out the amount in pounds. This is the expense of private car use. This includes fuel, a share of wear and tear, expendables, and tax.

There are two key arguments.

First, the amount claimed is not *reasonable*. Secondly, the expenses were not *solely* for the purpose of attending a hearing.

1. Reasonable

Where travel expenses appear to be unusually high, a suspiciously round figure, or both, a party can request to see evidence.

In any event, cross-examination may be fruitful.

For example, a successful claimant claims the cost of staying the night in a Central London hotel. Her evidence is that this is for the purpose of attending a final hearing at the County Court at Central London. She *lives* in Central London. This may *not* be reasonable.

2. Purpose

For example, a witness drove her car to court. She picked up something from her office on the journey. From her home address, court is South. Her office is North. The route was *in*direct.

Her journey North was *not* for the purpose of attending a hearing. It was for an *un*related purpose. That part cannot be awarded.

e. Expert

Fees cannot exceed £750 (CPR 27.14(2)(f) and PD 27 at [7.3]).

f. Lay representative

CPR 27.14 applies to lay representatives' fees (CPR 27.14(4)).

g. Personal injury

Stage 1 fixed costs, and where relevant Stage 2 fixed costs, under CPR 45.18, may be claimed on the following four conditions.

First, the claim was within the scope of the Pre-Action Protocol for Low Value Personal Injury Claims in Road Traffic Accidents, or the Pre-Action Protocol for Low Value Personal Injury (Employers' Liability and Public Liability) Claims.

Secondly, the claimant reasonably believed that the claim was valued at more than the small claims track limit, in accordance with the relevant protocol. Thirdly, the defendant admitted liability within the protocol process. Fourthly, the defendant has not already paid these costs.

h. Appeal

CPR 27.14 applies to the costs of an appeal (*Akhtar v Boland* [2014] EWCA Civ 943, [2014] CP Rep 41 at [7]).

i. Re-allocation

There are separate rules when a claim has been re-allocated.

i. After leaving the small claims track

CPR 27.14 does *not* apply *after* re-allocation to another track. The rules that apply to the *new* track are applicable (CPR 27.15).

ii. Before re-allocation to the small claims track

The rules that apply to the track *before* re-allocation apply up to the *date of reallocation*. CPR 27.14 applies *thereafter*. The exception is where the court orders otherwise (CPR 46.13(2)).

24. Unreasonable behaviour

If a party has "behaved unreasonably", the other party may recover *substantial* costs. This can be of fundamental importance.

a. Further costs

CPR 27.14(2)(g) provides (with emphasis added) that:

> The court may not order a party to pay a sum to another party in respect of that other party's costs, fees and expenses, including those relating to an appeal, except *such further costs* as the court may assess by the summary procedure and order to be paid by a party who has *behaved unreasonably* …

This requires a finding that a party has 'behaved unreasonably'.

The court may then find that 'further costs' are payable.

b. Definition

There is no definition in the CPR of "behaved unreasonably".

So, we look to authority for guidance. If real doubt remains, the dictionary is a well-established aid to statutory interpretation.

i. Authority

The following provides guidance on the words "behaved unreasonably", "unreasonable", and "unreasonable conduct".

1. Behaved unreasonably

There are three recent authorities.

a. Dammermann

In *Dammermann v Lanyon Bowdler LLP* [2017] EWCA Civ 269, [2017] 2 Costs LR 393 ("*Dammermann*"), Longmore and McFarlane LJJ gave the following guidance (with emphasis added):

> "[30]   … We doubt if we can usefully give general guidance in relation to the circumstances in which it will be appropriate for a court to decide whether a party 'has behaved unreasonably' since *all such cases must be highly fact-sensitive.* In the somewhat different context of the jurisdiction to order a party's legal (or other) representative to meet what are called 'wasted costs' (defined as costs incurred 'as a result of any improper, unreasonable or negligent act or omission' of such representative), the court speaking through Sir Thomas Bingham MR said:
>
> > 'conduct cannot be described as unreasonable simply because it leads in the event to an unsuccessful result or because other more cautious legal representatives would have acted differently. *The acid test is whether the conduct permits of a reasonable explanation.* If so, the course adopted may be regarded as optimistic and as reflecting in a practitioner's judgment, but it is not unreasonable.'
>
> See *Ridehalgh v Horsefield* [1994] Ch 205, 232F.
>
> [31]   While we would not wish to incorporate all the learning about wasted costs orders into decisions under CPR Part 27.14(2)(g), we think that *the above*

dictum should give sufficient guidance on the word 'unreasonably' to district judges and circuit judges dealing with cases allocated to the Small Claims Track. *Ridehalgh* was, of course, dealing with acts or omissions of legal representatives but *the meaning of 'unreasonably' cannot be different when applied to litigants in person in small claims cases. Litigants in person should not be in a better position than legal representatives but neither should they be in any worse position than such representatives.*

[32]   The only other thing we can usefully add is that it would be unfortunate if litigants were too easily deterred from using the Small Claims Track by the risk of being held to have behaved unreasonably and thus rendering themselves liable for costs. ..."

This can be summarised into three points.

First, cases are fact-sensitive. Secondly, the test is *whether the conduct permits of a reasonable explanation*. Thirdly, the meaning of "unreasonably" is not dependent on legal representation.

b. Gempride Ltd

In *Gempride Ltd v Bamrah & Anor* [2018] EWCA Civ 1367, [2019] 1 WLR 1545 at [26], Hickinbottom LJ (with whom Davis LJ agreed) provided further guidance, albeit in the context of wasted costs.

First, mistake, error of judgment, or negligence, without more, will be *in*sufficient to amount to unreasonable conduct.

Secondly, although the conduct of the relevant legal representative *must* amount to a breach of duty owed by that representative to the court, the conduct does *not* have to be in breach of any formal professional rule, or amount to dishonesty.

Thirdly, the burden of proof lies on the *applicant*.

Fourthly, even where the threshold criteria are satisfied, the court *still* has a discretion whether to make an order.

Fifthly, if the court finds "unreasonable behaviour", the sanction must be proportionate to the misconduct in all the circumstances.

c. Lastminute.com

In *Lastminute.com v Tatiana Moskalevitch* [2019] EWHC 1091 (QB), there were two issues.

First, costs of the final hearing. Secondly, costs on appeal.

The submission on the first was that, once the statement accompanying the defence had gone in, the claimant ought to have recognised that the claim could not succeed. It should have been discontinued. Therefore, costs after that date were recoverable.

At paragraph 26, Yip J disposed of the first issue in these terms:

> "I do not accept that that comes close to unreasonable behaviour. If that were the position, then essentially every defended action where a full defence is put forward, and where the claimant then proceeds, would give rise to a costs order, and that would wholly defeat the usual principle that costs on the small claims track are not recoverable. …"

On the second, the "usual rule" is that an unsuccessful respondent pays the court fees, and costs of reasonably obtaining a transcript.

Yip J took an "unusual course", however, for these reasons.

First, the court has a discretion whether to follow the usual rule. Secondly, unusual circumstances. Thirdly, the erroneous order was made on the court's own initiative. The unsuccessful respondent was not responsible. Fourthly, the court had to do justice between the parties. Neither party was to blame.

Fifthly, the successful appellant could have raised the issue of whether the respondent wished to defend the appeal, and explain that costs of appealing would be incurred. The appellant had legal representation. Resolution could have been sought outside of court, but this failure did not amount to behaving unreasonably.

2. Unreasonable

In *Associated Provincial Picture Houses Ltd v Wednesbury Corp* [1948] 1 KB 223 (CA) at 229, the then Master of the Rolls famously said (with emphasis added) that:

> "Lawyers familiar with the phraseology commonly used in relation to the exercise of statutory discretions often use the word 'unreasonable' in a rather comprehensive sense. It has frequently been used and is frequently used as a general description of the things that must not be done. For instance, a person entrusted with a discretion must, so to speak, direct himself properly in law. He must call his own attention to the matters which he is bound to consider. He must exclude from his consideration matters which are irrelevant … If he does not obey the rules, he may truly be said, and often is said, to be acting 'unreasonably.'"

3. Unreasonable conduct

In *Croydon v Greenham (Plant Hire) Ltd* [1978] ICR 415, the Employment Appeal Tribunal ("EAT") considered section 21(1) of the Employment Appeal Tribunal Rules 1976:

> Where it appears to the appeal tribunal … that there has been … unreasonable conduct in bringing or conducting the proceedings, the tribunal may order the party at fault to pay to any other party the whole or such part as it thinks fit of the costs or expenses incurred by that other party in connection with the proceedings.

At 417-418, the EAT reasoned (with emphasis added) that:

"Another basic feature of the jurisdiction ... is that it is only in exceptional circumstances defined in the appropriate rules that we are empowered to award costs to the successful party. *The award of costs, when appropriate, is primarily with the object of minimising the financial detriment to the successful party which has occurred by reason of him being made a party to the proceedings by the unsuccessful party.* But there is another element which is also important: *it is only by the award of costs against the unsuccessful litigant that you have any safeguard at all against completely irresponsible litigation.* One of the reasons why ... there is less irresponsible litigation than under some systems is that in the superior courts in England, if you lose you have to pay the other side's costs, and therefore you think twice, if you have any sense, before bringing a case unless you have a very strong prospect of winning it, and unless what is involved in the case bears some sensible relation to the expense of bringing it."

It was held that the employee's conduct in failing to attend the hearing of his appeal was "unreasonable conduct in conducting the proceedings". He was ordered to pay towards the costs of the appeal incurred by the employers. They had attended the hearing.

There are many material distinguishing facts of this case.

First, the county court is not one of the superior courts in England and Wales. Secondly, the small claims track is not concerned with employment appeals. Thirdly, an award of further costs is not dependent on section 21(1) of the Employment Appeal Tribunal Rules 1976. Fourthly, the threshold is not "unreasonable conduct".

Nonetheless, it exemplifies the following possible submissions.

First, an award of costs should have the primary object of minimising the financial detriment to the successful party. In other words, not punishment. An award of costs must be *causally connected* to the finding that a party has behaved unreasonably.

Secondly, there is a public interest in safeguarding against irresponsible litigation, and therefore making an *appropriate, justified* finding that a party has behaved unreasonably. There is *no* requirement for a causal connection. Finding that a party has behaved unreasonably is merely the peg on which costs hang.

ii. Statutory construction

The CPRs are secondary legislation (SI 1998/3132).

When interpreting legislation, where there is any real doubt as to its ordinary meaning, a dictionary may be consulted.

In *R (on the Application of Mawbey) v Lewisham London Borough Council* [2019] EWCA Civ 1016, [2020] PTSR 164 at [22], Lindblom LJ (with whom Holroyde and King LJJ agreed) said that:

> "If there were any real doubt as to the ordinary relevant meaning of the word, I can see no reason why one should not turn to dictionaries to dispel it. This is a well-established technique of statutory construction, …".

"Unreasonably" is defined in the Oxford English Dictionary (2nd edn, Clarendon Press, Oxford 1989) as follows:

1   In a manner at variance with reason; without due observance of reason or good judgment.

2   To an unreasonable extent; excessively, immoderately.

"Unreasonable" is defined as follows:

1   Not endowed with reason; irrational.

2   Not acting in accordance with reason or good sense; not reasonable in conduct, demands, expectations etc.

3   Not in accordance with reason; not based upon sound reason or good sense.

4   Going beyond what is reasonable or equitable; excessive in amount or degree.

c. Relevant circumstances

The court *will* have regard to all the circumstances.

In particular, this includes the following (CPR 44.2(4)).

First, the conduct of *all* parties. Secondly, whether a party has succeeded on *part* of its case, even if that party has not been wholly successful. Thirdly, any admissible offer to settle, which is drawn to the court's attention.

Conduct of the parties includes the following (CPR 44.2(5)).

First, conduct *before*, as well as *during*, proceedings. In particular, the extent to which the parties have followed the Practice Direction – Pre-Action Conduct ("the Practice Direction"), or any relevant pre-action protocol (see appendix E).

Secondly, whether it was reasonable for a party to *raise, pursue,* or *contest,* a particular allegation, or issue.

Thirdly, the *manner* in which a party has pursued, or defended, a particular allegation, or issue.

Fourthly, whether a claimant who has succeeded, in whole or in part, *exaggerated* her claim.

i. Pre-action Protocols & Practice Direction

Pre-action Protocols and the Practice Direction explain the conduct, and the steps, that the court would normally expect parties to take, before commencing proceedings (see chapter 4).

1. Non-compliance

Non-compliance in *substance* will be taken into account. Not *minor* or *technical* infringements (the Practice Direction at [13]).

There may be non-compliance in the following circumstances.

First, failure to provide sufficient information to enable the objectives of pre-action conduct to be achieved. Secondly, unreasonably refusing a form of alternative dispute resolution.

For example, on numerous occasions before proceedings are commenced, the defendant requested a key document. This may be an invoice evidencing the sum claimed.

This evidence would have enabled the defendant to understand the strength of any potential claim. A decision could then have been made as to how to proceed. A genuine attempt to settle may have been made without the need for, and cost of, proceedings.

Unreasonable failure to provide this invoice may amount to a failure to comply. Sufficient information has not been provided to enable the objectives of pre-action conduct to be achieved.

This will likely amount to a failure to take reasonable and proportionate steps before commencing proceedings.

2. Evidence

Ahead of the hearing, a *professional* client may settle a very *short* witness statement setting out substantial non-compliance. Where appropriate, relevant correspondence should be exhibited.

There is no requirement to file and serve a witness statement for the purpose of costs before a hearing. In practice, it often assists to do so. It shows transparency. It also provides the other party with an opportunity to respond. Ambush cannot be asserted.

Having had the benefit of notice, where no persuasive response is forthcoming, this will only strengthen your position.

In any event, the correspondence that you are relying on must be available to all court actors when making an application for costs on the basis that a party has behaved unreasonably.

iii. Issues raised, pursued or contested

Unreasonably raising, pursuing, or contesting, issues, show a party's failure to help the court to further the overriding objective.

The case will not have been dealt with justly, and at proportionate cost, so far as practicable. This includes the following (CPR 1.1(2)).

First, saving expense. Secondly, ensuring that it is dealt with expeditiously and fairly. Thirdly, allotting to it an appropriate share of the court's resources, while taking into account the need to allot resources to other cases.

1. Abuse of process

A statement of case that is struck out as an abuse of process *should* attract a finding that a party has behaved unreasonably.

Abuse reflects a *grievous* breach of the duty to help the court to further the overriding objective. This includes ensuring that a case is dealt with expeditiously and fairly.

Breach of a CPR, PD, or court order, is unnecessary (see chapter 17(e) (ii)(2)(a)).

2. Summary judgment

A claim or defence which is summarily judged to have no real prospect of success *may* attract a finding that a party has behaved unreasonably. The statement of case was unarguable.

The court is likely to require something more, however, before making a finding that a party has behaved unreasonably.

It will be remembered that, in *Dammermann* at paragraph 32, Longmore and McFarlane LJJ said that "it would be unfortunate if litigants were too easily deterred from using the Small Claims Track by the risk of being held to have behaved unreasonably and thus rendering themselves liable for costs".

There is a *qualitative* difference between an *abusive* statement of case, and one that merely has *no prospects of success.*

Where the party with the offending statement of case had legal representation, this may constitute a material circumstance.

a. Represented

Where there has been a failure to comply with a CPR or PD, in general, it is not a good reason that that failure may be solely attributable to a legal representative (see chapter 17(i)(iii)(2)).

b. Unrepresented

Permission is more likely to be granted to amend a statement of case. This must bring a reasonable prospect of success.

In any event, the court is likely to hesitate before finding that an *un*represented party, drafting her *own* statement of case, has behaved unreasonably because there is no real prospect of success.

3. Manner in which a case is pursued

There are two scenarios in which the *manner* that a party has conducted her case may amount to behaving unreasonably.

First, where there are *additional factors* surrounding failure to accept a reasonable, and timely, offer to settle, in light of the amount awarded following judgment.

Secondly, *non-attendance* of a party, or a key witness, where there has been no written notice, and no good reason for absence.

a. Offers

Rejecting an offer is not a sufficient condition (CPR 27.14(3)):

> A party's rejection of an offer in settlement will not of itself constitute unreasonable behaviour … but the court may take it into consideration …

Relevant circumstances around an offer include the following.

First, who made it? Claimant or defendant?

Secondly, when was it made? Pre-action, early on in proceedings, or on the day of the final hearing?

Thirdly, was it more or less than the judgment sum?

The mere fact that an offer was rejected is *not* sufficient for the court to find that a party has acted unreasonably. Add in three relevant circumstances, however, and it may be.

For example, the *claimant* made the offer. It was *before* she issued the claim. It was *twice* the judgment sum.

In any event, before making a submission that a party has behaved unreasonably, identify *at least* one circumstance, in addition to the mere fact that there has been a rejection of an offer to settle.

b. Non-attendance

Non-attendance is capable of forming the basis of a submission that the manner in which a party has pursued her case means that she has behaved unreasonably.

The following will often be determinative.

First, whether there was written notice. Secondly, the importance of the likely evidence that the witness is able to give. Thirdly, whether there has been a breach of a CPR, PD, or court order.

i. Party

A party may have behaved unreasonably if she does not attend, and does not give written notice (see chapter 19(c)(i)).

If a claimant does not attend a final hearing, and does not give written notice, the court may strike out her claim.

If a defendant does not attend a final hearing, the court may decide the claim on the basis of the claimant's evidence alone. That is, provided that written notice was not given, and the claimant either attended the hearing, or gave written notice.

ii. Witness

In principle, there is *no* requirement to serve a hearsay notice where a witness cannot attend trial (CPR 27.2(1)(c)).

In practice, where that witness is vital, the other party has not been notified, and a good reason has not been given for the absence, the court may find that a party has behaved unreasonably.

For example, in cases where liability is in dispute following a road traffic collision, absence may determine liability.

The parties are under an obligation to help the court to further the overriding objective (CPR 1.3).

This includes the following (CPR 1.1(2)).

First, saving expense. Secondly, allotting to the case an appropriate share of the court's resources, while taking into account the need to allot resources to other cases. Thirdly, enforcing compliance with court orders.

Standard directions includes a time estimate. The notice of allocation will usually include the following direction: 'If a party is aware of a reason why this estimate might be substantially inaccurate, that party must notify the court immediately.'

If so, there is a breach of the CPR, and a court order.

4. Exaggeration

This is important for two reasons.

First, exaggerated claims mean higher costs and disbursements.

For example, if the claim form is served by the court, the legal representative's fee is £80 where the amount claimed is £5,000; and £100 where the amount claimed is more than £5,000. The online issue fee is £185 if the amount claimed is £5,000; and £410 where the amount claimed is £5,000.01 to £10,000.

A case is not dealt with justly and at proportionate cost by ordering the defendant to pay *exaggerated* costs and disbursements. It is irrelevant whether or not the defence succeeded.

Secondly, exaggeration makes it difficult for a defendant to *assess* the true value of a claim, and to *settle* at an earlier stage.

Whilst there is no distinction in the rules between intentional and unintentional exaggeration, the former *must* be considered in any assessment of costs (*Painting v University of Oxford* [2005] EWCA Civ 161, [2005] 3 Costs LR 394 at [22]).

5. Unnecessary applications

The parties are under an obligation to help the court to further the overriding objective (CPR 1.3).

This includes the following (CPR 1.1(2)).

First, saving expense. Secondly, ensuring that the matter is dealt with expeditiously and fairly. Thirdly, allotting the case an appropriate share of the court's resources, taking into account the need to allot resources to other cases.

Take a written application to strike out a defence. It may have been necessary to incur the cost of a skeleton argument to counter. The application, and then the claim, may have been dismissed.

Of itself, this is unlikely to attract a finding that a party has behaved unreasonably. Coupled with *another* circumstance, however, and this unnecessary application may tip the balance.

6. Communications

Any communication with the court *must* be disclosed.

If it is in writing, whether paper or electronic, it *must* be copied to the other party (CPRs 27.2(1)(h) and 39.8).

This applies to any matter of *substance* or *procedure*.

There are three exceptions.

First, for purely routine, uncontentious, and administrative, correspondence. Secondly, where there is a compelling reason for not doing so, and this is clearly stated in the communication. Thirdly, where authorised by a CPR, or PD.

Correspondence to the court must state three matters.

First, that it is being copied to the other party. Secondly, the identity of the author. Thirdly, her capacity. For example, 'legal representative and solicitor for the claimant'.

Unless the court otherwise directs, failure to do so will result in the court returning the correspondence, without being considered, but with a brief explanation as to why it is being returned.

Where there has been a failure to disclose, and to copy to the other party, any communication on a matter of substance or procedure, the court will hear from the parties. Having done so, the court may impose sanctions, or exercise its powers of case management.

Corresponding with the court, so as to deprive the other party of an opportunity to respond, amounts to "a serious procedural irregularity" (*National Westminster Bank Plc v Rushmer* [2010] EWHC 554 (Ch), [2010] 2 FLR 362 at [35]).

The overriding objective includes ensuring that the parties are on an equal footing. This is not achieved if one party corresponds with the court on a matter of substance or procedure, without notice to the other party, so that the other party cannot respond.

7. Opportunism

Opportunistically resisting an application that is bound to succeed requires "heavy costs sanctions" to be imposed (*Denton & Ors v TH White Ltd & Ors* [2014] EWCA Civ 906, [2015] 1 All ER 880 at [43]).

This is contrary to the duty of the parties to help the court to further the overriding objective. It frustrates the court's duty to actively case-manage. In particular, to encourage cooperation.

d. Summary assessment

In principle, costs should be summarily assessed at the end of the hearing, unless there is a good reason not to do so (PD 44 at [9.2]).

In practice, the exception will be rare.

For example, where the party who has behaved unreasonably shows *substantial* grounds for disputing the amount of costs.

e. Statement of costs

Parties and their legal representatives must assist the court to make a summary assessment of costs.

To do so, a written "statement of costs" should be prepared.

In principle, it should follow Form N260 as closely as possible. In practice, this form is used. In any event, it must be signed, either by the party, or that party's legal representatives (PD 44 at [9.5]).

i. Particulars

The following should be in a separate schedule (PD 44 at [9.5(2)]).

First, number of hours. Secondly, hourly rate. Thirdly, grade of fee earner. Fourthly, amount and nature of any disbursement (other than counsel's fee for appearing at the hearing). Fifthly, amount of legal representative's costs to be claimed for attending, or appearing at, the hearing. Sixthly, counsel's fees. Seventhly, any VAT.

1. Grade & number of hours

Be prepared to justify the number of hours that are claimed.

Reasonableness will likely depend on two factors. First, *extent* and *complexity* of the procedural history. Secondly, *grade* of fee earner.

If there are a number of previous applications, the number of hours invested in the case is likely to be high.

In a straightforward claim for the cost of repairs following a road traffic collision, absent pre-final hearing applications, however, the court will expect a modest number of hours.

It is hard to justify a grade 'A' fee earner.

Where the claim or defence is abusive, there is a stronger argument that the issues are more complex, requiring a guiding, experienced hand.

There is, of course, a limit. There is also a balance.

A *lower* grade of fee earner means a *larger* number of hours.

2. Rate

Solicitors' guideline hourly rates can be found online at www.gov.uk/guidance/solicitors-guideline-hourly-rates.

See appendix I for the rates as of 1 November 2020.

a. London

Grade 1 encompasses the City of London EC1-EC4.

Grade 2 encompasses Central London W1, WC1, WC2, and SW1.

Grade 3 encompasses all other, outer London postcodes.

b. National

Grade 1 encompasses: Aldershot, Farnham, Bournemouth (including Poole); Birmingham Inner; Bristol; Cambridge City, Harlow; Canterbury, Maidstone, Medway, Tunbridge Wells; Cardiff (Inner); Chelmsford South, Essex, East Suffolk; Fareham, Winchester; Hampshire, Dorset, Wiltshire, Isle of Wight; Kingston, Guildford, Reigate, Epsom; Leeds Inner (within two kilometres of City Art Gallery); Lewes; Liverpool, Birkenhead; Manchester Central; Newcastle (City Centre) (within 2 metres of St Nicholas Cathedral); Norwich City; Nottingham City; Oxford, Thames Valley; Southampton, Portsmouth; Swindon, Basingstoke; and Watford.

Grade 2 encompasses: Bath, Cheltenham, Gloucester, Taunton, Yeovil; Bury; Chelmsford North, Cambridge County, Peterborough, Bury St Edmunds, Norfolk, Lowestoft; Chester; North Wales; Coventry, Rugby, Nuneaton, Stratford, Warwick; Exeter, Plymouth; Hull (City); Leeds Outer, Wakefield, Pontefract; Leigh; Lincoln; Luton, Bedford, St Albans, Hitchin, Hertford; Manchester Outer, Oldham, Bolton, Tameside; Newcastle (other than City Centre); Nottingham, Derbyshire; Sheffield, Doncaster, South Yorkshire; Southport; St Helens; Stockport, Altrincham, Salford; Swansea, Newport, Cardiff Outer;

Wigan; Wolverhampton, Walsall, Dudley, Stourbridge; and York, Harrogate.

Grade 3 encompasses: Birmingham Outer; Bradford, Dewsbury, Halifax, Huddersfield, Keighley, Skipton; Cumbria; Devon, Cornwall; Grimsby, Skegness; Hull Outer; Kidderminster; Northampton, Leicester; Preston, Lancaster, Blackpool, Chorley, Accrington, Burnley, Blackburn, Rawenstall, Nelson; Scarborough, Ripon; Stafford, Stoke, Tamworth; Teesside; Worcester, Hereford, Evesham, Redditch; Shrewsbury, Telford, Ludlow, Oswestry; and South and West Wales.

ii. Notice

The statement of costs must be filed at court, and a copy must be served on the other party, as soon as possible. In any event, this should be not less than 24 hours before the hearing.

Without reasonable excuse, failure to do so will be taken into account when deciding what order to make (PD 44 at [9.6]).

It is prudent to have a spare copy of the statement of costs. The correspondence evidencing filing and service mitigates against any dispute over the same. In practice, such disputes are common.

iii. Absence

Where there is no statement of costs, practice managers, or professional clients, should be able to confirm counsel's fee.

This sum plus any applicable VAT is often awarded. It deals with the issue of costs swiftly, without the need for a further hearing.

25. Appeals

It is part of your implied instructions to make an oral application for permission to appeal where properly arguable.

a. Court

The "appeal court" is the court to which an appeal must be made.

The "lower court" is the court from whose decision an appeal is brought (CPR 52.1(3)(b) and (c)).

For a first appeal, the appeal court from a (deputy) district judge is the circuit judge at the same county court.

In the rare circumstance that a circuit judge heard the claim, the appeal court is a High Court judge.

It does not depend on whether the decision was interim, or final.

For a second appeal, the appeal court is the Court of Appeal (PD 52A at [3.4], [3.5], and Table 1).

b. Centre

Appeals must be brought in the appropriate "appeal centre".

All other notices, such as the respondent's notice, must also be filed at that appeal centre.

The venue for an appeal will be determined by the Designated Civil Judge. This may be different to the appeal centre (PD 52B at [2.2] and Table A).

c. Permission

Permission is needed to appeal.

There are two tests. First appeals and second appeals.

An oral, or a written, application, can be made. The latter requires four documents, grounds of appeal, and an appeal bundle.

Two further applications can be made.

First, for a stay of the lower court's order. Secondly, for an extension of time in which to file an appellant's notice.

i. Need

Any party wishing to appeal requires permission (CPR 52.3(1)).

This includes where a party wishes to appeal against an order made without a hearing, or in that party's absence in accordance with her request (PD 27 at [8.2]).

In principle, an application for permission to appeal may be made to the lower court that made the decision being appealed (CPR 52.3(2)). In practice, this is often refused.

Further application must be to the appeal court (CPR 52.3(3)).

ii. Test

The test is different for first and second appeals.

1. First appeal

Permission *may* only be given in two circumstances (CPR 52.6(1)).

First, the court considers that the appeal would have a *real prospect of success*. Secondly, there is some *other compelling reason* for the appeal to be heard.

Permission is *not* granted as of right, even where the test is satisfied. The court has a *discretion*. This is clear from the word "may".

In practice, the first limb of the test is most frequently relied upon.

In *R (A Child)* [2019] EWCA Civ 895, [2019] FLR 1033 at [31], Peter Jackson LJ (with whom Baker LJ agreed) said that "there must be a realistic, as opposed to a fanciful, prospect of success. There is no requirement that success should be probable, or more likely than not."

2. Second appeal

The Court of Appeal *will not* give permission, unless it considers that one of the following is satisfied (CPR 52.7(2)).

First, the appeal would have a real prospect of success *and raise an important point of principle or practice*. Secondly, there is some other compelling reason *for the Court of Appeal* to hear it.

From a decision of the county court, which was itself made on appeal, only the Court of Appeal can give permission (CPR 52.7(1)).

Permission is *not* granted as of right. Even where the test is met.

In practice, the first limb of the test is most frequently relied upon.

The *first* part of the *first* limb of the second appeal test is the same as the *first* limb of the *first* appeal test.

The *second* part of the *first* limb – that is, an important point of practice or principle is raised – means one "that has not yet been established". This was confirmed by McCombe LJ (with whom Richards LJ agreed) in *BS (Congo) & Ors v Secretary of State for the Home Department* [2015] EWCA Civ 639 at [17].

iii. Oral application

After judgment and costs, an oral application may be made.

Reasons for the application should be clear, and concise.

It is part of your implied instructions to make an oral application for permission to appeal where properly arguable. If you do not, an opportunity to gain permission will have been lost.

A written application attracts a fee. An oral application does not.

iv. Appellant's notice

Where permission is sought from the appeal court, it must be in the form of an "appellant's notice".

This is Form N164 (PDs 27 at [8A] and 52B at [4.1]).

Guidance is available in Form N161A.

As a general rule, it must be filed at the appeal court within 21 days of the date of the decision of the lower court. The period may be longer, or shorter, as ordered by the lower court.

CPRs and PDs regarding time limits apply (PD 52D).

Unless the appeal court orders otherwise, it must be served on each respondent as soon as practicable. In any event, it must be no later than seven days after it is filed.

1. Fee

It must be accompanied by the fee of £120, a fee remission application, or certificate (PD 52B at [4.1] and Form EX50).

2. Documents

The following must be filed with the notice (PD 52B at [4.2]).

First, three copies of the appellant's notice, and one additional copy for each respondent.

Secondly, a copy of the sealed order under appeal.

Thirdly, where an application was made to the lower court for permission to appeal, a copy of any order granting or refusing permission, together with a copy of the reasons, if any, for allowing, or refusing, permission.

Fourthly, grounds of appeal.

3. Grounds

Grounds of appeal *must* be set out on a *separate* sheet and *attached* to the appellant's notice. They *must* set out why the decision of the lower court was one (or both) of the following (CPR 52.21(3)).

First, *wrong*. Secondly, *unjust* because of a serious procedural, or other, irregularity.

Language used must be simple, clear and concise.

4. Transcript

There is no requirement for a transcript of the judgment of the lower court, or other record of reasons (PD 52B at [6.2]).

In practice, it will likely assist the appeal court.

v. Respondent's notice

A respondent *may* file and serve a "respondent's notice".

This is Form N162.

Guidance is available in Form N162A.

It must be filed in two circumstances (CPR 52.13(2)).

First, where permission to appeal is sought from the *appeal* court by the *respondent*. Secondly, the respondent wishes to ask the appeal court to uphold the decision of the lower court for reasons *different* from, or *additional* to, those given by the lower court.

1. Permission

Where permission is sought from the appeal court, it *must* be in a respondent's notice.

It *must* be filed within such period as directed by the lower court, or 14 days after the "relevant date".

Where permission to appeal was *granted* by the *lower* court, or permission to appeal is *not* required, the relevant date is when the respondent is *served* with the appellant's notice.

When the *respondent* is served with notification that the *appeal* court has *given* the appellant permission, this is the relevant date.

When the *respondent* is served with notification that the *application* for permission to appeal and the *appeal* itself are to be heard together, this is the relevant date.

2. Service

Unless otherwise ordered by the appeal court, the respondent's notice *must* be served on the appellant, and any other respondent, as soon as practicable, and no later than seven days after filing.

d. Skeleton arguments

Skeleton arguments should *not* be relied on as a matter of course.

They should only be used in two circumstances (PD 52B at [8.3]).

First, where they are *justified* on the basis of the *complexity* of the issues of fact, law, or evidence, in the appeal.

Secondly, they would otherwise assist the court in respects that are *not readily apparent from the documents* in the appeal.

In general, costs are not recoverable (see below).

e. Appeal bundle

As soon as practicable, but in any event, within 35 days of filing the appellant's notice, the appellant must file an appeal bundle.

It must contain *only* those documents relevant to the appeal. This is subject to any order made by the court.

It *must* be paginated and indexed (PD 52B at [6.3]).

i. Relevant

There are six "relevant" documents (PD 52B at [6.4(1)]).

First, the appellant's notice. Secondly, any respondent's notice. Thirdly, any skeleton argument. Fourthly, the order under appeal.

Fifthly, the order of the lower court, granting or refusing permission to appeal, with a copy of the judge's reasons (if any). Sixthly, a copy of any order allocating the case to the small claims track.

Relevant documents obtained, or created, after the appeal bundle has been filed, should be added to the appeal bundle as soon as practicable. In any event, this must be no less than seven days before the hearing of the appeal, or any application (PD 52B at [6.6]).

ii. May be relevant

Where relevant, include the following (PD 52B at [6.4(2)]).

First, statements of case. Secondly, application notices. Thirdly, other orders made in the case. Fourthly, chronology of events.

Fifthly, witness statements made in support of any application in the appellant's notice. Sixthly, other witness statements. Seventhly, documents that a party considers would assist the court.

iii. Service

The appeal bundle must be served as follows (PD 52B at [6.5]).

Where permission to appeal was *granted* by the *lower* court, at the same time as filing the appeal bundle.

Where the *appeal* court has *granted* permission to appeal, as soon as practicable after notification, and, in any event, within 14 days of the grant of permission.

Where the *appeal* court directs that the *application* for permission to appeal will be heard on the *same* occasion as the *appeal*, as soon as practicable, and, in any event, within 14 days after notification of the hearing date.

iv. Respondent's documents

Where a respondent considers that relevant documents have been omitted, she may file and serve on all parties a "respondent's supplemental appeal bundle".

It should contain these omitted documents. It *must* be filed and served as soon as practicable, and, in any event, no less than seven days before the hearing (PD 52B at 8.2).

f. Applications

Applications should be made to the *lower* court.

Where the time limit for filing an appellant's notice has expired, they should be made to the *appeal* court.

i. Stay

Application can be made to stay the order of the lower court.

This should be in the appellant's notice. Any application for a transcript at public expense should be in this notice (PD 52B at [4.3]).

ii. Extension

Application can be made for an extension of time to file an appellant's notice.

It must be made at the same time as the appellant applies to the lower court for permission to appeal (PD 52B at [3.1]).

Where the time limit for filing an appellant's notice has expired, the appellant must include an application within the appellant's notice (PD 52B at [3.2] and [4.3]).

It *must* state the following (PD 52B at [3.2]).

First, the *reason* for delay. Secondly, the *steps taken* before making the application.

The court *may* make an order granting, or refusing, an extension of time. This may be with or without a hearing.

Where it is without a hearing, a party seeking to set aside, or vary, the order, may apply for a hearing within 14 days of service of the order (PD 52B at [3.3]).

g. Determination

Applications may be determined with, or without, a hearing. This includes an application for permission to appeal (PD 52B at [7.1]).

Where permission to appeal is refused without a hearing, a party may *request* this to be reconsidered at a hearing.

Where the court determines any other application without a hearing, any party affected by that determination may *apply* to have the order set aside, or varied.

In any event (PD 52B at [7.4]):

First, the request or application *must* be made within seven days of service of notification of the determination upon the party making the application. Secondly, a copy of the request, or application, *must* be served on *all other parties* at the *same* time. Thirdly, the court *will* give directions for the determination of the application.

Where an appeal is allowed, the appeal court will, if possible, dispose of the case at the *same* time. That is, *without* ordering a further hearing in the lower court. The court may do so without hearing further evidence (PD 27 at [8.3]).

h. Costs

The costs regime under CPR 27.14 applies to appeals.

In *Akhtar v Boland* [2014] EWCA Civ 943, [2014] CP Rep 41 at [7], Sir Stanley Burnton (with whom Floyd and Gloster LJJ agreed) said (with emphasis added) that:

> "If I could, I would order the appellant to pay the respondent's costs of his appeal to this Court. However, the power of this Court to make a costs order is constrained by the CPR. *The wording of CPR 27.14 is clear, and extends to the costs of an appeal,* and I see no basis for construing that as inapplicable to an appeal to this Court. ... Regrettably, therefore, I would make no order for costs on the appeal to this Court, on the ground that any such order is precluded by CPR r.27.14."

In *Dammermann v Lanyon Bowdler LLP* [2017] EWCA Civ 269, [2017] 2 Costs LR 393 at [15], Longmore and McFarlane LJJ said (with emphasis added) that:

> "The first point to note about *the provisions in Part 27.14* is that they *apply to an appeal.* Ms Tildesley was therefore right to draw the provision to the judge's attention ... see *Akhtar v Boland* [2014] EWCA Civ 943."

26. Attendance notes

An attendance note ("a note") may be condensed, or contain a complete, word-for-word alternative to a transcript.

In any event, the practice of writing a couple of sentences on a back sheet is dying out for a number of reasons.

There are no set rules for notes, albeit there are pieces of information that any note should strive to contain.

This includes the name of the court, judge, legal representative (if there is one), and the terms of any order.

In a competitive market, professional clients repeatedly instruct counsel where there is evidence (a note) of the following.

First, ability to foresee problems, take prompt action to flag them up, and mitigate against any unavoidable hurdles. Secondly, gain the trust and confidence of witnesses in a pre-hearing conference. Thirdly, ability to deliver sound legal submissions, which, on looking at the reasoning in the judgment, have had the desired impact.

a. Utility

Notes are helpful. For counsel, those instructing, and the party who they represent. In different ways, and for different reasons.

i. Counsel

For counsel, it offers an opportunity to make a clear, contemporaneous, comprehensive note of what has been said, complete with any relevant context.

For example, the time that a conference started, that the witness had an opportunity to read an unmarked copy of her statement, and that she confirmed the truth of it, without any suggested amendments.

During cross-examination, the witness may admit in oral evidence that, for example, she was not wearing a seat belt. This may conflict with her written evidence.

The note may provide that the witness did not take the opportunity in conference to correct her written evidence. If this inconsistency is cited in the judgment as a reason that the credibility of this witness was un-dermined, then, the note may provide counsel with reassurance that they gave the witness an opportunity to re-read the statement, and amend it, ahead of the final hearing.

If there is any dispute as to what was said, perhaps days, months, or even *years*, later, a detailed note provides the answer.

ii. Professional client

For a professional client, the following are vital.

First, what points were successful, and the reasons why. Secondly, what points were not successful, and the reasons why. Thirdly, the total amount of the judgment sum. Fourthly, a breakdown of the amounts awarded for each head of loss. Fifthly, any payment terms. For example, payment within 21 (as opposed to 14) days.

If your lay client asks your professional client what was discussed in conference, what oral evidence was given, or what were the reasons for judgment against them, your professional client is able to respond. Promptly, in detail, and with confidence.

This is a reason that your note should be received by your professional client promptly. They must be able to field questions from their client. This is often shortly after a hearing.

A professional client will not appreciate being kept in the dark.

It may compromise their relationship with their client. *In*ability to answer questions, advise on next steps, or prospects of successfully appealing, is *not* conducive to building trust and confidence.

iii. Lay client

For a party, they may wish to confirm, for example, the reasoning in the judgment. They may have been held to be an unreliable historian of events. If so, what was the factual basis?

A comprehensive note of the judgment will enable a professional client to inform a party of the reasoning in the judgment and the factual basis for it.

After the hearing, it is prudent to *telephone* your professional client to relay the result. They may need to revert to their client *promptly.* Even if you take time to proofread your note before emailing it, your professional client will be able to revert to her client, if the result has been promptly relayed over the telephone.

It will also enable a party to instruct counsel to advise whether or not there are prospects of successfully appealing, without having to wait for, and to incur the cost of, a transcript.

Remember that your lay client may reasonably request to see your note. This may inform whether you wish to include, for example, your mobile telephone number. It may also inform whether or not you include a candid view of the reasonableness of your lay client, their credibility, and their witnesses.

This is not code to conceal.

It is a reason to take a professional note.

b. Fundamentals

At the top of the note, it is helpful to set out the following details.

First, the names of the parties as they appear on the statements of case. Secondly, the claim number. Thirdly, the name of the court. Fourthly, the number of the courtroom. Fifthly, the title, and the name of the judge. Sixthly, the date of the hearing.

Seventhly, the type of hearing (preliminary or final). Eighthly, the title, surname, and status (counsel or solicitor) of any advocate representing the other party. Ninthly, the contact details of your professional client, including her name, firm, and email address.

c. Outcome

The outcome should be on the first page.

Usually, this will be the terms of the order. If the hearing has been adjourned, and the party represented by you has been directed to do something, this should be **emboldened** so that it stands out. It should also be clear in the email to which your note is attached.

d. Correspondence

It is prudent to note any material correspondence.

This includes correspondence with your *professional* client, instructions taken in conference from your *lay* client, or issues raised by the *other party*.

This is especially helpful where, for example, an offer to settle is made. It is useful to have a note of the terms of that offer after the hearing, when the issue of costs is decided, and for your professional client to assess quantum in future, similar cases.

i. Professional client

For counsel, it may be helpful to record that a key document, such as an invoice, has been requested from a professional client ahead of the hearing via *email;* and followed up with a *telephone* call.

If the head of loss to which that invoice relates is then dismissed, there is a note that counsel has discharged her duty to *foresee* obvious problems, and *promptly* attempt to resolve them.

The terms of any offer to settle (including provision for costs) should be noted, including when it was made, and who made it.

The note should also provide when you relayed that offer to your professional client, your advice as to whether or not it was in your client's interests to accept that offer, and any instructions from your professional client.

If an offer to settle is made, and you advise your professional client that, the *best* alternative to a settlement out of court is judgment for the same, or even *less* than that offer, and your client does not beat that offer after a final hearing, the question *why* that offer was not accepted may reasonably arise.

If you are able to set out the above, and that you did not have authority to accept the offer, despite receipt of your advice, counsel has discharged her professional duty.

ii. Lay client

Instructions taken in conference should be noted.

What time the conference started, when the witness read an unmarked copy of her statement, and whether she confirmed the contents of that statement without any suggested amendment.

If that witness changes a material part of her written evidence under cross-examination, thereby undermining her credibility, so that the case that you are instructed to present is dismissed, counsel cannot be criticised in this respect.

The *exact* words of any suggested amendment should be noted, and the *paragraph* of the statement to which they relate.

It is often helpful for a witness to read the other party's statement(s), and to take a note of what that witness says in *response* to material evidence conflicting with the case of the party who you represent.

First, to understand the case that you are instructed to present. Especially in cases following a road traffic collision, witness statements can be sparse, lacking the necessary detail as to the exact location of the collision, where the impact occurred in respect of each vehicle, and the mechanism of collision.

Secondly, when cross-examining, you know what facts are in dispute, and what the witness for the party who you represent has to say about them.

iii. Other party

When you speak to the other party before the hearing, summarise the material points that arose out of that discussion.

As well as offers to settle, the issues that are in dispute, and any procedural issues, are helpful to note.

First, to have at your fingertips during the hearing, especially if you are representing the claimant, and summarising the issues in dispute at the outset. Secondly, so that you can speak to your professional client, relay the same *accurately*, and take *precise* instructions. Thirdly, so that your professional client is able to understand the other party's position *ahead* of the hearing, and compare that to the judgment, *after* the hearing.

e. Tactical & strategic decisions

Any *tactical* or *strategic* decision before a hearing should be noted.

For example, the defendant is required to make an application for relief from sanctions due to failure to serve a key document, such as an invoice. The claimant wishes to rely on video footage of the collision that has not been served until the day of the final hearing.

On instructions, and on receipt of your advice, the decision is taken not to resist the claimant relying on this video. The reason is that this will assist the defendant's application for relief from sanctions. If instructions were taken over the telephone, the time of that call, and the person giving these instructions, may be noted.

The video may feature heavily in the reasoning of the judgment *against the party who you represent*. Succinctly summarising the circumstances in which this decision was made can be helpful for counsel, those instructing, and the lay client.

This is because, if the question is asked why there was no resistance to the video going into evidence, say, a week after the final hearing – when memories have faded, and oral recollections appear less credible – the answer is in a contemporaneous note.

f. Additional instructions

Additional instructions to those in the brief to counsel, whether obtained over the telephone, or via email, should be noted.

This is so that, in days, months, or years to come, if there is a question as to why something was, or was not agreed, admitted, or submitted, there is a contemporaneous note recording the reason.

For example, you may have deleted the email, instructing you not to pursue a counterclaim, in accordance with your privacy policy.

g. During hearing

Some advocates make an accurate, word-for-word note of the hearing. Others summarise. Either way, oral evidence, submissions, judgment, and the terms of the order, are useful to note.

i. Shorthand

In case of appeal, where a transcript of the hearing may be requested, the time that the hearing was called on may be helpful.

Counsel for the claimant, Ms Smith, may be shortened to "S".

Whenever Ms Smith addresses the court, a note can be made using shorthand. For example: 'S: this is a claim for credit hire, where need, period, and rate, are the issues that are in dispute.'

The judge can be shortened to "J".

In the above example, if the defendant agrees that these are the issues in dispute, the court will not then allow the defendant to cross-examine on, for example, enforceability. This is why an accurate note of what was said during proceedings is important.

ii. Evidence

In case of appeal, the time that a witness was called may be helpful, in the event that a transcript of the hearing is requested.

The oral evidence given by a witness should be noted carefully.

Instead of noting question and answer, they can be combined.

Take the question: "You could have used public transport?" And the answer: "I have a disabled mother, who I often take to the hospital." This can be combined: "I could not use public transport as I have a disabled mother, who I often take to the hospital."

If a witness makes a concession in your cross-examination, and you wish to refer to it in your closing submissions, you can **embolden** it. There are two reasons to do so.

First, it can be easily found. Secondly, it is more persuasive to quote the *actual words* used, rather than paraphrase.

If your witness says something on which you wish to re-examine, again, you can embolden it, so that you can quickly navigate to it.

Sometimes, the judge will comment on a piece of evidence, submission, or the conduct of a party. If it assists your case, again, it can be emboldened, for ease of reference. Then, it can be incorporated into your closing submissions, or application for costs on the basis that a party has behaved unreasonably, or both.

For example, the judge may strike out a claim, on the basis that it is abusive. If so, the reasoning of the judge may be usefully relayed when making submissions that costs should be awarded on the basis that the claimant has behaved unreasonably.

You may submit that, *given the reasoning for dismissing the claim,* the only consistent ruling on costs is that the claimant has behaved unreasonably.

If the judge asked the other party a question, it may be a point that you would like to address in submissions. If so, emboldening it will enable you to find it, and answer it at the appropriate time.

iii. Submissions

Note the other party's closing submissions for three reasons.

First, if there is anything that you need to address, this will remind you to do so. Secondly, if a concession is made, you can rely on it in your closing submissions. Thirdly, to demonstrate internal inconsistency, and inherent unlikelihood.

iv. Judgment

A word-for-word note of the judgment is helpful for four reasons.

First, to explain to your lay client why, for example, her case was dismissed, she was not awarded the full amount that was claimed, or the reasons that the judge found that the credibility of a witness was compromised.

Secondly, to advise on prospects of successfully appealing, or resisting an appeal. Where there may be prospects of appeal, the relevant sentence, paragraph, or passage, can be emboldened, so that it stands out from the rest of the judgment.

Thirdly, so that you, and your professional client, have evidence of what submissions succeeded, failed, and did not feature in the reasoning of the judgment. This is so that, in future cases, you can hone your submissions.

Both professional client and counsel are thereby able to fulfil professional duties to further *clients'* best interests, and help the *court* to further the overriding objective.

Fourthly, if the order is incompatible with the judgment, there may be an error. If so, this can be corrected using the slip rule.

Without an accurate note of the judgment, you are in a weaker position to advise whether there has been an error; and what the order *should* read, so that it accurately reflects the judgment.

v. Order

The terms of the order should be set out on the first page.

You may also wish to copy and paste the same into the email to your professional client, attaching the note, for two reasons.

First, the convenience for your *professional* client.

Secondly, so that your *practice manager*, who is unlikely to open your note, will see whether or not your client has been successful.

h. Next steps

If the hearing was preliminary, after which the court made case management directions, this is the place to note them.

Any summary advice on next steps should be included. Usually, there is no reason that it should be longer than a paragraph.

You may have seen the evidence in support of the claim. If so, you may also have advised that an offer for that sum should be made, together with the relevant fixed costs that have been incurred.

Your professional client is then in a position to act on your advice, make the offer, and attempt to settle the matter out of court.

i. Travel expenses

Some advocates set out their travel expenses for two reasons.

First, your practice manager may have agreed with your professional client that they should be billed, in addition to the brief fee, especially where the court is some distance from your chambers.

Secondly, when working out your expenses for tax purposes, your notes provide a convenient, contemporary record.

This is a failsafe if you are not as fastidious in going through your expenses every month or so. When you do come around to it, you should then be able to see your travel expenses in detail.

Train tickets should still be retained for tax purposes.

To this end, if you are practising in London, a record of your journeys using a registered Oyster card can be downloaded as a PDF.

j. Contact details

At the bottom of a note, the name of your practice manager, her contact details, and your professional address should be set out, in case your professional client wishes to contact you.

Remember that your lay client may reasonably request your note, so bear this in mind if you provide your mobile telephone number.

k. Telephone

Speak to your professional client after the hearing.

First, to relay the result *promptly*, so that your *professional* client is able to answer questions, should the *lay* client telephone. You may take some time proofreading your note.

Secondly, this is an *opportunity to build rapport* with a professional client, who may be based at the other end of the country.

It is easier to build rapport over the telephone than in writing.

l. Email

Once completed, email your note to your professional client.

Ideally, on the day of the hearing. In any event, this should be within 24 hours. Professional clients choose repeatedly to instruct counsel who promptly send notes.

Copy your practice manager into this email for three reasons.

First, she will know that the case can be billed.

Secondly, if there is a further hearing, but, due to another professional commitment, you are unable to attend, your practice manager is able to forward your note to counsel who will attend.

Thirdly, if your professional client contacts your practice manager to say that they have not received your note, your practice manager can forward on your note, *without* having to revert to you.

27. Tools

A number of tools are useful to a junior advocate.

A smart phone, laptop, and access to online, electronic legal resources are invaluable. They enable you to correspond, type up attendance notes, orders, and look up an authority that has arisen just before, during, or after, a hearing.

The rapid rise in remote working, telephone and audio-visual hearings, have also given increased importance to software.

a. Smart phone

Most carry a mobile telephone.

It is necessary to swiftly send requests for, and to rapidly receive, instructions, from your professional client.

For example: to relay that a witness is late; and to receive instructions that the good reason for this is that that witness was admitted to an accident and emergency department of a hospital.

It is also necessary to urgently update your practice manager.

For example: to relay that your train has been delayed; or to receive the notification that, in fact, the in-person hearing has been vacated whilst making your way to court.

Offers to settle must *promptly* be relayed to professional clients.

This is so that instructions can swiftly be taken as to whether to accept. The terms of a last-minute counter-offer may need to be relayed before the case is called on.

A *smart phone* is helpful for in person hearings.

First, to check train times, buy tickets, and plan your route to and from court, using the full range of public transport options. This includes tube, train, and bus.

Secondly, to use online navigation software, and find the court.

Thirdly, so that you can tether your smart phone to your laptop.

This enables access to the internet. Online legal resources may need to be considered. For example, so as to confirm whether an authority has received negative judicial consideration.

b. Laptop

A laptop and the software to utilise it efficiently are invaluable.

A laptop charger guards against running out of battery. It is especially important when your case is on an unassigned list.

You may be waiting for *hours,* while getting on with other work, as the prospects increase of running out of battery.

i. Hardware

For *remote* hearings, a computer is necessary. It need not be portable. Desktop computers suffice.

Two electronic devices are preferable. One to access the hearing. Another to access electronic copies of the documents.

A preliminary issue may arise as to whether a document has been filed or served. Many professional clients file and serve documents by sending an email, to both the court and the other side, attaching the document to that email. Frequently, the court and the other party are recipients of the same email.

If so, this email can be forwarded to counsel in advance of the hearing. On the occasion that the issue of filing or service arises, that email can be forwarded from counsel to the court, and the other party. The date and time of the email, and any attachment, can then swiftly be determined.

Or, an authority may arise just before, or during, a remote hearing. This can swiftly be emailed to all court actors when they have a computer, internet, and email.

A laptop is invaluable for *in person* hearings for three reasons.

First, so that you have an electronic copy of the documents. You may have to hand up your spare, hard copy to the court, or it may be needed as a witness bundle.

Secondly, so that you can take an accurate note of the hearing, swiftly proofread, and promptly email it to those instructing.

Thirdly, so that you can send and receive emails, access online, electronic legal resources, and view an online diary.

ii. Software

Software enables you to be effective, and time-efficient.

1. Read Aloud

Read Aloud reads your document.

It is available for Windows, macOS and iOS.

For example, in Microsoft Word on macOS, press 'Review' then 'Read Aloud'. Controls are simple. 'Play'. 'Pause'.

To change paragraphs, press 'Previous' or 'Next'. To exit, press 'x'. Using the icon that looks like a gear on top of a speaker, the reading speed and voice can be changed.

It is useful for rapid assimilation, and proofreading.

2. Speech

Speech enables PDFs to be selected and read on macOS.

To activate, select 'System Preferences' then 'Accessibility'. Select 'Speech' and tick 'Speak selected text when the key is pressed'. You can change the key by selecting 'Change Key'.

Reading speed and voice can be changed in 'Speech'.

Speech is for PDFs what Read Aloud is for Word documents.

3. Adobe Acrobat

The main benefit over PDF Expert is that a document can be converted into a searchable digital file.

Optical Character Recognition ("OCR") converts images of typed, handwritten, or printed, text, into digital text.

A photocopied bundle will arrive as a photograph. If it is clear enough, text can be converted by OCR into digital text. This enables you to search the document for words, or phrases.

To convert a bundle, open it. Select 'Tools', 'Scan & OCR', 'Recognise Text', 'In This File', 'All Pages', 'English UK', and 'Recognise Text'.

To search that bundle, open it. Select 'Edit', 'Advanced Search', insert the word or phrase, and 'search'.

You can also press 'command' and 'F' to search.

4. PDF Expert

This is *excellent* for constructing bundles.

Documents may be inserted or removed from an existing bundle. Pages may be rearranged. They can be paginated, indexed, and bookmarked.

Bundles may be annotated with comments, underlining, and highlighting. These may be exported, and printed.

For OCR, use Adobe Acrobat, and open the file in PDF Expert.

To search a converted bundle, open it in PDF Expert. Use the search bar in the top, right-hand corner.

c. Online resources

Access to an electronic version of a professional text will save you from carrying a hard copy to in person hearings.

Professional texts may be saved electronically, however, online access is preferable.

First, the number of professional texts, and authorities, that you can access online. This has the corresponding impracticality of taking hard copies to an in person hearing, or of saving electronic copies to your electronic device.

Secondly, when accessed, you can be confident that you are reading a version that is likely to be more up to date. A printed copy, or one that has been saved electronically, may be out of date.

You may recall an authority that assists your case. The legal principle that it is authority for has only been raised during submissions. Therefore, you do not have a copy of the authority.

If you have online access to an electronic database, you can find the name, citation, and relevant paragraph. The reason for not providing a copy in advance can be stated. The best interests of your client can then be served, whilst also assisting the court to further the overriding objective.

This includes dealing with the matter justly, and at proportionate cost, without the need for an adjournment, or an appeal.

d. Notepad

A notepad and a black, ball-point pen are often useful.

First, in case your laptop is unworkable. Secondly, to draft consent orders that may be signed when attending an in person hearing.

A consent order may be scanned, emailed to you, and sent to your professional client, or just stored on your external, encrypted hard drive. In either case, the hard copy can be disposed of confidentially. This assists your practice to become paperless. It therefore also furthers the objectives of data protection.

Writing should be in black ink. Text should be in capital letters.

When scanned, and photocopied, it will then remain legible.

e. Disk drive

A disk may be included in your instructions.

It may store a video captured by a dashboard camera. This may show the weather conditions, road layout, location, and perhaps even the mechanism of a collision.

If so, it is likely to either assist, or undermine, a claim.

If it assists your client's case, it is in her interests to rely on it. If it undermines her case, it is likely that the other party will seek to rely on it. If it cannot be played, there is a risk that the case will be adjourned. If your client goes on to lose the case, she will have incurred time and cost through *your* inability to play the video.

Disk drives no longer come as standard in many new, slimline laptops. If your laptop does not have an in-built disk drive, consider purchasing an external one. The chances are that you will come to view it as a necessary investment.

f. Tablet

A tablet is useful for three reasons.

First, playing a video following a road traffic collision during an in person hearing, so that all court actors can see it. Secondly, so that it can be used as an electronic witness bundle. Thirdly, during a remote hearing, to navigate around an electronic bundle.

In the likely event that you are required to cross-examine on a video, it is not possible to play the video, and simultaneously take a note of the evidence, on a single electronic device.

All too often, separate witness bundles that have been filed in good time do not make it to an in person hearing. If so, the bundle may be accessed using your professional email address and a tablet.

It is preferable to have two electronic devices for remote hearings.

One to access the hearing. Another to access the documents.

g. The Highway Code

Where liability is in dispute, *The Highway Code* is essential for final hearings following a road traffic collision.

It is the starting point for identifying the standard of care that is expected of a reasonable driver (see chapter 20(e)).

h. Judicial College Guidelines

Where there is a claim for personal injury, the *Judicial College Guidelines for the Assessment of General Damages in Personal Injury Cases* (15th edn, OUP 2019) is essential (see chapter 20(f)).

i. Props

In cases following a road traffic collision, toy, or model, cars, may be useful for conferences. They may also assist with oral evidence.

Reasons include that a witness can demonstrate the mechanism of collision, point of impact, and corresponding damage.

Other items may also be used. For example, highlighters.

j. External encrypted vault

Electronic devices should promptly be sanitised of confidential material, in accordance with your privacy policy.

Once a case is concluded, there is no good reason to retain confidential material relating to it on a *portable* electronic device.

To comply with data protection and privacy laws, external hard drives containing confidential material *must* be encrypted.

There are two forms of encryption. Hardware and software.

In general, hardware encryption is preferable. This means that a keypad requires a numerical code to be entered before the hard drive will be re-cognised, files can be accessed, or transferred.

One encrypted, external hard drive is *vital.* Two is preferable.

The first can be kept under lock and key in chambers.

The second can be kept at another location. For example, your home. This may also be under lock and key.

The first should be periodically updated onto the second.

The second functions as a secure "vault". This shows reasonable steps to mitigate against the worst-case scenario. Fire or theft.

28. Dress

There is recent guidance on court dress, and emblems of faith.

a. Guidance

'Court dress' (reviewed July 2020) ("the 2020 guidance") recommends appropriate court dress to barristers.

It is 'intended to provide a ready guide as to what clothing will generally be expected and acceptable'.

Unless 'court dress' is required, 'business attire' is to be worn.

'Court dress' means 'wigs, gowns, wing-collars and bands or collarettes.'

'Business attire' means 'smart dark office wear.' This 'will usually mean a black, dark grey or dark suit with tie for men, and, for women, a similarly coloured jacket and either skirt or trousers'.

Business attire should be worn for all applications, appeals from applications, and final hearings in the county court.

The 2020 guidance is not intended to affect any change.

It does not provide guidance on dress for appeals from final hearings, however, 'Court dress: Revised Guidance from the Chairman of the Bar Council' (2 June 2009), suggests court dress.

The 2020 guidance prescribes an exception for *remote* hearings, where court dress need not be worn.

b. Emblems of faith

The 2020 guidance strikes a balance between 'reflecting the seriousness of the function Counsel perform in Court, the role of Court dress as the uniform of the profession, and the need for such uniform to be inclusive of different religious practice.'

As a general rule, 'clothing that is worn as a requirement or emblem of faith is permitted'. The exception is where 'the clothing in question may affect the just determination of proceedings.'

Four common examples are provided.

First, jewellery bearing crosses or other symbols of religious belief is permitted. Secondly, kippahs may be worn, including under wigs. Thirdly, sober-coloured headscarves may be worn, and Muslims who wear headscarves need not wear wigs. Fourthly, sober-coloured turbans may be worn, and Sikhs who wear turbans need not wear wigs.

29. Ethics

Practising barristers and solicitors are bound by their respective codes of conduct. They are taken as read for the purposes of this guide, however, there is some *practical* guidance below.

a. Confidants

Prepare in advance of an ethical issue.

It is helpful, and comforting, to store the mobile telephone numbers, and the email addresses of several *appropriately* experienced, reliable, and trustworthy, colleagues.

Queen's Counsel is unlikely to be appropriate.

Ideally, they should not be so senior that they are likely to be unfamiliar with claims that are allocated to the small claims track.

You should be confident that, if they can, they will answer your call, or otherwise revert to you, as soon as practicable.

They should have your confidence so that you can confide in them.

Many advocates in claims that are allocated to the small claims track are pupils, or otherwise junior advocates. They will be grateful that their questions are not passed on to colleagues.

Often, a telephone call can be the quickest means of relaying an issue, receiving guidance, and reassurance.

If all of the telephone numbers that you have are engaged, or you cannot otherwise speak to a colleague, send an email.

If time is of the essence, another option is to speak to your practice manager, enquire whether any of your colleagues are available, and request to be put through to the one who is most appropriate.

b. Ethical Enquiries Services

If it is not possible to speak to a colleague, the Bar Council provides an Ethical Enquiries Service.

It provides confidential assistance to *barristers,* and, where appropriate, their *clerks and other members of staff* connected with barristers' professional practices.

It does so by assisting to *identify, interpret, and comply with, professional obligations,* under the BSB Handbook.

Monday to Friday, from 09:15 to 17:15, it is available by calling 020 7611 1307. Emails can be sent to ethics@barcouncil.org.uk.

A response should be within four working days.

It is confidential. All information provided through this service, and any assistance given, will be kept confidential.

There are two exceptions.

First, where you consent. Secondly, where the law provides.

Assistance is not 'guidance' for the purposes of the BSB Handbook.

Barristers are personally responsible for their own conduct, ethics, and decisions. The service 'assists'. It does not 'decide'.

An important benefit of seeking assistance is that, in the event of a complaint against you, it may be easier to explain your decisions, where you can show that you have sought assistance, and taken into account any response, before making a decision.

To this end, a note should be made of any oral assistance, and confirmed with the advisor within a week. Calls are not recorded.

In any event, you must not disclose the identity of the advisor without her prior consent, or that of the Chairman of the Ethics Committee. The exception is when you are responding to a complaint made to the BSB, or the Legal Ombudsman.

30. Etiquette

Etiquette goes hand in hand with professional ethics.

A core duty of counsel is not to behave in a way that is likely to diminish the trust and confidence that the public place in *you,* and generally, in the *profession.*

Failure to show respect and courtesy to court actors, for example, through following the appropriate etiquette, may breach this duty.

a. Outside court

Punctuality, use of an advocates' room, secure disposal of confidential documents, and formal correspondence, are consistent with the customary code of polite, professional behaviour.

i. Punctuality

For an in person hearing, plan to arrive in the right *place*, at the right *time*, with the right *tools*, and the right *attitude*.

Public transport may be delayed, listings can go awry, and personal circumstances may conspire against you.

The ethical question is often not *whether* you are late, but the *reason* why, and what you have done to *mitigate* the effects of it.

If there is a reasonable prospect that you will be late, correspond with your practice manager, professional client, and *ensure that the court is notified.*

If you are late, apologise. *Unreservedly.*

To your professional client, lay client, opponent, and the court.

Briefly explain why you are late.

Let your practice manager, and your instructing solicitor, know that you have arrived. Keep them updated of any complications.

If you need more time to hold a conference before a hearing is called on, inform the usher, and outline the reason why.

Cases are often listed together at 10:00, or 14:00.

The court may be able to accommodate a request for more time by hearing another matter before the one that you are instructed in.

ii. Coats, umbrellas & bags

Advocates should not take unnecessary items into the courtroom.

If they are unnecessary for the hearing, they are unnecessary.

One of the reasons for an advocates' room is so that legal representatives do not have to take unnecessary items into court. There is somewhere that they can be left securely.

If there is an advocates' room, and it is *lockable,* it should be used.

Documents and electronic devices containing confidential material, however, should *never* be left unattended. Even where there is a locked room. Keep it to hand.

iii. Disposal

Her Majesty's Courts and Tribunals Service ("HMCTS") met with the Bar Council to confirm the correct position as to who has responsibility for documents after hearings.

In a joint notice, it was agreed that *only those documents (or bundles) belonging to legal representatives* should be removed by the legal representatives.

If they are not, and they contain 'special category (formerly sensitive) personal data', HMCTS 'may consider it necessary to report that a personal data breach has occurred pursuant to the General Data Protection Regulation and Data Protection Act 2018.'

Documents filed with the court should not be removed by legal representatives. They are not data processors for the court.

iv. Correspondence

When corresponding with court, professional clients, or practice managers, follow formalities, revert promptly, be professional.

1. Judge

Generally, any communication with the court on a matter of substance, or procedure, *must* be served on the other party.

It is etiquette. It is also a CPR (CPRs 27.2(1)(h) and 39.8).

The court may ask a party to draw up a draft minute of order.

If so, the legal representative for the claimant, or applicant, will usually have "carriage" (see chapter 22(a)(i)).

This means that they are responsible for three actions.

First, drafting. Secondly, ensuring that it is an accurate reflection of the court's order, as prescribed in open court. Thirdly, handing the draft minute of order to the court's usher if it is handwritten, or emailing it to the court if it is electronic.

In practice, it is usually emailed to a judicial email address.

If so, the email should start: "Dear Judge".

It *must* state that it is being copied to the other party, her identity, and capacity. For example, solicitor for the claimant.

It should end with the title and surname of the legal representative sending the correspondence, and the party who they represent.

Do not copy in your *lay* client.

Having sent the email, it can be forwarded to your *professional* client, so that they are aware of the date and time that the email was sent, its content, and any attachments.

2. Ushers & other court staff

Be courteous.

First, and most importantly, they deserve it. Secondly, they speak to the judges. Thirdly, there may be a time when they can assist by calling another case before the one that you are instructed in. Fourthly, if you would like a photocopy of an order, or forgotten to print out a vital document, they may be more inclined to assist.

3. Professional client

Be courteous. Revert promptly. Stick to deadlines.

There is nothing that a client hates more than missing a deadline.

Where there is a potential problem, do not put your head in the sand. Speak to your practice manager.

When a professional client instructs counsel, they are putting their neck on the line. They have an enormous stake in the case.

If your professional client is unavailable, it is often possible to take instructions from another member of her team.

4. Practice manager

There should be implicit trust and confidence between counsel and practice manager.

Counsel look after their practice manager's wellbeing. Practice managers look after their barristers. There is reciprocity.

Emotional intelligence, considered correspondence, and flexibility, are key. They nurture confidence in practice managers when corresponding with you, other members of chambers, and your professional clients.

b. Inside court

The key etiquette *in* court surrounds submissions, and encompasses ethics. In particular, criticism of other professionals.

i. Mobile telephones

During in-person hearings, keep a smart phone on 'silent'.

First, to tether to your laptop, where the court does not provide a reliable internet connection. Secondly, to use a calculator function, so as to work out damages, interest, and costs. Thirdly, to use a calendar function, so as to work out what the date will be, for example, 21 days from the hearing.

ii. Entering & exiting

For an in-person hearing, wait for the names of the parties to be called by the usher before moving to the door of the courtroom.

As long as you have signed in, the matter will not go ahead without you. Unless you have left the court building.

On entering and exiting the courtroom, it is etiquette to bow.

In practice, this is a modest nod of the head, rather than the greeting that one imagines may be used when meeting the Queen.

When exiting the courtroom, you should not leave the judge sitting in court with the other side. All parties should leave together. That may mean waiting for the other side to gather their belongings.

Never leave the judge with a litigant in person.

Frequently, after the matter has concluded, the judge will say "good morning / afternoon". It is normal to repeat the greeting.

For an in-person hearing, this is your cue that you may leave the courtroom. For a remote hearing, you may then hang up the telephone, or leave the audio-visual hearing.

After an in person hearing, you may ask to be excused.

This is very formal. It may take a judge by surprise.

Asking to be excused may originate from the practice that you should not leave court before a judge has risen.

Accordingly, an alternative is to enquire whether the court is rising. Most judges will then understand that you are alluding to this custom. They are likely to stay in court and excuse you.

iii. Seating

For in person hearings, most courtrooms are of an average, or slightly bigger than average, size.

Judges are not elevated. All court actors are at the same eye-level.

Frequently, there are only three in-built architectural features, so as to convey the authority of the decision-maker.

First, a royal crest above the judge. Secondly, a pronounced gap between where the parties sit, and where the judge sits. Thirdly, a vertical panel in front of the judge's desk, so that the parties cannot see what she is writing.

In other courts, the rooms are larger, and the judge sits higher-up, so that the parties have to look up to catch the judge's eye.

On occasion, in the County Court at Central London, judges sit in courtrooms used by the High Court. Frequently, in the Queen's Building, or the West Green Building. If so, it is preferable to stand, so as to catch the judge's eye, and so not to appear discourteous.

There are conventions surrounding where legal representatives, witnesses, and non-court actors, are located in the courtroom.

The layout will dictate.

When a person is disabled, the courts usually permit that person to fulfil her role in the position in which she is most comfortable. You can identify whether to make such a request on behalf of that person in the conference before an in-person hearing.

1. Parties

Legal representatives sit at the front tables.

Usually, the claimant sits on the left. The defendant sits on the right. In some courts, however, this is reversed. If so, there will be signs denominating which party is to sit at which table.

A litigant in person also sits at the respective front table.

2. Witnesses

Witnesses usually sit at a table behind the legal representative for the party who calls them to give evidence.

When giving evidence, witnesses usually move to another table.

Often, it is in between the legal representatives' and the judge's table. Usually, it is off to one side, so that all court actors can comfortably see and hear the witness.

A witness bundle will give away the witness table.

In absence of a separate table, however, witnesses sit at the table at which the legal representatives (or unrepresented parties) sit.

Witnesses should only be able to see an unmarked witness bundle.

Care should be taken not to appear to give any visual cues, or otherwise project body language, when a witness is giving evidence.

This may require a concerted effort.

3. Non-court actors

Pupils and mini-pupils should sit at the back of the courtroom.

It should be clear that they are not a court actor. They have no role in the case. They are not a legal representative, party, or witness.

Introduce non-court actors before the hearing to the other party, and at the start of the hearing for the benefit of the court.

iv. Submissions

There are conventions surrounding the way in which court actors introduce the case, address other court actors, and interruptions.

Do not make a positive submission unless you have instructions to do so, the evidence in support; or if it is a matter of law, you reasonably believe it to be correct.

Be careful not knowingly to mislead the court by appearing to endorse a proposition of law to which you are not able to agree.

1. Forms of address

In the unlikely event that you are before a recorder, or a circuit judge, they should be referred to as "Your Honour".

Deputy district judges, and full district judges should be referred to as "Madam" or "Sir".

Alternatively, judges can be referred to as "the court".

This is preferable for three reasons.

First, it is formal. Secondly, it guards against the perception that you are over-familiar with the judge. Thirdly, it indicates that the judge is the court actor with authority as decision-maker.

The convention is that counsel refer to one another as "my learned friend". Counsel refer to solicitors as "my friend".

The latter can appear old-fashioned, however, so counsel often refer to a solicitor using title and surname.

There are two ways to refer to a party.

First, "claimant" or "defendant". Secondly, title and surname.

Witnesses are referred to using title and surname.

Ushers are referred to as "Madam Usher" or "Mister Usher".

2. Introduction

As a general rule, the claimant speaks first.

It is the claimant's case. Even where there is a counterclaim, if there is an introduction, the claimant usually speaks first.

Where the hearing is listed to dispose of an application, the applicant speaks first because it is the applicant's application.

It is safer to wait for the judge to invite you to speak before addressing the court. If the judge is writing when you enter the courtroom, she may be finalising the order of the previous matter.

Usually, the judge will introduce the case for the recording.

For an in person hearing, you will have signed in with the usher.

Sometimes, case-management forms have been completed before the hearing. If so, the names of the parties, legal representatives, and witnesses will have been noted.

Accordingly, the judge is likely to state the names of the parties, case number, name of any advocate, and the parties who they represent, before the hearing begins.

If the judge does not state the names of the advocates, it is etiquette to introduce the legal representative for the other side.

Title and surname, followed by the party who they represent.

Introduce yourself, using your surname, followed by the party who you represent. There is no need to include your title.

In the event that a non-court actor is observing to gain experience, introduce them, for the benefit of all court actors.

3. Issues

The judge will usually ask what issues are in dispute.

So as to respond, it is invaluable to speak to the other party before the hearing to confirm the following (see chapter 15(g)).

First, the documents that have been filed, served, and the parties wish to rely upon.

Secondly, which heads of loss are still pursued; in respect of each, whether it is admitted, denied, or agreed subject to liability; and the issues relating to each head of loss in dispute.

Thirdly, whether quantum is agreed; and, if so, the sum for each head of loss.

Fourthly, what authority (if any) is relied upon.

This will dictate whether or not there are any preliminary issues.

Having *defined* and *confined* the issues that are in dispute, if you try to raise an issue that has not been flagged up at the outset, you will likely be stopped by the court for three reasons.

First, the court is under a duty to further the overriding objective. This includes ensuring that the parties are on an equal footing and ensuring that the case is dealt with fairly and expeditiously.

Secondly, the court is under a duty to actively manage cases. This includes identifying the issues at an early stage and fixing timetables, or otherwise controlling the progress of the case.

Thirdly, etiquette. The other party has a legitimate expectation that the issues will not expand throughout the hearing.

4. Interrupting

Do not interrupt another court actor, unless there is a *good* reason.

Judge, counsel, or witness.

If the judge, or another legal representative interrupts you, yield, and wait. If the interruption is unjustified, you will have the opportunity to explain the reason why. The impact of your explanation will not diminish having demonstrated common courtesy.

An obvious exception is where a witness strays into relaying what was said during a conference. This is privileged.

5. Humility

If you cannot assist the judge on a particular issue, say so.

You should do your best to acquire such knowledge of the facts and the law, so as to understand the facts that are in dispute, applicable law, and what you are inviting the court to do.

But you must not mislead the court, knowingly, or recklessly.

Better to show *reasonable* humility, and *appropriate* deference, than to invite, or otherwise to encourage, the court to do something against CPRs, PDs, or authority, which is appealable.

6. Gestures

No matter your instinctive reaction to the evidence, submission, order, or judgment, try to retain your composure.

Let a witness be discourteous. It will undermine her evidence.

When a weak submission is made, an effective way to neutralise it may be to demonstrate that it is not persuasive using the evidence, and submissions on the law.

If it is *inherently* weak, the judge is likely to have perceived that it is an unsustainable reason on which to base her judgment. She may not necessarily flag it up, however, it may be unnecessary to give verbose submissions on why it is inherently weak.

Orders *will* be made, and judgments *will* be given, with which you do not agree. They are the *responsibility* of the *judge*.

Not counsel, or solicitor.

If it is arguably susceptible to an appeal, an application for permission to appeal can be made at the end of the hearing.

You are likely to be instructed in many more cases before *that* judge. You will undermine your professional reputation with that judge, and perhaps also her colleagues, the usher, and court staff, if you visibly show your disapproval.

7. Criticism

Criticism should be *measured, reasoned,* and, unless there is a good reason, on *instructions*. The hearing will be recorded.

a. Experts

Criticism of experts, and their reports, should be carefully considered, and without good reason, only with *written* instructions.

There may be an "expert" report on diminution in the value of a vehicle following a road traffic collision, over and above the reasonable cost of repair.

If there is no permission to rely on expert evidence, the following three submissions can be effective, and time-efficient, without criticising the expert personally, or her report.

First, no expert may give evidence at a hearing, whether oral or written, without the permission of the court (CPR 27.5).

Secondly, the court is under a duty to restrict expert evidence (CPRs 27.2(1)(e) and 35.1).

Thirdly, if the party seeking to rely on expert evidence has indicated that they wish to do so in their directions questionnaire, the court has already had notice of the request, and it has been refused. Alternatively, if that party has failed to indicate that they wish to rely on expert evidence, there has been a failure to complete the directions questionnaire accurately.

In the case of the former, an application should have been made for permission to rely on an expert. In the case of the latter, the overriding objective will be compromised if permission is granted.

The parties will no longer be on an equal footing. The case will not have been dealt with fairly. Compliance with the direction to complete directions questionnaires accurately has not been enforced.

Whether or not there is permission to rely on an expert, the author of an expert report is unlikely to attend a hearing. If so, she will not give oral evidence. There is no opportunity to respond to any criticism, as it will not be put in cross-examination.

In practice, this means that it is often difficult to persuade a judge that an "expert" report is unreliable. To do so, the *reasoning* behind the conclusion should be addressed in cogent submissions.

b. Legal representatives

Attacks on the conduct of a legal representative should also be *carefully* considered, and, unless there is a good reason, only with *explicit*, written instructions.

The conduct of legal representatives is relevant for deciding what order to make as to costs.

For example, in responding to requests for key documents, such as invoices, so as to narrow, and potentially settle, the issues.

When identified ahead of the hearing, a *very* short witness statement from your professional client, setting out any non-compliance, can assist. Relevant correspondence may be exhibited.

If there is legitimate criticism to be made as to the manner in which a legal representative has litigated, it may also be possible expressly to state that no criticism is made of counsel. If so, say so.

Appendix A
CPR 1.1
The Overriding Objective

(1) These Rules are a new procedural code with the overriding objective of enabling the court to deal with cases justly and at proportionate cost.

(2) Dealing with a case justly and at proportionate cost includes, so far as is practicable—

   (a) ensuring that the parties are on an equal footing;

   (b) saving expense;

   (c) dealing with the case in ways which are proportionate—

       (i) to the amount of money involved;

       (ii) to the importance of the case;

       (iii) to the complexity of the issues; and

       (iv) to the financial position of each party;

   (d) ensuring that it is dealt with expeditiously and fairly;

   (e) allotting to it an appropriate share of the court's resources, while taking into account the need to allot resources to other cases; and

   (f) enforcing compliance with rules, practice directions and orders.

Appendix B
CPR 1.4
Court's Duty To Manage Cases

(1) The court must further the overriding objective by actively managing cases.

(2) Active case management includes—

(a) encouraging the parties to co-operate with each other in the conduct of the proceedings;

(b) identifying the issues at an early stage;

(c) deciding promptly which issues need full investigation and trial and accordingly disposing summarily of the others;

(d) deciding the order in which issues are to be resolved;

(e) encouraging the parties to use an alternative dispute resolution procedure if the court considers that appropriate and facilitating the use of such procedure;

(f) helping the parties to settle the whole or part of the case;

(g) fixing timetables or otherwise controlling the progress of the case;

(h) considering whether the likely benefits of taking a particular step justify the cost of taking it;

(i) dealing with as many aspects of the case as it can on the same occasion;

(j) dealing with the case without the parties needing to attend at court;

(k) making use of technology; and

(l) giving directions to ensure that the trial of a case proceeds quickly and efficiently.

Appendix C
CPR 27
The Small Claims Track

CPR 27.1 — Scope of this Part

(1) This Part—

  (a) sets out the special procedure for dealing with claims which have been allocated to the small claims track under Part 26; and

  (b) limits the amount of costs that can be recovered in respect of a claim which has been allocated to the small claims track.

(Rule 27.14 deals with costs on the small claims track.)

(2) A claim being dealt with under this Part is called a small claim.

(Rule 26.6 provides for the scope of the small claims track. A claim for a remedy for harassment or unlawful eviction relating, in either case, to residential premises shall not be allocated to the small claims track whatever the financial value of the claim. Otherwise, the small claims track will be the normal track for—

• any claim which has a financial value of not more than £10,000 subject to the special provisions about claims for personal injuries and housing disrepair claims;

• any claim for personal injuries which has a financial value of not more than £10,000 where the claim for damages for personal injuries is not more than £1,000; and

• any claim which includes a claim by a tenant of residential premises against his landlord for repairs or other work to the premises where the estimated cost of the repairs or other work is not more than £1,000 and the financial value of any other claim for damages is not more than £1,000.)

CPR 27.2 — Extent to which other Parts apply

(1) The following Parts of these Rules do not apply to small claims—

(a) Part 25 (interim remedies) except as it relates to interim in-junctions;

(b) Part 31 (disclosure and inspection);

(c) Part 32 (evidence) except rule 32.1 (power of court to con-trol evidence);

(d) Part 33 (miscellaneous rules about evidence);

(e) Part 35 (experts and assessors) except rules 35.1 (duty to re-strict expert evidence), 35.3 (experts—overriding duty to the court), 35.7 (court's power to direct that evidence is to be given by single joint expert) and 35.8 (instructions to a single joint expert);

(f) Subject to paragraph (3), Part 18 (further information);

(g) Part 36 (offers to settle); and

(h) Part 39 (hearings) except rule 39.2 (general rule—hearing to be in public) and rule 39.8 (communications with the court).

(2) The other Parts of these Rules apply to small claims except to the extent that a rule limits such application.

(3) The court of its own initiative may order a party to provide further information if it considers it appropriate to do so.

CPR 27.3 — Court's power to grant a final remedy

The court may grant any final remedy in relation to a small claim which it could grant if the proceedings were on the fast track or the multi-track.

CPR 27.4 — Preparation for the hearing

(1) After allocation the court will—

(a) give standard directions and fix a date for the final hearing;

(b) give special directions and fix a date for the final hearing;

(c) give special directions and direct that the court will consider what further directions are to be given no later than 28 days after the date the special directions were given;

(d) fix a date for a preliminary hearing under rule 27.6; or

(e) give notice that it proposes to deal with the claim without a hearing under rule 27.10 and invite the parties to notify the court by a specified date if they agree the proposal.

(2) The court will—

(a) give parties at least 21 days' notice of the date fixed for the final hearing, unless the parties agree to accept less notice; and

(b) inform them of the amount of time allowed for the final hearing.

(3) In this rule—

(a) "standard directions" means—

(i) a direction that each party shall, at least 14 days before the date fixed for the final hearing, file and serve on every other party copies of all documents (including any expert's report) on which he intends to rely at the hearing; and

(ii) any other standard directions set out in Practice Direction 27; and

(b) "special directions" means directions given in addition to or instead of the standard directions.

CPR 27.5 — Experts

No expert may give evidence, whether written or oral, at a hearing without the permission of the court.

CPR 27.6 — Preliminary hearing

(1) The court may hold a preliminary hearing for the consideration of the claim, but only—

(a) where—

  (i) it considers that special directions, as defined in rule 27.4, are needed to ensure a fair hearing; and

  (ii) it appears necessary for a party to attend at court to ensure that he understands what he must do to comply with the special directions; or

 (b) to enable it to dispose of the claim on the basis that one or other of the parties has no real prospect of success at a final hearing; or

 (c) to enable it to strike out a statement of case or part of a statement of case on the basis that the statement of case, or the part to be struck out, discloses no reasonable grounds for bringing or defending the claim.

(2) When considering whether or not to hold a preliminary hearing, the court must have regard to the desirability of limiting the expense to the parties of attending court.

(3) Where the court decides to hold a preliminary hearing, it will give the parties at least 14 days' notice of the date of the hearing.

(4) The court may treat the preliminary hearing as the final hearing of the claim if all the parties agree.

(5) At or after the preliminary hearing the court will—

 (a) fix the date of the final hearing (if it has not been fixed already) and give the parties at least 21 days' notice of the date fixed unless the parties agree to accept less notice;

 (b) inform them of the amount of time allowed for the final hearing; and

 (c) give any appropriate directions.

CPR 27.7 — Power of court to add to, vary or revoke directions

The court may add to, vary or revoke directions.

CPR 27.8 — Conduct of the hearing

(1) The court may adopt any method of proceeding at a hearing that it considers to be fair.

(2) Hearings will be informal.

(3) The strict rules of evidence do not apply.

(4) The court need not take evidence on oath.

(5) The court may limit cross-examination.

(6) The court must give reasons for its decision.

CPR 27.9 — Non-attendance of parties at a final hearing

(1) If a party who does not attend a final hearing—

(a) has given written notice to the court and the other party at least 7 days before the hearing date that he will not attend;

(b) has served on the other party at least 7 days before the hearing date any other documents which he has filed with the court; and

(c) has, in his written notice, requested the court to decide the claim in his absence and has confirmed his compliance with paragraphs (a) and (b) above, the court will take into account that party's statement of case and any other documents he has filed and served when it decides the claim.

(2) If a claimant does not—

(a) attend the hearing; and

(b) give the notice referred to in paragraph (1),

the court may strike out the claim.

(3) If—

(a) a defendant does not—

(i) attend the hearing; or

(ii) give the notice referred to in paragraph (1); and

(b) the claimant either—

(i) does attend the hearing; or

(ii) gives the notice referred to in paragraph (1),

the court may decide the claim on the basis of the evidence of the claimant alone.

(4) If neither party attends or gives the notice referred to in paragraph (1), the court may strike out the claim and any defence and counterclaim.

CPR 27.10 — Disposal without a hearing

The court may, if all parties agree, deal with the claim without a hearing.

CPR 27.11 — Setting judgment aside and re-hearing

(1) A party—

> (a) who was neither present nor represented at the hearing of the claim; and

> (b) who has not given written notice to the court under rule 27.9(1),

may apply for an order that a judgment under this Part shall be set aside and the claim re-heard.

(2) A party who applies for an order setting aside a judgment under this rule must make the application not more than 14 days after the day on which notice of the judgment was served on him.

(3) The court may grant an application under paragraph (2) only if the applicant—

> (a) had a good reason for not attending or being represented at the hearing or giving written notice to the court under rule 27.9(1); and

> (b) has a reasonable prospect of success at the hearing.

(4) If a judgment is set aside —

> (a) the court must fix a new hearing for the claim; and

(b) the hearing may take place immediately after the hearing of the application to set the judgment aside and may be dealt with by the judge who set aside the judgment.

(5) A party may not apply to set aside a judgment under this rule if the court dealt with the claim without a hearing under rule 27.10.

(Rules 27.12 and 27.13 are revoked.)

CPR 27.14 — Costs on the small claims track

(1) This rule applies to any case which has been allocated to the small claims track.

(Rules 46.11 and 46.13 make provision in relation to orders for costs made before a claim has been allocated to the small claims track.)

(2) The court may not order a party to pay a sum to another party in respect of that other party's costs, fees and expenses, including those relating to an appeal, except—

(a) the fixed costs attributable to issuing the claim which—

(i) are payable under Part 45; or

(ii) would be payable under Part 45 if that Part applied to the claim;

(b) in proceedings which included a claim for an injunction or an order for specific performance a sum not exceeding the amount specified in Practice Direction 27 for legal advice and assistance relating to that claim;

(c) any court fees paid by that other party;

(d) expenses which a party or witness has reasonably incurred in travelling to and from a hearing or in staying away from home for the purposes of attending a hearing;

(e) a sum not exceeding the amount specified in Practice Direction 27 for any loss of earnings or loss of leave by a party or witness due to attending a hearing or to staying away from home for the purpose of attending a hearing;

(f) a sum not exceeding the amount specified in Practice Direction 27 for an expert's fees;

(g) such further costs as the court may assess by the summary procedure and order to be paid by a party who has behaved unreasonably;

(h) the Stage 1 and, where relevant, the Stage 2 fixed costs in rule 45.18 where—

    (i) the claim was within the scope of the Pre-Action Protocol for Low Value Personal Injury Claims in Road Traffic Accidents ("the RTA Protocol") or the Pre-action Protocol for Low Value Personal Injury (Employers' Liability and Public Liability) Claims ("the EL/PL Protocol");

    (ii) the claimant reasonably believed that the claim was valued at more than the small claims track limit in accordance with paragraph 4.1(4) of the relevant Protocol; and

    (iii) the defendant admitted liability under the process set out in the relevant Protocol; but

    (iv) the defendant did not pay those Stage 1 and, where relevant, Stage 2 fixed costs; and

(i) in an appeal, the cost of any approved transcript reasonably incurred.

(3) A party's rejection of an offer in settlement will not of itself constitute unreasonable behaviour under paragraph (2)(g) but the court may take it into consideration when it is applying the unreasonableness test.

(4) The limits on costs imposed by this rule also apply to any fee or reward for acting on behalf of a party to the proceedings charged by a person exercising a right of audience by virtue of an order under section 11 of the Courts and Legal Services Act 1990 (a lay representative).

CPR 27.15 — Claim re-allocated from the small claims track to another track

Where a claim is allocated to the small claims track and subsequently reallocated to another track, rule 27.14 (costs on the small claims track) will cease to apply after the claim has been re-allocated, and the fast track or multi-track costs rules will apply from the date of re-allocation.

Appendix D
PD 27
Small Claims Track

Judges

[1] The functions of the court described in Part 27 which are to be carried out by a judge will generally be carried out by a District Judge but may be carried out by a Circuit Judge.

Case management directions

[2.1] Rule 27.4 explains how directions will be given, and rule 27.6 contains provisions about the holding of a preliminary hearing and the court's powers at such a hearing.

[2.2] Appendix A sets out details of the case that the court usually needs in the type of case described. Appendix B sets out the Standard Directions that the court may give. Appendix C sets out Special Directions that the court may give.

[2.3] Before allocating the claim to the Small Claims Track and giving directions for a hearing the court may require a party to give further information about that party's case.

[2.4] A party may ask the court to give particular directions about the conduct of the case.

[2.5] In deciding whether to make an order for exchange of witness statements the court will have regard to the following—

(a) whether either or both the parties are represented;

(b) the amount in dispute in the proceedings;

(c) the nature of the matters in dispute;

(d) whether the need for any party to clarify his case can better be dealt with by an order under paragraph 2.3;

(e) the need for the parties to have access to justice without undue formality, cost or delay.

Representation at a hearing

[3.1] In this paragraph—

(1) a lawyer means a barrister, a solicitor or a legal executive employed by a solicitor or any other person authorised under the Legal Services Act 2007 to act as a litigator or advocate; and

(2) a lay representative means any other person.

[3.2]

(1) A party may present his own case at a hearing or a lawyer or lay representative may present it for him.

(2) The Lay Representatives (Right of Audience) Order 1999 provides that a lay representative may not exercise any right of audience—

(a) where his client does not attend the hearing;

(b) at any stage after judgment; or

(c) on any appeal brought against any decision made by the District Judge in the proceedings.

(3) However the court, exercising its general discretion to hear anybody, may hear a lay representative even in circumstances excluded by the Order.

(4) Any of its officers or employees may represent a corporate party.

Small claim hearing

[4.1] [Omitted.]

[4.2] A hearing that takes place at the court will generally be in the judge's room but it may take place in a courtroom.

[4.3] Rule 27.8 allows the court to adopt any method of proceeding that it considers to be fair and to limit cross-examination. The judge may in particular—

(1) ask questions of any witness himself before allowing any other person to do so;

(2) ask questions of all or any of the witnesses himself before allowing any other person to ask questions of any witnesses;

(3) refuse to allow cross-examination of any witness until all the witnesses have given evidence in chief;

(4) limit cross-examination of a witness to a fixed time or to a particular subject or issue, or both.

Recording evidence and the giving of reasons

[5.1] A hearing that takes place at the court will be tape recorded by the court. A party may obtain a transcript of such a recording on payment of the proper transcriber's charges.

[5.2] Attention is drawn to section 9 of the Contempt of Court Act 1981 (which deals with the unauthorised use of tape recorders in court) and to the Practice Direction ([1981] 1 WLR 1526) which relates to it.

[5.3]

(1) The judge may give reasons for his judgment as briefly and simply as the nature of the case allows.

(2) He will normally do so orally at the hearing, but he may give them later at a hearing either orally or in writing.

[5.4] Where the judge decides the case without a hearing under rule 27.10 or a party who has given notice under rule 27.9(1) does not attend the hearing, the judge will prepare a note of his reasons and the court will send a copy to each party.

[5.5] Nothing in this practice direction affects the duty of a judge at the request of a party to make a note of the matters referred to in section 80 of the County Courts Act 1984.

Non-attendance of a party at a hearing

[6.1] Attention is drawn to rule 27.9 (which enables a party to give notice that he will not attend a final hearing and sets out the effect of his giving such notice and of not doing so), and to paragraph 3 above.

[**6.2**] Nothing in those provisions affects the general power of the court to adjourn a hearing, for example where a party who wishes to attend a hearing on the date fixed cannot do so for a good reason.

Costs

[**7.1**] Attention is drawn to rule 27.14 which contains provisions about the costs which may be ordered to be paid by one party to another.

[**7.2**] The amount which a party may be ordered to pay under rule 27.14(2)(b) (for legal advice and assistance in claims including an injunction or specific performance) is a sum not exceeding £260.

[**7.3**] The amounts which a party may be ordered to pay under rule 27.14(3)(c) (loss of earnings) and (d) (experts' fees) are—

> (1) for the loss of earnings or loss of leave of each party or witness due to attending a hearing or staying away from home for the purpose of attending a hearing, a sum not exceeding £95 per day for each person; and

> (2) for experts' fees, a sum not exceeding £750 for each expert.

(As to recovery of pre-allocation costs in a case in which an admission by the defendant has reduced the amount in dispute to a figure below £10,000, reference should be made to paragraph 7.4 of Practice Direction 26 and to paragraph 7.1(3) of Practice Direction 46.)

Appeals

[**8.1**] Part 52 deals with appeals and attention is drawn to that Part and Practice Direction 52.

[8A] An appellant's notice in small claims must be filed and served in Form N164.

[8.2] Where the court dealt with the claim to which the appellant is a party—

(1) under rule 27.10 without a hearing; or

(2) in his absence because he gave notice under rule 27.9 requesting the court to decide the claim in his absence,

an application for permission to appeal must be made to the appeal court.

[8.3] Where an appeal is allowed the appeal court will, if possible, dispose of the case at the same time without referring the claim to the lower court or ordering a new hearing. It may do so without hearing further evidence.

Appendix A — Information and Documentation the Court Usually Needs in Particular Types of Case

ROAD ACCIDENT CASES (where the information or documentation is available)

- witness statements (including statements from the parties themselves);
- invoices and estimates for repairs;
- agreements and invoices for any car hire costs;
- the Police accident report;
- sketch plan which should wherever possible be agreed;
- photographs of the scene of the accident and of the damage.

BUILDING DISPUTES, REPAIRS, GOODS SOLD AND SIMILAR CONTRACTUAL CLAIMS (where the information or documentation is available)

- any written contract;

- photographs;

- any plans;

- a list of works complained of;

- a list of any outstanding works;

- any relevant estimate, invoice or receipt including any relating to repairs to each of the defects;

- invoices for work done or goods supplied;

- estimates for work to be completed;

- a valuation of work done to date.

LANDLORD AND TENANT CLAIMS (where the information or documentation is available)

- a calculation of the amount of any rent alleged to be owing, showing amounts received;

- details of breaches of an agreement which are said to justify withholding any deposit itemised showing how the total is made up and with invoices and estimates to support them.

BREACH OF DUTY CASES (negligence, deficient professional services and the like)

Details of the following:

- what it is said by the claimant was done negligently by the defendant;

- why it is said that the negligence is the fault of the defendant;

- what damage is said to have been caused;

- what injury or losses have been suffered and how any (and each) sum claimed has been calculated;

- the response of the defendant to each of the above.

Appendix B — Standard Directions

(For use where the district judge specifies no other directions)

The Court Directs:

1. Each party must deliver to every other party and to the court office copies of all documents on which he intends to rely at the hearing no later than [...] [14 days before the hearing]. (These should include the letter making the claim and the reply.)

2. The original documents must be brought to the hearing.

3. [Notice of hearing date and time allowed.]

4. The parties are encouraged to contact each other with a view to trying to settle the case or narrow the issues. However the court must be informed immediately if the case is settled by agreement before the hearing date.

5. No party may rely at the hearing on any report from an expert unless express permission has been granted by the court beforehand. Anyone wishing to rely on an expert must write to the court immediately on receipt of this Order and seek permission, giving an explanation why the assistance of an expert is necessary.

   NOTE: Failure to comply with the directions may result in the case being adjourned and in the party at fault having to pay costs.

The parties are encouraged always to try to settle the case by negotiating with each other. The court must be informed immediately if the case is settled before the hearing.

Appendix C — Special Directions

The … must clarify his case.

He must do this by delivering to the court office and to the … no later than … [a list of …] [details of …]

The … must allow the … to inspect by appointment within … days of receiving a request to do so.

The hearing will not take place at the court but at …

The … must bring to court at the hearing the …

Signed statements setting out the evidence of all witnesses on whom each party intends to rely must be prepared and copies included in the documents mentioned in paragraph 1. This includes the evidence of the parties themselves and of any other witness, whether or not he is going to come to court to give evidence.

The court may decide not to take into account a document [or video] or the evidence of a witness if these directions have not been complied with.

If he does not [do so] […] his [Claim] [Defence] [and Counterclaim] will be struck out and (specify consequence).

It appears to the court that expert evidence is necessary on the issue of … and that that evidence should be given by a single expert to be instructed by the parties jointly. If the parties cannot agree about who to choose and what arrangements to make about paying his fee, either party MUST apply to the court for further directions. The evidence is to be given in the form of a written report. Either party may ask the expert questions and must then send copies of the questions and replies to the other party and to the court. Oral expert evidence may be allowed in exceptional circumstances but only after a further order of the court. Attention is drawn to the limit of [£750] on expert's fees that may be recovered.

If either party intends to show a video as evidence he must –

(a)   contact the court at once to make arrangements for him to do so, because the court may not have the necessary equipment, and

(b)   provide the other party with a copy of the video or the opportunity to see it at least … days before the hearing.

Appendix E
PD — Pre-Action Conduct & Protocols

Introduction

[1] Pre-action protocols explain the conduct and set out the steps the court would normally expect parties to take before commencing proceedings for particular types of civil claims. They are approved by the Master of the Rolls and are appendixed to the Civil Procedure Rules (CPR). (The current pre-action protocols are listed in paragraph 18.)

[2] This Practice Direction applies to disputes where no pre-action protocol approved by the Master of the Rolls applies. A person who knowingly makes a false statement in a pre-action protocol letter or other document prepared in anticipation of legal proceedings may be subject to proceedings for contempt of court.

Objectives of pre-action conduct and Protocols

[3] Before commencing proceedings, the court will expect the parties to have exchanged sufficient information to—

    (a) understand each other's position;

    (b) make decisions about how to proceed;

    (c) try to settle the issues without proceedings;

    (d) consider a form of Alternative Dispute Resolution (ADR) to assist with settlement;

(e) support the efficient management of those proceedings; and

(f) reduce the costs of resolving the dispute.

Proportionality

[4] A pre-action protocol or this Practice Direction must not be used by a party as a tactical device to secure an unfair advantage over another party. Only reasonable and proportionate steps should be taken by the parties to identify, narrow and resolve the legal, factual or expert issues.

[5] The costs incurred in complying with a pre-action protocol or this Practice Direction should be proportionate (CPR 44.3(5)). Where parties incur disproportionate costs in complying with any pre-action protocol or this Practice Direction, those costs will not be recoverable as part of the costs of the proceedings.

Steps before issuing a claim at court

[6] Where there is a relevant pre–action protocol, the parties should comply with that protocol before commencing proceedings. Where there is no relevant pre-action protocol, the parties should exchange correspondence and information to comply with the objectives in paragraph 3, bearing in mind that compliance should be proportionate. The steps will usually include—

(a)   the claimant writing to the defendant with concise details of the claim. The letter should include the basis on which the claim is made, a summary of the facts, what the claimant wants from the defendant, and if money, how the amount is calculated;

(b)   the defendant responding within a reasonable time—14 days in a straight forward case and no more than 3 months in a very complex one. The reply should include confirmation as to whether the claim is accepted and, if it is not accepted, the reasons why, together with an explanation as to which facts and parts of the claim are disputed and whether the defendant is making a counterclaim as well as providing details of any counterclaim; and

(c)   the parties disclosing key documents relevant to the issues in dispute.

Experts

[7] Parties should be aware that the court must give permission before expert evidence can be relied upon (see CPR 35.4(1)) and that the court may limit the fees recoverable. Many disputes can be resolved without expert advice or evidence. If it is necessary to obtain expert evidence, particularly in low value claims, the parties should consider using a single expert, jointly instructed by the parties, with the costs shared equally.

Settlement and ADR

[8] Litigation should be a last resort. As part of a relevant pre-action protocol or this Practice Direction, the parties should consider whether negotiation or some other form of ADR might enable them to settle their dispute without commencing proceedings.

[9] Parties should continue to consider the possibility of reaching a settlement at all times, including after proceedings have been started. ... offers may be made before proceedings are issued.

[10] Parties may negotiate to settle a dispute or may use a form of ADR including—

(a) mediation, a third party facilitating a resolution;

(b) arbitration, a third party deciding the dispute;

(c) early neutral evaluation, a third party giving an informed opinion on the dispute; and

(d) Ombudsmen schemes.

Information on mediation and other forms of ADR is available in the Jackson ADR Handbook (available from Oxford University Press) or at—

- http://www.civilmediation.justice.gov.uk/

[11] If proceedings are issued, the parties may be required by the court to provide evidence that ADR has been considered. A party's silence in response to an invitation to participate or a refusal to participate in ADR might be considered unreasonable by the court and could lead to the court ordering that party to pay additional court costs.

Stocktake and list of issues

[12] Where a dispute has not been resolved after the parties have followed a pre-action protocol or this Practice Direction, they should review their respective positions. They should consider the papers and the evidence to see if proceedings can be avoided and at least seek to narrow the issues in dispute before the claimant issues proceedings.

Compliance with this Practice Direction and the Protocols

[**13**] If a dispute proceeds to litigation, the court will expect the parties to have complied with a relevant pre-action protocol or this Practice Direction. The court will take into account non-compliance when giving directions for the management of proceedings (see CPR 3.1(4) to (6)) and when making orders for costs (see CPR 44.3(5)(a)). The court will consider whether all parties have complied in substance with the terms of the relevant pre-action protocol or this Practice Direction and is not likely to be concerned with minor or technical infringements, especially when the matter is urgent (for example an application for an injunction).

[**14**] The court may decide that there has been a failure of compliance when a party has—

(a) not provided sufficient information to enable the objectives in paragraph 3 to be met;

(b) not acted within a time limit set out in a relevant protocol, or within a reasonable period; or

(c) unreasonably refused to use a form of ADR, or failed to respond at all to an invitation to do so.

[**15**] Where there has been non-compliance with a pre-action protocol or this Practice Direction, the court may order that:

(a) the parties are relieved of the obligation to comply or further comply with the pre-action protocol or this Practice Direction;

(b) the proceedings are stayed while particular steps are taken to comply with the pre-action protocol or this Practice Direction;

(c) sanctions are to be applied.

[16] The court will consider the effect of any non-compliance when deciding whether to impose any sanctions which may include—

(a) an order that the party at fault pays the costs of the proceedings, or part of the costs of the other party or parties;

(b) an order that the party at fault pay those costs on an indemnity basis;

(c) if the party at fault is a claimant who has been awarded a sum of money, an order depriving that party of interest on that sum for a specified period, and / or awarding interest at a lower rate than would otherwise have been awarded;

(d) if the party at fault is a defendant, and the claimant has been awarded a sum of money, an order awarding interest on that sum for a specified period at a higher rate, (not exceeding 10% above base rate), than the rate which would otherwise have been awarded.

Limitation

[17] This Practice Direction and the pre-action protocols do not alter the statutory time limits for starting court proceedings. If a claim is issued after the relevant limitation period has expired, the defendant will be entitled to use that as a defence to the claim. If proceedings are started to comply with the statutory time limit before the parties have followed the procedures in this Practice Direction or the relevant pre-action protocol, the parties should apply to the court for a stay of the proceedings while they so comply.

Protocols in force

[18] The table sets out the protocols currently in force and from which date.

Protocol	Came into force
Personal Injury	6 April 2015
Resolution of Clinical Disputes	6 April 2015
Construction & Engineering	9 November 2016 (second edition)
Defamation	2 October 2000
Professional Negligence	16 July 2000
Judicial Review	6 April 2015
Disease & Illness	8 December 2003
Housing Disrepair	6 April 2015
Possession Claims by Social Landlords	6 April 2015
Possession Claims for Mortgage Arrears	6 April 2015
Dilapidation of Commercial Property	1 January 2012
Low Value Personal Injury Road Traffic Accident Claims	30 April 2010 extended from 31 July 2013
Low Value Personal Injury Employers' & Public Liability Claims	31 July 2013
Debt Claims	1 October 2017
Resolution of Package Travel Claims	7 May 2018

Appendix F
Issue Fees

Amount claimed	Issue fee	
	Paper	Online
Not more than £300	£35	£25
£300.01 to £500	£50	£35
£500.01 to £1,000	£70	£60
£1,000.01 to £1,500	£80	£70
£1,500.01 to £3,000	£115	£105
£3,000.01 to £5,000	£205	£185
£5,000.01 to £10,000	£455	£410
£10,000.01 to £100,000	5% of the claim	4.5% of the claim

To calculate five percent of the amount claimed, multiply it by 0.05, and round the sum to the nearest penny.

Appendix G
Hearing Fees

Amount claimed	Hearing fee
Not more than £300	£25
£300.01 to £500	£55
£500.01 to £1,000	£80
£1,000.01 to £1,500	£115
£1,500.01 to £3,000	£170
More than £3,000	£335

Appendix H
Legal Representative's Costs

Amount claimed	A	B	C
£25 to £500	£50	£60	£15
£500.01 to £1,000	£70	£80	£15
£1,000.01 to £5,000*	£80	£90	£15
More than £5,000	£100	£110	£15

A: Where the claim form is served by the court, or by any other method, other than personal service by the claimant.

B: Where the claim form is served personally by the claimant, and there is only one defendant.

C: Where there are multiple defendants, for each additional defendant personally served at a separate address by the claimant.

* This is the relevant row where the only claim is for delivery of goods, and no value is specified on the claim form.

Appendix I
Guideline Hourly Rates

Band	Fee earner	Grade					
		London			National		
		1	2	3	1	2	3
A	Solicitors & legal executives over eight years' experience	£409	£317	£229-£267	£217	£201	£201
B	Solicitors & legal executives over four years' experience	£296	£242	£172-£229	£192	£177	£177
C	Other solicitors or legal executives & fee earners of equivalent experience	£226	£196	£165	£161	£146	£146
D	Trainee solicitors, paralegals & other fee earners	£138	£126	£121	£118	£111	£111

MORE BOOKS BY
LAW BRIEF PUBLISHING

A selection of our other titles available now:-

'Covid-19, Homeworking and the Law – The Essential Guide to Employment and GDPR Issues' by Forbes Solicitors
'Covid-19, Force Majeure and Frustration of Contracts – The Essential Guide' by Keith Markham
'Covid-19 and Criminal Law – The Essential Guide' by Ramya Nagesh
'Covid-19 and Family Law in England and Wales – The Essential Guide' by Safda Mahmood
'Covid-19 and the Implications for Planning Law – The Essential Guide' by Bob Mc Geady & Meyric Lewis
'Covid-19, Residential Property, Equity Release and Enfranchisement – The Essential Guide' by Paul Sams and Louise Uphill
'Covid-19, Brexit and the Law of Commercial Leases – The Essential Guide' by Mark Shelton
'Covid-19 and the Law Relating to Food in the UK and Republic of Ireland – The Essential Guide' by Ian Thomas
'A Practical Guide to the General Data Protection Regulation (GDPR) – 2nd Edition' by Keith Markham
'Ellis on Credit Hire – Sixth Edition' by Aidan Ellis & Tim Kevan
'A Practical Guide to Working with Litigants in Person and McKenzie Friends in Family Cases' by Stuart Barlow
'Protecting Unregistered Brands: A Practical Guide to the Law of Passing Off' by Lorna Brazell
'A Practical Guide to Secondary Liability and Joint Enterprise Post-Jogee' by Joanne Cecil & James Mehigan

'A Practical Guide to Chronic Pain Claims' by Pankaj Madan
'A Practical Guide to Claims Arising from Fatal Accidents' by James Patience
'A Practical Guide to Subtle Brain Injury Claims' by Pankaj Madan

These books and more are available to order online direct from the publisher at www.lawbriefpublishing.com, where you can also read free sample chapters. For any queries, contact us on 0844 587 2383 or mail@lawbriefpublishing.com.

Our books are also usually in stock at www.amazon.co.uk with free next day delivery for Prime members, and at good legal bookshops such as Wildy & Sons.

We are regularly launching new books in our series of practical day-to-day practitioners' guides. Visit our website and join our free newsletter to be kept informed and to receive special offers, free chapters, etc.

You can also follow us on Twitter at www.twitter.com/lawbriefpub.

Printed in Great Britain
by Amazon

21208259R00228